Windows Server 2012 Hyper-V: Deploying Hyper-V Enterprise Server Virtualization Platform

Building Hyper-V infrastructure with secured multitenancy, flexible infrastructure, scalability, and high availability

Zahir Hussain Shah

professional expertise distilled

BIRMINGHAM - MUMBAI

Windows Server 2012 Hyper-V: Deploying Hyper-V Enterprise Server Virtualization Platform

First published: March 2013

Production Reference: 2210313

Published by Packt Publishing Ltd.
Livery Place
35 Livery Street
Birmingham B3 2PB, UK.

ISBN 978-1-84968-834-5

www.packtpub.com

Cover Image by Neha Rajappan (neha.rajappan1@gmail.com)

Credits

Author
Zahir Hussain Shah

Reviewers
Niklas Akerlund

Lai Yoong Seng

Acquisition Editor
Mary Jasmine Nadar

Lead Technical Editor
Sweny M. Sukumaran

Technical Editors
Prasad Dalvi

Devdutt Kulkarni

Copy Editors
Brandt D'Mello

Insiya Morbiwala

Aditya Nair

Laxmi Subramanian

Ruta Waghmare

Project Coordinator
Abhishek Kori

Proofreader
Chris Smith

Indexer
Rekha Nair

Graphics
Aditi Gajjar

Production Coordinator
Shantanu Zagade

Cover Work
Shantanu Zagade

About the Author

Zahir Hussain Shah is a Microsoft Most Valuable Professional who has worked with businesses from small- to medium-sized organizations to gigantic multinational companies, providing IT consultancy and solution delivery. He has been working in the IT industry for over 7 years now. Currently he is working with UAE's prestigious oil and gas sector for providing solution designs and delivery using Microsoft Hyper-V, clustering, Active Directory, Exchange Server, Lync Server, and System Center.

He has also been honored with the industry's most prestigious **Microsoft Most Valuable Professional** (**MVP**) award in the year 2011/2012, for his excellent contribution in the Microsoft server systems technical communities. Apart from the daily office life, Zahir is an author, public speaker, and a blogger. He owns a successful blog (`http://zahirshahblog.com`) on Microsoft private cloud, messaging, unified communications, and systems infrastructure solutions. He also has CISSP, MCSE, MCITP, MCTS, and CCNA certifications.

I want to dedicate this book and my thanks to my parents and family, and especially to my father Amir Asghar Shah, who always showed trust in me and supported me for every little thing in my life. I also want to thank my book reviewers, friends, colleagues, and teachers for their support. And last but not least, I can't forget to give sincere thanks to my beautiful wife Aynah, for her support and love.

About the Reviewers

Niklas Akerlund is a Product Manager at Lumagate. His focus is on private clouds and Microsoft System Center. Niklas has been working with Microsoft infrastructure solutions since 1998. He has quite a lot of experience in virtualization projects with consolidation planning and migrations from physical to virtual. Niklas has done both project management and technical design in Hyper-V upgrades and new installations. He started working with Hyper-V as a former employee in the TAP program for Windows Server 2008, and has great interest in automation and optimization of virtual machines and hosts. He was also responsible for the TAP program engagement for System Center Virtual Machine Manager 2012 at RTS. Niklas has been on TechNet TV in Sweden and has been working as an MCT at a local learning center for a long time. He is also a VMware vExpert 2012 and a VCI.

Lai Yoong Seng has been a **Microsoft Most Valuable Professional (MVP)** in virtual machines since 2010. He has more than 10 years of experience in IT and started his career as a Hyper-V and System Center specialist for Redynamics in Malaysia. He started specializing in Microsoft virtualization and started blogging (www.ms4u.info) and presenting for local and regional events. He is the founder of **Malaysia Virtualization User Group (MVUG)**, which has provided a one-stop center to people who want to learn about Hyper-V and System Center. Lai has also actively participated in **Microsoft Technology Adoption Program (TAP)** in System Center Virtual Machine Manager 2012 and System Center 2012 SP1.

Reviewing a book takes a lot of effort and is a difficult process. It would not have been possible without the help of my family, girlfriend, colleagues, and friends. I would like to thank my parents, and girlfriend Elizabeth Seow for understanding me, being patient, and helping to keep all the other stuff together while I was reviewing the book. In addition, a very special thanks to Packt Publishing for giving me an opportunity to contribute to this book.

www.PacktPub.com

Support files, eBooks, discount offers and more

You might want to visit www.PacktPub.com for support files and downloads related to your book.

Did you know that Packt offers eBook versions of every book published, with PDF and ePub files available? You can upgrade to the eBook version at www.PacktPub.com and as a print book customer, you are entitled to a discount on the eBook copy. Get in touch with us at service@packtpub.com for more details.

At www.PacktPub.com, you can also read a collection of free technical articles, sign up for a range of free newsletters and receive exclusive discounts and offers on Packt books and eBooks.

http://PacktLib.PacktPub.com

Do you need instant solutions to your IT questions? PacktLib is Packt's online digital book library. Here, you can access, read and search across Packt's entire library of books.

Why Subscribe?

- Fully searchable across every book published by Packt
- Copy and paste, print and bookmark content
- On demand and accessible via web browser

Free Access for Packt account holders

If you have an account with Packt at www.PacktPub.com, you can use this to access PacktLib today and view nine entirely free books. Simply use your login credentials for immediate access.

Instant Updates on New Packt Books

Get notified! Find out when new books are published by following @PacktEnterprise on Twitter, or the *Packt Enterprise* Facebook page.

Table of Contents

Preface

The only thing which is not constant is change; change provides new ideologies and methodologies for getting things done in more efficient and cost-effective ways. We all have been seeing a drastic shift of industry where every single product and IT system being supported is migrated to a virtualized server platform also known as a virtual machine. This new virtualized platform or virtual machine provides a handy way of maximizing the usage of underlying infrastructure and getting the most out of your investment.

Hyper-V is a hypervisor and a Microsoft implementation of a server virtualization and consolidation product, where Hyper-V is a native server role available in the Windows Server operating system. At the time of writing this book, the current version is Windows Server 2012 Hyper-V, which is the most robust and extremely well-equipped hypervisor product for server virtualization platforms.

This book is built upon the building-blocks strategy, where we start with introducing Hyper-V, and then we move along with adding necessary blocks of knowledge that provide the base platform for upcoming chapters and feature sets. This book covers all features and functionalities of Hyper-V as a hypervisor and discusses them in detail to ensure that readers get the information they need to set up the same technology in the real world. In addition to all this, each chapter of this book contains specific best practices, tips, and recommendations from a real-world standpoint and experience.

We hope after reading this book, you will become experienced in deploying and managing Hyper-V for enterprise-wide server virtualization and consolidation.

What this book covers

Chapter 1, Getting to Know Microsoft Hyper-V, introduces Windows Server 2012 Hyper-V, and provides deep information about Hyper-V deployment scenarios, architecture, requirements, VMMS, and last but not least, feature set comparison.

Chapter 2, Planning, Designing, and Implementing Microsoft Hyper-V, provides Hyper-V planning and designing guidelines, and instruction steps for upgrading legacy Hyper-V servers and installing new Hyper-V server for GUI and core server installations. It also covers basic Hyper-V server settings and new virtual machine creation.

Chapter 3, Setting Up Hyper-V Replication, introduces the Hyper-V Replica feature, explains deployment scenarios for Hyper-V Replica along with a technical overview, and also covers monitoring best practices and step-by-step configuration of Hyper-V Replica.

Chapter 4, Understanding Hyper-V Networking, covers a technical overview Hyper-V virtual switch, and gathers new features of Windows Server 2012 Hyper-V extensible virtual switch. It also provides guidelines for configuring various types of Hyper-V virtual switch configuration, and discusses best practices and configuration settings for the built-in NIC teaming feature.

Chapter 5, A New World of Hyper-V Automation with PowerShell, digs inside of PowerShell 3.0, discusses PowerShell's innate capabilities for managing Windows Server 2012 Hyper-V, and also provides examples for accomplishing common Hyper-V management tasks with PowerShell 3.0.

Chapter 6, Insight into Hyper-V Storage, delivers knowledge about all types of Hyper-V storage implementation scenarios, and goes deeper into discussing each type of storage in detail. It also covers virtual machine storage settings and last but not least concludes with Hyper-V storage best practices.

Chapter 7, Managing Hyper-V with System Center Virtual Machine Manager, gives an SCVMM overview and describes what's new in SCVMM 2012, provides step-by-step instructions for installing and configuring SCVMM for managing the Hyper-V environment, and covers virtual machine management and automation.

Chapter 8, Building Hyper-V High Availability and Virtual Machine Mobility, provides an overview of Hyper-V high availability and what's new in Windows Server 2012 for Hyper-V HA. It discusses Hyper-V HA and failover clustering core components, and delivers step-by-step instructions for preparing, creating, and configuring Hyper-V failover clusters. Finally, this chapter provides knowledge about virtual machine mobility and migrations.

Chapter 9, Hyper-V Security Hardening – Best Practices, covers Hyper-V and virtualization security pillars, and also delivers security hardening best practices for Hyper-V base operating systems, Hyper-V virtual network switch, Hyper-V management, Hyper-V storage, and most importantly safeguarding of guest virtual machines.

Chapter 10, Performing Hyper-V Backup and Recovery, discusses Hyper-V backup methodologies, and provides Hyper-V backup considerations and best practices. It also provides deep understanding of Hyper-V backup and recovery implementation for Windows Server Backup Feature and System Center Data Protection Manager 2012.

Appendix A, SCVMM 2012 New Features and Enhancements, covers all new features and enhancements added into System Center Virtual Machine Manager 2012 for Hyper-V and virtual machine management and automation.

Appendix B, SCVMM Management Console Configuration Settings, sums up all the configuration settings for System Center Virtual Machine Manager 2012 to configure it for basic and advanced settings.

What you need for this book

This book discusses and provides knowledge about various Microsoft server systems technology around the virtualization domain. For an example, if you want to try out scenario and configuration steps provided in this book in a real-world deployment scenario or in the lab, you will need the following software:

- Microsoft Windows Server 2012
- Microsoft System Center Virtual Machine Manager 2012, SP1
- Microsoft System Center Data Protection Manager 2012, SP1

Who this book is for

This book is for all types of audience from a new system engineer who is exploring the native virtualization capabilities of Windows Server to an expert Hyper-V and virtualization engineer, and also for IT management personnel who want to get insight into Hyper-V capabilities as an enterprise-wide hypervisor for server virtualization and consolidation projects. This book expects that you should be familiar with the Microsoft Windows Server operating system but not necessarily be an expert in it. This book is an ideal choice for both Hyper-V beginners and experts, because it takes you from the basic level to the advanced level with the help of step-by-step processes, and discusses all aspects of Hyper-V virtualization.

Conventions

In this book, you will find a number of styles of text that distinguish between different kinds of information. Here are some examples of these styles, and an explanation of their meaning.

Code words in text, database table names, folder names, filenames, file extensions, pathnames, dummy URLs, user input, and Twitter handles are shown as follows: "If you don't change the default path, the Hyper-V Manager on this server will present the default path, which is `C:\Users\Public\Document\Hyper-V\Virtual Hard Disks`, whenever you create a new VHD/VHDX file."

New terms and **important words** are shown in bold. Words that you see on the screen, in menus or dialog boxes for example, appear in the text like this: " On the **New Virtual Machine Wizard** window, click on **Next**."

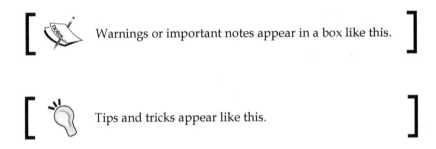

Warnings or important notes appear in a box like this.

Tips and tricks appear like this.

Reader feedback

Feedback from our readers is always welcome. Let us know what you think about this book—what you liked or may have disliked. Reader feedback is important for us to develop titles that you really get the most out of.

To send us general feedback, simply send an e-mail to `feedback@packtpub.com`, and mention the book title via the subject of your message.

If there is a topic that you have expertise in and you are interested in either writing or contributing to a book, see our author guide on `www.packtpub.com/authors`.

Customer support

Now that you are the proud owner of a Packt book, we have a number of things to help you to get the most from your purchase.

Errata

Although we have taken every care to ensure the accuracy of our content, mistakes do happen. If you find a mistake in one of our books—maybe a mistake in the text or the code—we would be grateful if you would report this to us. By doing so, you can save other readers from frustration and help us improve subsequent versions of this book. If you find any errata, please report them by visiting http://www.packtpub.com/submit-errata, selecting your book, clicking on the **errata submission form** link, and entering the details of your errata. Once your errata are verified, your submission will be accepted and the errata will be uploaded on our website, or added to any list of existing errata, under the Errata section of that title. Any existing errata can be viewed by selecting your title from http://www.packtpub.com/support.

Piracy

Piracy of copyright material on the Internet is an ongoing problem across all media. At Packt, we take the protection of our copyright and licenses very seriously. If you come across any illegal copies of our works, in any form, on the Internet, please provide us with the location address or website name immediately so that we can pursue a remedy.

Please contact us at copyright@packtpub.com with a link to the suspected pirated material.

We appreciate your help in protecting our authors, and our ability to bring you valuable content.

Questions

You can contact us at questions@packtpub.com if you are having a problem with any aspect of the book, and we will do our best to address it.

Introduction

We welcome you on board to our journey of discovering Microsoft Windows Server 2012 Hyper-V. As we speak, the current version of Hyper-V is Windows Server 2012. In this book we will cover all aspects of Hyper-V as an enterprise server virtualization platform. Since Hyper-V is a server role inside the Windows Server operating system, while we make our journey of discovering Hyper-V basic fundamentals and new features, we will also be covering numerous new features added into Windows Server 2012. Throughout this book our goal will be not only to cover the theory of Hyper-V or Windows Server, but also to provide you with knowledge about real-world scenarios, best practices, tips, and last but not least recommendations from field experience. In addition to all this, we will see the screenshots of step-by-step setting of Hyper-V basic and advanced configuration. This will provide you enough guidance to start your first server virtualization and consolidation project with Hyper-V. Or if you are already running an existing virtualization platform with Hyper-V, after completing this book you will become capable of upgrading your existing Hyper-V server to new Windows Server 2012 for utilizing various brand-new out-of-the-box server-virtualization features, which currently none of the other hypervisor products deliver.

Okay, we now know what we are going to see in this book, and before we go deeper in Hyper-V and discuss all its bits and pieces, let's first get introduced to few of the basic concepts and theories on which we build server virtualization. I would like to first introduce you to a few of the important concepts such as virtualization, server consolidation, and cloud computing. All these concepts are essential for us to build our underlying understanding for moving forward with each new chapter that we cover in this book.

What is virtualization?

Virtualization is a broad term in general but when we use it in the IT world, we use it to say we will virtualize our applications, networks, servers, storage or even client workstation. Virtualization is a technology that allows an IT administrator to utilize the same hardware to run multiple software or operating systems by allocating or dedicating the underlying physical hardware resources of a computer or server. On the other side we see that the same hardware can run a single operating system and can be used for a single host or identity, like a web server that is hosting our internal finance department web application. But if we use virtualization technology here, we could install server virtualization software (a hypervisor) on the same piece of hardware, and we could then run multiple independent virtual instances of many web servers or any type of operating system or application instance. These completely different instances that we create on the physical server are referred to as guest or virtual machines; they exist virtually and so they are known as virtual machines.

Although virtual machines use the same physical resources among all their other siblings on the same piece of hardware, virtualization software, which is also referred to as a hypervisor, ensures that the **trusted computing base** (**TCB**) concept is always enforced and doesn't allow the virtual machine to see what data and communication it's doing with the physical resources. This means that if there are two virtual machines running on the same physical hardware, each doesn't know what the other virtual machine running on it is up to or which data the other virtual machine is providing or taking from the processor and RAM. When the administrator creates a virtual machine using a hypervisor, it can dedicate a chunk of physical RAM and processor cycles to the virtual machine; this allocation can be either static or dynamic. When we configure static RAM for a virtual machine, let's say 1,024 MB, the virtual machine is restricted to always show its virtual RAM as 1 GB. However, on the other side, if we want we can configure dynamic memory for the virtual machine, so we could set the startup RAM of 1,024 MB and allow the virtual machine to go up to 10,240 MB. In the same way, we can configure the virtual machine to have either one logical processor or four logical processors.

Okay, we discussed virtual RAM and processors for a virtual machine; what about the hard disk or storage of a virtual machine? Here you go; just like virtual RAM and processor, we create **virtual hard disk** (**VHD**) in the Hyper-V case. VHD is a file-based storage for a virtual machine. It gets added or associated to a virtual machine, and then the virtual machine sees this VHD file associated to a virtual machine instance as its hard disk. The more VHDs you create and associate to a virtual machine, the more virtual hard disk space will be assigned to that virtual machine. We could also dedicate a physical disk to a virtual machine, so if we don't create a file-based virtual hard disk for a virtual machine, then we can associate a physical hard disk or SAN LUN associated on the virtualization server to the virtual machine. Virtualization can be set up in the form of a shared service where we configure the identical type of virtualization servers (a cluster), and this shared form of virtualization server allows us to migrate virtual machines from one server to another, in case one virtualization server goes down or the administrator wants to perform maintenance on the physical server. How to create a virtual machine and manage the hypervisor for server virtualization is discussed in detail in the upcoming chapters, so stay tuned.

Why virtualization?

An organization that doesn't follow the latest trend of virtualizing its server workloads will often see its existing hardware investment as under utilized from the resource utilization prospective. This means a majority of physical hardware boxes don't reach to their capacity even twice a month. These under-utilized hardware boxes utilize rack space, cooling, power, and most importantly annual server maintenance cost if your server is out of the supplier's original warranty of 3 years.

The notion of virtualization allows us to consolidate multiple workloads on a single server, which ensures that existing server hardware investment gets fully utilized. This concept also supports the green IT slogan where the IT department tries to save power, cooling, as well as space to maintain the same level of service delivery but with less utilization of these natural resources. Often we see it is difficult to scale in and scale out an application server running on a physical server, while on the other side with the help provided by virtualization, we can scale in and scale out an application very easily. This helps an administrator to dynamically increase the resources for a virtual machine whenever it is needed; with the help of a server virtualization management platform, such as SCVMM we can even automate this. So whenever the hypervisor comes to know that there is more load, it can dynamically add more instances of an application, and when there is no load, the same extra provisioned instances get removed from the environment on the fly.

Let's try to simplify this question of why virtualization is needed by laying out few of the reasons, which immensely strengthen the need for virtualization:

- Among all other benefits of virtualization the most exciting benefits an organization gets from it, are server consolidation and cost reduction. This means an organization can run multiple different IT application systems on a single hardware server, where without virtualization it has to have dedicated hardware equipment for these multiple application instances, which means a larger required amount of rack space, cooling, power, and associated maintenance cost has to be paid for. On the flip side, without virtualization, the majority of the server systems run in an under-utilized state, which means the organization cannot get the most from its investments, where by utilizing virtualization it can use its systems to their maximum capacity.

- Virtualization allows an organization to run its legacy application systems on the latest hardware. This reduces the extra burden to maintain the old server equipment, which is out of warranty and is very expensive to maintain due to the unavailability of service and spare parts.

- Being an IT professional, virtualization is like an old school buddy who helps you learn and always be on top of new technologies and expertise. With virtualization it is much easier to build a research and development environment again and again. And by using a virtual machine, we can build a new server along with OS installed in just a minute. As we all know, testing requires us to build various test cases where rebuilding the same environment is needed from time to time, so virtualization helps you save your time and get things done in a much easier way.

- Virtualization is one of the methods for converting a physical machine to a virtual machine, which allows you to maintain the existing physical server operating system settings and convert it into a virtual machine. Usually, this gets done when there is an old hardware server on which you are running an application, which you would like to run on a virtual machine, but you don't want to install from the scratch and want to maintain the existing configuration. So in this case all we need to do is to perform the conversion and we can run the same application as a virtual machine with everything untouched.

- Another essential reason why virtualization is needed in our datacenter is that, with virtualization, applying dynamics and optimization becomes much easier. As we mentioned previously, with some sort of virtualization orchestration and management tools you can configure real-time dynamics for applications to scale out and scale in whenever there is a load for application. And virtualization as a base layer provides the computing platform for these dynamically expending application platforms.

Types of virtualization

Virtualization is a broad term, and addresses a wide range of core-computing elements, but here we will mainly discuss three major types of virtualization, which are as follows:

- Server virtualization
- Network virtualization
- Storage virtualization

Server virtualization

In the first type of virtualization, we build virtual computers on a physical computer that is running virtualization software. Now let's elaborate this to better understand the concept here. This means the need of a computer that mainly comprises hard disk, processor, and RAM and other hardware components is fulfilled virtually on a physical computer with the help of the virtualization software that we call the hypervisor. By doing this we try to create as many virtual computers as is possible on a physical computer so that we can take advantage of and utilize the physical computer's installed resources and also save power, cooling, and space requirement by virtually hosting these computers.

Network virtualization

Network virtualization is when all of the separate resources of a network are combined, allowing the network administrator to share them out amongst the users of the network. This is done by splitting the resources' bandwidth into channels and allowing the administrator to assign these resources as and when required. This allows each user to access all of the network resources from his/her computer. These resources can be files and folders on the computer, printers or hard drives, and so on. This streamlined approach makes the life of the network administrator much easier, and it makes the system seem much less complicated to the human eye than it really is.

Storage virtualization

Storage virtualization has two distinct objectives, where the first objective is to separate the logical storage from the physical storage regardless of where data is stored. This allows the storage administrator to create partitions and manage data storage in a much more meaningful fashion. For an example, being a storage administrator you would like to keep fast storage disks for your ERP and Business Intelligence system, while slower disks can be allocated for file servers where speed and performance might not be needed.

Another objective of storage is to provide file-based access to data no matters where the actual data is stored. This enhances the performance and optimizes storage usage. In both ways when the storage virtualization is performed, it allows the administrator to effectively utilize the storage by taking advantage of storage automation and scalability features. Another example of storage migration is the tier-based architecture in which we divide stored data based on its classification and usage needs. So with the help of the fast cache feature, data can be moved from a slower SATA disk to a fast **solid-state drive (SSD)** when the I/O requirement increases from the user side.

Server consolidation

Server consolidation is a term more frequently used in connection with virtualization, where virtualization helps organizations to consolidate various IT workloads while running independently on a single hardware. What this consolidation mainly does is to achieve cost reduction by getting rid of running dedicated hardware for one application. Other than the cost factor, server consolidation greatly helps to ensure that existing hardware equipment does not stay underutilized and it is utilized in a more productive way.

It is extremely important to analyze the existing environment before going forward with a server consolidation and virtualization project, because we don't just randomly pick up the application server and decide to either convert it into a virtual machine or migrate existing server applications to a virtualized server application instance. Without proper analysis of our workload placement and sizing of underlying infrastructure, we might run into a problem where consolidated and virtualized instances suffer from availability and performance issues. Therefore, we recommend that organizations should perform proper sizing and planning exercises to evaluate all types of computing resources to see whether the same virtualized instance of the existing physical server would be enough to take over the load and scale of the service.

Cloud computing

If you are new to cloud computing, you might be wondering why we are discussing cloud computing as our next hop right after virtualization. The answer to your question is that cloud computing is a guy in the market, which boomed virtualization with one step ahead, as it introduced virtualization as a base infrastructure component of cloud computing. Cloud computing is more about combining people, processes, and technologies towards providing IT as a service; and in this journey of cloud computing, virtualization provides a platform on which cloud computing builds its architecture to use pools of hardware resources and share them, whenever it is required with orchestration and provide self service to its customers.

If you have been around the IT field for some time now, you must have heard about this term. Cloud computing is a way to deliver IT services in a more dynamic and self-service way, where someone can request for a virtual machine or a software environment to set up or build their own application, or use a publically hosted service. The cloud service provider and its customer relationship are tightly synchronized with each other, where on one side the party hosting the service needs to provide all these types of computing services to its end users with some sort of self-service style. And on the other side, depending on the user's needs, he/she can request a service and the service gets provisioned without any intervention. Another important aspect of this service is that it should be flexible enough so that if the service needs to be scaled out, it has enough scalability to cater for the request load.

Because cloud computing is an extremely diversified field of technology, all vendors, suppliers, and technology providers phrase their definition in their own way to explain their cloud offerings.

NIST (National Institute of Standards and Technology) provided its standard definition as a common understanding for everyone. So instead of understanding and creating our own cloud computing definition let's take a look at the definition of cloud computing provided by NIST. Visit the following URL for the definition:

`http://csrc.nist.gov/publications/nistpubs/800-145/SP800-145.pdf`

1
Getting to Know Microsoft Hyper-V

In the previous section of the book, we tried to get ourselves familiar with virtualization, server consolidation, and cloud computing concepts. These concepts play a vital role in today's virtualized infrastructure of every organization, whether it's a small to medium size organization or a multinational enterprise. We also saw how server consolidation helps organizations to tailor their needs to consolidate their widespread server farm from underutilized to a consolidated few physical servers (hypervisors). Server consolidation also provides another way of allowing legacy applications to be run on the newer hardware and efficiently migrating the legacy server to run as a **virtual machine** (**VM**), which is called **physical-to-virtual** (**P2V**) migration.

Cloud computing is a journey, or can better be called a practice of managing IT in an organization. The major players for an organization to build their own private cloud, or start offering public cloud services, are people, processes, and technology. Server virtualization and consolidation is one element of cloud computing and provides the base platform for computing requirements in an economic way.

To understand more about cloud computing, we will go deeper into it and see the definitions for different types of clouds and their services, in this chapter.

In this first chapter, we will elaborate the Microsoft Hyper-V as a hypervisor and a server virtualization platform. After completing this chapter, we will understand the following concepts:

- Hyper-V deployment scenarios
- Hyper-V architecture
- Features of Hyper-V
- Hyper-V system and hardware requirements

Introducing Hyper-V

In the year 2008, Microsoft released the RTM version of Microsoft Windows Server 2008, which had Hyper-V as its first version free of cost; but this was not the first virtualization product Microsoft introduced for operating system or application-level virtualization. Prior to the release of Hyper-V, Microsoft provided Virtual PC, which was a desktop application for end users to install on the base operating system and run as a secondary operating system, to enjoy the concept of virtualization. Using this, a user was able to have two copies of the same or different operating systems running on his/her PC. Later, Microsoft went one step further and released Microsoft Virtual Server 2005 in the year 2006. Virtual Server was the first initiative where Microsoft jumped into server-side virtualization, and this journey later continued with the release of Microsoft Windows Server 2008. In this release of the Windows Server operating system, Microsoft introduced its first true x64 hardware-based hypervisor, known as Hyper-V. In this version of the Microsoft virtualization solution, Microsoft also introduced the flexibility to make virtual machines highly available, with the use of **Microsoft Cluster Service (MSCS)**. This high-availability feature for virtual machines was called quick migration. In this, all the virtual machines are located on a shared cluster storage, and if one Hyper-V cluster node fails, all the virtual machines running on this failed Hyper-V cluster node get migrated to another available Hyper-V cluster node, with some downtime. We will learn more about quick migration and other virtual machine migration within Hyper-V failover cluster, in *Chapter 8, Building Hyper-V High Availability and Virtual Machine Mobility*, where we will cover Hyper-V and the virtual machine high availability feature in detail.

Later, in 2009, Microsoft released Windows Server 2008 R2, which was the second release of Windows Server 2008 as an operating system. In this release Microsoft fixed a couple of bugs found in the earlier release of Hyper-V, but most importantly added a few new enhancements to the product, such as live migration of virtual machines and **Cluster Shared Volumes (CSV)**. These new features for virtual machines — High Availability and Mobility — gained huge appreciation from customers, and the industry in particular. The first version of Hyper-V gained a lot of attention from those Windows Server 2008 users who found Hyper-V interesting as a native Windows server feature available for a true 64-bit compatible hypervisor. This first version of the product provided all the generic and standard features for 64-bit OS virtualization. As an IT professional, when I started using Hyper-V within Windows Server 2008, I personally found it a handy way of running a virtual machine for virtualizing applications to utilize the hardware resources more effectively, and for building research and development environments. Initially, we had to install and manage virtual machines either with VMware or Microsoft Virtual Server 2005 for setting up the testing environment for real-world **proof of concepts (POCs)**, and since both these solutions were not available as native features of the operating system, it was a bit time consuming.

In the second release of Windows Server 2008 (R2), Microsoft included a series of new features and functionalities to the Hyper-V role that made it popular among companies to roll out Hyper-V as a hypervisor for their server consolidation and application virtualization needs. At this time, Hyper-V really started gaining confidence from its customers, and on the other side there were series of Microsoft enterprise applications such as Exchange Server and SQL Server that officially started supporting the virtualization of these types of workloads. So, at this stage of the product, Hyper-V was not only hosting R&D virtual workloads, but also started hosting the first-tier and middle-tier of applications with High Availability setup, where live migration was added in addition to quick migration. Live migration was another milestone for the product in becoming an enterprise hypervisor. Live migration provided for a single virtual machine to be seamlessly migrated to another Hyper-V host in the event of planned migration. We will get to know more about different types of Hyper-V HA deployment scenarios in the upcoming chapters.

Let's take our journey with Hyper-V to the next level — when Microsoft released Windows Server 2008 R2 Service Pack 1. In Windows Server 2008 R2 Service Pack 1, Microsoft added a number of enhancements to Hyper-V; Dynamic Memory and RemoteFX were two of the major enhancements. These two value-added features changed how Hyper-V used to work earlier, and also helped Hyper-V as a hypervisor to provide a base platform for environments such as Dynamic Data Centers. With the Dynamic Memory feature, Hyper-V allowed its customers to configure memory settings dynamically for the workloads. With dynamic memory, we configure the virtual machine to have "startup RAM" along with a reserved buffer, and a "max RAM". The startup RAM plus reserved buffer will be a dedicated allocation of RAM to the virtual machine, while the remaining max threshold limit value will allow the virtual machine to grab more memory from the physical server's available memory pool on the fly, whenever it is needed by the virtual machine. With this new era, the process of assigning and configuring memory for virtual machines was changed completely, where the Dynamic Memory feature helped administrators to efficiently utilize the physical resources among multiple workloads running on the same Hyper-V host server.

The second major enhancement introduced with Service Pack 1 was RemoteFX. Microsoft RemoteFX was a new feature that was included in Windows Server 2008 R2 Service Pack 1. It introduced a set of end user experience enhancements for **Remote Desktop Protocol (RDP)** that enable a rich desktop environment within your corporate network.

Hyper-V deployment scenario

In this section we will discuss how customers can take advantage of Hyper-V as a base hypervisor for the virtualization stack and server consolidation. And in addition to this, we will see how and where Hyper-V can contribute as a Microsoft native Windows Server hypervisor product.

The following are the scenarios in which Microsoft Hyper-V can contribute efficiently as a hypervisor:

- Server consolidation
- Physical-to-virtual and virtual-to-virtual conversions
- Research and development
- Business continuity and disaster recovery
- Cloud computing

Now, in the following section, we will discuss each Hyper-V deployment scenario in detail, which may be one of your server virtualization project's main requirements.

Server consolidation

As we have been seeing over a decade, computer technology is getting micro—with great enhancements for computer processing power and increased memory and storage capacity. These new changes are allowing new computers to process more data in less time, with less overhead. One of the great examples of these new enhancements is the inclusion of multiple cores in a physical processor, where a single processor chip socket virtually holds multiple processors, and thus we can have more processor cycles and more physical RAM in a single box.

These highly intelligent and fast beasts can handle an immense amount of workload, so running a single application role that might not be a resource-hungry application may result in the hardware box being underutilized. This is not a single commodity loss, because it might also make your other investments underutilized, and that would also result in bad **return on investment** (**ROI**). This is a situation where the customer is not making the most of his/her investment.

Virtualization allows a server administrator to consolidate server workloads in the form of virtual machines. This allows an organization to fully utilize its servers with multiple operating systems running on the same box.

On one side, server consolidation gives the benefit of utilizing hardware resources to their utmost capacity, and on the other side it also helps to reduce the power consumption and keeps the datacenter environment less occupied with issues of cooling and loaded racks. Imagine a system's infrastructure without virtualization and server consolidation concepts: where for each single application frontend tier, we have to keep a physical server in the rack; where combining power, cooling, and rack space management would result in high maintenance costs from all aspects of datacenter management. Thanks to virtualization technology, which helps to reduce the maintenance cost by consolidating these multiple applications boxes and running them on a single physical box as virtual machines, we produce more with less cost and overhead while equally using our underutilized resources across the infrastructure.

Physical-to-virtual and virtual-to-virtual conversions

Physical-to-virtual, also known as P2V, is one of the most demanding features of any server consolidation and datacenter consolidation project, where client requirements are to convert the running physical boxes regardless of the operating system or installed applications, and convert them into VMs. There is also the opposite possibility, **virtual-to-physical** (**V2P**), but it hardly comes as a requirement to a hypervisor administrator.

P2V allows legacy application servers to be converted into virtual machines and run on newer hardware, which is one of the features of server consolidation. This helps an organization to get rid of the legacy hardware, which consumes space in the racks, generates a huge amount of heat, and most importantly consumes a lot of power. So you can imagine removing these physical application boxes and converting them into a virtual machine, which can save a lot of your money and datacenter resources. On one end, P2V benefits from server consolidation concepts, and on the other side it provides a flexible platform for migrated servers and applications, by allowing dynamic memory and flexibility to add additional processors and hard disk drives, which is very difficult to do if you run a physical server.

Okay, we talked about P2V, but what about **virtual-to-virtual (V2V)**? This is also a growing requirement, especially with the availability of native Windows Server hypervisor (Hyper-V), and its fast growth and high demand. Nowadays, most of the customers that are running their Microsoft platform want to migrate their virtual workloads from a third-party hypervisor to Microsoft Hyper-V. This move gives them a lot of flexibility and saves costs, and since the release of Windows Server 2012, where Hyper-V 3.0 provides a number of features and functionalities that no other third-party hypervisor product provides within the industry, many of them have this requirement of converting third-party virtual machines into Hyper-V virtual machines.

Microsoft has made this conversion easier for its customers by providing a handy way of converting these third-party virtual machines into Hyper-V virtual machines using Microsoft Virtual Machine Converter. For example, this allows Hyper-V customers to convert VMware virtual machines into Hyper-V virtual machines. Microsoft Virtual Machine Converter is a part of the Microsoft Solution Accelerator suite, which can be downloaded and used from the Microsoft Solution Accelerator website (`http://technet.microsoft.com/en-us/library/hh967435.aspx`).

Research and development

This is one is my favorites, where Hyper-V gives you immense flexibility in building R&D and testing environments with the luxury of many features that help you to test different product applications on different operating systems. Hyper-V admins can also script the creation of virtual machines based on their test cases, which expedites the process of building the R&D environment. We all know that during the testing phase, especially for developers, sometimes it is necessary to reformat the operating system. Hyper-V gives you the snapshot facility, where a Hyper-V administrator can take a snapshot of a VM at any given time and restore it later at any stage of the test cycle, which will take the virtual machine to the exact same state as when the snapshot was initially created. Running multiple OSs with a limited amount of physical RAM has always been a bottleneck, and therefore to provide a handy way to administrators to deal with such cases, Hyper-V provides the virtual machine state saving feature, where you can save or resume the virtual machine to the same state, and at the same time continue with other testing activities.

Business continuity and disaster recovery

Business continuity or **business continuity planning (BCP)** allows an organization to survive major catastrophic situations, and makes sure that business continuity and operation will not be affected if the primary facility is unavailable. Hyper-V provides sound business continuity support for an organization whose mission-critical application is running in a virtualized mode. Microsoft Windows Server 2012 Hyper-V provides BCP capabilities for virtualized workloads by allowing them to replicate to a disaster recovery site, where a primary site Hyper-V server can as act as primary server and a Hyper-V server sitting in the disaster recovery site can get all the VM-related replication from its primary instance.

Hyper-V also allows customers to configure VSS backups for the virtual machines, where VSS writers for Hyper-V virtual machines make it possible for VSS-based software solutions to take virtual machine backups while the virtual machine is up and running.

So let's say you are taking your Hyper-V VM's backup, and unfortunately your entire primary datacenter goes down. In this case, you can get your off-site backup tape drives and restore the virtual machine to any point in time on the same or a different host. We will be covering Hyper-V backup and recovery concept in details in *Chapter 10, Performing Hyper-V Backup and Recovery*.

The other feature that Hyper-V supports for the BCP concept is VM migration. Hyper-V provides two flavors of VM migration, quick migration and live migration. In quick migration, which came into existence with the first release of Hyper-V Windows Server 2008, a Windows failover cluster is configured with shared cluster storage, on which the **virtual hard disks (VHDs)** are stored. So, if a failure occurs and one Hyper-V host node goes offline, the cluster senses and moves the VM's workload to another Hyper-V host. In quick migration, while the migration happens, the virtual machine's state (more importantly, the storage VM state) is paused till the time the failover of other resources occurs. Once all the resources get up and running for the second running cluster node, the virtual machine gets resumed on this node. Since quick migration was a cluster failover based migration feature, it introduced some delay in a few user-centric applications.

The other migration solution provided to Hyper-V was live migration, which had come with Windows Server 2008 R2. Live migration was more mature than quick migration, and, as it sounds, it was a live migration of VM workload from one Hyper-V node to another. Live migration of virtual machines provides great flexibility for planned migration, where an administrator, while patching the physical Hyper-V hosts, can migrate a guest virtual machine to other available Hyper-V hosts without any disruption in the machine's availability on the network. While performing the migration, the Hyper-V server creates a secure session from the source Hyper-V host to the destination Hyper-V host where the virtual guest machine is intended to be migrated, as part of the migration plan. During the live migration process, the source Hyper-V server starts copying the memory pages to the destination Hyper-V server, and once all of the memory pages are copied to the destination Hyper-V server, the VM moves and starts on the secondary Hyper-V node. This process is network resource intensive, where the memory pages get copied to the destination Hyper-V server over the network. And for this reason, it would be advisable to have a dedicated NIC card for the live migration process. We will go deeper into the Hyper-V migration strategies in the coming chapters, so stay tuned.

Cloud computing

It is quite cloudy here today! In the beginning of the book, we gave an introduction about cloud computing after introducing virtualization. In the cloud services delivery model, the service provider provides computing capabilities, also called a pool of resources, such as network, servers, storage, and applications. These services are highly elastic and flexible with the users' needs. Let's see how a hypervisor works hand in hand with cloud computing. Hyper-V as a hypervisor provides the base virtualization layer of cloud computing, on which the cloud computing builds its underlying infrastructure and provides computing resources. Hyper-V as a base hypervisor in cloud computing solution delivery works with Microsoft System Center 2012 product suite, and covers end-to-end cloud delivery, where the Microsoft System Center 2012 product provides self-service portal, cloud service request, orchestration, operations monitoring, and virtual workload management as well.

Hyper-V architecture

After the extensive information gathering from virtualization as a technology, and server consolidation as a technique to take advantage of virtualization, let's move on to the next section of this chapter. Here we will discuss Hyper-V architecture, and will go deeper to understand how different Hyper-V architectural components work together to provide hardware-assisted virtualization.

Before we jump in to discuss the core elements of Hyper-V architecture, let's first quickly see the definition of a hypervisor, and its available types, to better understand the Hyper-V architecture as a hypervisor.

Hypervisor

Hypervisor is a term used to describe the software stack, or sometimes operating system feature, that allows us to create virtual machines by utilizing the same physical server's resources. Based on the hypervisor type, some hypervisors run on the operating system layer, and some go underneath the operating system and directly interact with the hardware resources, such as processor, RAM, and NIC. We will understand these different types of hypervisors shortly — in the coming topics.

Hypervisor is not a new term that rose with VMware or Microsoft. If you see the history of this term, it takes you back to the year 1965, when IBM first upgraded the code for its 360 mainframe system's computing platform to support memory virtualization. By evolving this technique, they provided great enhancements to computing as a technology, by addressing different architectural limitations of mainframes.

Now let's discuss the various available hypervisor types, which may be categorized as shown next.

Type 1 (bare metal) hypervisors

Type 1, or bare metal, hypervisors run on the server hardware. They get more control over the host hardware, thus providing better performance and security. And guest virtual machines run on top of the hypervisor layer. There are a couple of hypervisors available on the market that belong to this hypervisor family, for example, Microsoft Hyper-V, VMware vSphere ESXi Server, and Citrix XenServer.

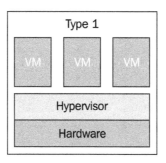

Type 2 (hosted) hypervisors

These second type of hypervisors run on top of the operating system as an application installed on the server. And that's why they are often referred to as hosted hypervisors. In type 2 hypervisor environments, the guest virtual machines run on top of the hypervisor layer.

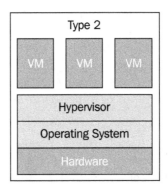

The preceding diagrams illustrate the difference between type 1 and type 2 hypervisors, where you can see that in the type 1 hypervisor architecture, the hypervisor is the first layer right after the base hardware. This allows the hypervisor to have more control and better access to the hardware resources.

While looking at the type 2 hypervisor architecture, we can see that the hypervisor is installed on top of the operating system layer, which doesn't allow the hypervisor to directly access the hardware. This inability to have direct access to the host's hardware increases overhead for the hypervisor, and thus the resources that you may run on the type 1 hypervisor are more while those on the type 2 hypervisor are less for the same hardware.

The second major disadvantage of type 2 hypervisors is that this hypervisor runs as a Windows NT service; so if this service is killed, the virtualization platform will not be available anymore. The examples of Type 2 hypervisor are Microsoft Virtual Server, Virtual PC, and VMware Player/VMware Workstation.

Monolithic hypervisors

The monolithic hypervisor is a subtype of the type 1 hypervisors. This type of hypervisor holds hypervisor-aware device drivers for guest-operating systems. There are some benefits of using monolithic hypervisors, but there are also a couple of disadvantages in using them. The benefit of using monolithic hypervisors is that they don't need a parent or controlling operating system, and thus they have direct control over the server hardware.

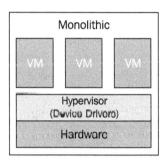

The first disadvantage of using monolithic hypervisors is that not every single hardware vendor may have device drivers ready for these types of hypervisors. This is because there are number of different motherboards and other devices. Therefore, to find a compatible hardware vendor who supports specific monolithic hypervisors could be a potentially hard task to do, before choosing the right hardware for your hypervisor. The same thing can also be counted as an advantage, because each of these drivers for the monolithic hypervisors are tested and verified by the hypervisor manufacturer.

The second disadvantage of a monolithic hypervisor is that it allows the hypervisor to get closer access to kernel (Ring 1) and hardware resources, which may open the door for the malicious activities taking advantage of this excessive privilege. The openness to this threat goes against the **trusted computing base (TCB)** concept. VMware vSphere ESXi Server is an example of this type of bare metal hypervisor.

Microkernel hypervisors

In this type of hypervisor, you have device drivers in the kernel mode (Ring 0), and also in the user mode (Ring 3) of the trusted computing base (OS). Along with this, only the CPU and memory scheduling happens in Ring 1.

The advantage of this type of hypervisor is that since the majority of hardware manufactures provide compatible device drivers for operating systems, with the microkernel hypervisor, finding compatible hardware is not a problem.

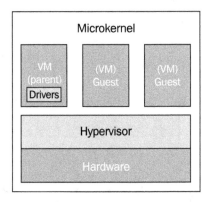

A microkernel hypervisor requires device drivers to be installed for the physical hardware devices in the operating system, which is running under the parent partition of a hypervisor. This means that we don't need to install the device drivers for each guest operating system running as a child partition, because when these guest operating systems need to access physical hardware resources on the host computer, they simply do this by communicating through the parent partition. One of the features of using microkernel-based hypervisors is that these hypervisors don't hurt the concept of TCB; thus, they work within the limited, privileged boundaries. The hardware-assisted virtualization Hyper-V that Microsoft implemented is an example of a microkernel-based hypervisor.

What is a trusted computing base?

You can find information about TCB at `http://csrc.nist.gov/publications/history/dod85.pdf`.

Insight into Hyper-V architecture

Now let's take a look at the Hyper-V architecture diagram, as follows:

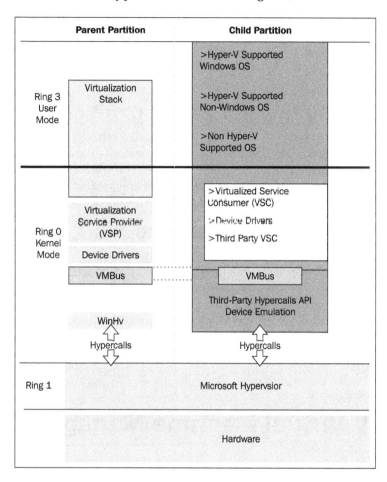

As you can see in the preceding diagram, Hyper-V behaves as a type 1 hypervisor, which runs on top of hardware. Running on top of the hypervisor are one parent partition and one or more child partitions. A partition is simply a unit of isolation within the hypervisor that is allocated physical memory address space and virtual processors. Now let's discuss the parent and child partitions.

Parent partition

The **Parent partition** is the partition that has all the access to hardware devices, and control over the local virtualization stack. The parent partition has the rights to create child partitions and manage all the components related to them.

Child partition

As we said in the preceding section, the child partition gets created by the parent partition, and all the guest virtual machine related components run under the child partition.

After seeing the two major elements of any hypervisor virtualization stack, we will now see some more elements related to Hyper-V virtual stack.

Understanding Hyper-V parent partition

When we install the Hyper-V role on supported hardware, right after we start the server to complete the installation of Hyper-V role, the parent partition gets created and the parent partition hypervisor itself goes underneath the operating system layer, and now Windows Server 2012 operating system runs on top of the hypervisor's parent partition layer. With the basic definition, we understood that the parent partition is the brain of Hyper-V virtual stack management, and all the components get installed in child partitions. The parent partition also makes sure that the hypervisor has adequate access to all the hardware resources; and while accessing these hardware resources, the trusted computing base concept will be used. In addition to all the tasks the parent partition performs, when you start your Hyper-V server, the parent partition is the first partition to get created; and while running the virtual machines on the Hyper-V server, it is the parent partition that provisions the child partitions on the hypervisor or Hyper-V server. The parent partition also acts as the middleman in between the virtual machines (child partitions) and hardware for accessing the resources.

Hyper-V Virtual Machine Management Service

Virtual Machine Management Service is the management engine of Hyper-V. **Virtual Machine Management Service (VMM Service** or **VMMS)** is responsible for the management of the virtual machine state for the child partitions. This includes making the right decision to change the virtual machine state, handling the creation of snapshots, and managing the addition or removal of devices. When a virtual machine in a child partition is started, the VMMS spawns a new VM worker process, which is used to perform the management tasks for that virtual machine.

Virtual devices

Virtual devices (**vDevices**) are the application interfaces that provide control over devices to the VMs. There are two types of vDevices, as follows:

- Core devices
    - Emulated devices
    - Synthetic devices
- Plugin devices

Let's see the difference between these devices.

Core devices (emulated devices)

These virtual devices emulate a specific hardware device, such as a VESA video card. Most core vDevices are emulated devices like this, and examples include BIOS, DMA, APIC, ISA bus, PCI bus, PIC device, PIT device, Power Management device, RTC device, Serial controller, Speaker device, 8042 PS/2 keyboard/mouse controller, Emulated Ethernet (DEC/Intel 21140), Floppy controller, IDE controller, and VGA/VESA video. Another aspect of the emulated devices is that they run in the user mode of the TCB concept and have less ability to interact with the server hardware.

Core devices (synthetic devices)

These virtual devices do not model specific hardware devices. Examples of synthetic devices include a synthetic video controller, synthetic **human interface device** (**HID**) controller, synthetic **network interface card** (**NIC**), synthetic storage device, synthetic interrupt controller, and memory service routines. These synthetic devices are available only to guest operating systems that support Integration Services.

As we saw previously, emulated devices run in Ring 3 (which is a user ring) and therefore cannot directly interact with the hardware resources; they thus have limited reliability and approachability. On the other hand, synthetic devices run under the kernel mode, which allows them to run faster and be more reliable.

Plugin devices

Plugin devices are different from other types of devices. These devices allow direct communications between the parent and the child partition. These devices can safely be removed and added whenever it is necessary. Examples of these types of devices are human interfaces and mass storage devices.

Virtual machine bus

The virtual machine bus is the communication medium between the parent partition (hypervisor) and the child partition (VM). VMBus is the backbone of the overall management and data transmission from parent to child, and vice versa. All the instructions go from the parent partition to the child partition via VMBus. If the VM needs to access the DVD-ROM on the hypervisor server, this request from the child partition (VM) to the DVD-ROM will go through VMBus.

Features of Hyper-V

After the introduction and architectural knowledge we gained from the previous topics, let's go forward and get some information about Windows Server 2012 Hyper-V features. We will first take a look at the general features Hyper-V provides as a hypervisor for your server virtualization needs, and then we will discover new features provided by Hyper-V 3.0 with Windows Server 2012.

All these general features were available in the previous version of Hyper-V; among these general features, a few of them have been overhauled and tweaked for better and more reliable service delivery.

Now let's take a look at the following general features, which were introduced with the first version of Hyper-V within Windows Server 2008:

* 64-bit native hypervisor-based virtualization
* Ability to run 32-bit and 64-bit virtual machines concurrently
* Uniprocessor and multiprocessor virtual machines
* Virtual machine snapshots, which capture the state of a running virtual machine
* Snapshots record the system state so that you can revert the virtual machine to a previous state
* Virtual LAN support
* **Microsoft Management Console** (**MMC**) 3.0 management tool
* Documented **Windows® Management Instrumentation** (**WMI**) interfaces for scripting and management
* Integrated cluster support for quick migration of virtual machines
* Virtual machine backups based on **Volume Shadow Copy Service** (**VSS**)
* Fixed (pass-through) disk support

The following are the features added in Windows Server 2008 R2:

- **Cluster Shared Volumes** (**CSV**): These were introduced as a special type of storage for the clustered virtual machine instance, with the support of live migration.

- In addition to quick migration, live migration was added to the inventory of features of Hyper-V, where virtual machines can seamlessly migrate from one host to another host without any network downtime for the VM.

- Dynamic virtual machine storage improvements for virtual machine storage include support for hot plugin and hot removal of the storage on a SCSI controller of the virtual machine. By supporting the addition or removal of virtual hard disks and physical disks while a virtual machine is running, it is possible to quickly reconfigure virtual machines to meet changing requirements.

- Enhanced processor support has up to 64 physical processor cores. This increased support has made it possible to run even more demanding workloads on a single host. In addition to this, Hyper-V also provides support for **Second Level Address Translation** (**SLAT**) and CPU Core Parking. CPU Core Parking allows Windows and Hyper-V to consolidate processing onto the fewest possible number of processor cores, and suspend inactive processor cores. SLAT adds a second level of paging below the architectural x86/x64 paging tables in x86/x64 processors.

- Enhanced networking support for jumbo frames has been extended and is now available on virtual machines (note that this was previously available only in nonvirtual environments). This feature enables VMs to use jumbo frames (up to 9,014 bytes in size) if the underlying physical network supports it.

Now let's take a look at the new features that are provided in Microsoft Windows Server 2012 Hyper-V.

Hyper-V automation with PowerShell

The earlier versions of Windows Server, such as Windows Server 2008 / 2008 R2, allowed administrators to automate various tasks with respect to managing Hyper-V environments using WMI and a portion of Windows PowerShell. But the problem with WMI is that it is designed for developers, and for a server administrator it was a bit difficult to work with. On the other side, PowerShell didn't provide end-to-end automation and support for Hyper-V and virtual machine management related features.

In Windows Server 2012, Microsoft provided full support, through Windows PowerShell, for automation of Hyper-V as the hypervisor and VM-related management tasks. Windows Server 2012 includes 164 built-in PowerShell cmdlets for administrators to work with and customize as per their needs.

Hyper-V dynamic memory improvements

Initially, the Dynamic Memory feature was introduced in Windows Server 2008 R2 SP1, which changed the way Hyper-V virtual machines were assigned virtual memory. And it also gave great flexibility to administrators to dynamically manage the physical server memory between the various virtual workloads in the datacenter.

With the dynamic memory improvements introduced in Windows Server 2012 Hyper-V version 3.0, you can now attain a higher level of consolidation with improved reliability for virtual machine restart operations. There are two main areas of dynamic memory that are improved in Hyper-V version 3.0.

The first one is the availability of the minimum memory feature. Before version 3.0 of Hyper-V, however, only the startup memory setting and maximum memory limit settings were available. Here, the unavailability of the minimum memory limit requires administrators to set the startup memory at a higher level because most of the server-side applications require more memory to be available. Once the virtual machine reaches the stable state and loads all its operations, this higher amount of memory, which is now accessed according to the needs of the virtual machine, stays idle with no utilization.

The problem of giving extra amount of memory to the virtual machine to supply required amount of RAM for the boot processes was addressed by Windows Server 2012 Hyper-V version 3.0, and with the ability to set the minimum RAM to a lower value we can have a separate startup RAM that could be higher. This new feature helped to save the extra memory from staying idle in the virtual machines.

The second major improvement that happened around the dynamic memory concept is second-level paging, which is a cure for problems such as memory shortage. Second-level paging provides an alternate for the memory on a disk, which can be used in case there is no available memory available to give a virtual machine its configured and required startup amount of RAM.

Improved network virtualization and multitenancy

Windows Server 2008 / 2008 R2 fulfilled virtual machine network isolation related requirements with the VLAN concept, but there were a series of problems associated with this solution because there were a number of limitations that made it difficult to provide true isolation between different machines in the cloud and dynamic datacenters. These limitations were as follows:

- Increased risk of an inadvertent outage due to cumbersome reconfiguration of production switches whenever virtual machines or isolation boundaries move in the dynamic datacenter.

- Limited scalability because typical switches support not more than a few thousands of VLAN IDs (maximum of 4,094).

- VLANs cannot span multiple logical subnets, which limits the number of nodes within a single VLAN and restricts the placement of virtual machines based on physical location. Even though VLANs can be enhanced or stretched across physical intranet locations, the stretched VLANs must all be on the same subnet.

In addition to the preceding limitations, there were a series of drawbacks of using VLANs for VM isolation requirements, which are as follows:

- Dynamic or cloud-based environments require readdressing virtual machines

- Security management of virtual machines and policies are based on the IP address of the VM

Windows Server 2012 addressed all these problems, and provided a true virtualized network isolation for virtual workload. Customers who are running Hyper-V in dynamic and cloud-based environments can even use overlapping IP addressing schemes between different VMs. It's a big topic, so we will discuss that in detail in the coming chapters.

Hyper-V data offloading improvements

In the earlier version of Hyper-V Windows Server 2008 / 2008 R2, the method of copying data requires data to be read from and written to different locations, which can be a time-consuming process. Windows Server 2012 introduced a new way to tackle this problem by supporting offloading data transfer operations so that these operations can be passed from the guest operating system to the host hardware. This ensures that the workload can use storage enabled for offloaded data transfer, as it would if it were running in a nonvirtualized environment. The Hyper-V storage stack also issues offloaded data transfer operations during maintenance operations for virtual hard disks, such as merging disks and storage migration meta operations where large amounts of data are moved.

Hyper-V virtual machine replication

This gets me excited, as this feature makes Hyper-V so different and unique from other hypervisors available on the market. This is a brand-new feature; it came with Hyper-V version 3.0. This allows the Hyper-V administrator to set a virtual machine to be replicated to another Windows Server 2012 Hyper-V instance regardless of its location and IP subnet. This feature also supports business continuity and disaster-recovery solutions to critical virtual workloads in virtualized environments.

Resource metering for Hyper-V virtual workloads

In the early days of Hyper-V Windows Server 2008 / 2008 R2, organizations had to implement chargeback mechanisms for Hyper-V virtual workloads using either a third-party or a self-developed solution, which would never be cheap or handy.

With Windows Server 2012, Microsoft introduced native functionalities in Hyper-V for chargeback calculation with historical information. This feature is called Hyper-V resource metering.

Hyper-V support for large-sector disks

With the recent improvements around the storage area, disks are now being shipped with the capabilities to read/write on disk sectors from 512-byte sectors to 4096-byte sectors (also known as 4 KB sectors). This feature enhances disk storage density and reliability. Earlier editions of Hyper-V and Windows Server didn't provide compatibility for this new enhancement, especially in the case of VHD drivers that assume a physical sector size of 512 bytes and issue 512-byte I/Os, which made them incompatible with these disks.

As a result, the current VHD driver cannot open VHD files on physical 4-KB sector disks. Hyper-V makes it possible to store VHDs on 4-KB disks by implementing a software **Read-Modify-Write** (**RMW**) algorithm in the VHD layer to convert the 512-byte access and update request to the VHD file to corresponding with 4-KB accesses and updates.

Virtual Fibre Channel for fabric connectivity

This is one of the coolest features, and one of my favorites. In the earlier versions of Hyper-V, if you wanted to provide a **storage area network** (**SAN**) or **logical unit number** (**LUN**) to a virtual machine, the only method available was to use iSCSI SAN or connect the LUN to the Hyper-V host using Fibre Channel or iSCSI, and from there take the LUN inside the VM using a pass-through disk. But this solution doesn't allow us to assign a LUN directly to the VM, therefore not leveraging the benefits from the Fibre Channel investment that was made.

Hyper-V Windows Server 2012 addressed this problem, and provided a new feature, where an administrator can take advantage of its Fiber Channel SAN, and directly connect the SAN fabric to a virtual machine. You can configure as many as four virtual Fiber Channel adapters on a virtual machine and associate each one with a virtual SAN. Each virtual Fiber Channel adapter connects with one **World Wide Name** (**WWN**) address or two WWN addresses to support live migration. You can set each WWN address automatically or manually.

New virtual hard disk format

In Windows Server 2008 R2 the maximum size of a VHD was 2 TB, but this size was not enough for mission-critical or media-related applications, which store huge amounts of data on a frequent basis. Windows Server 2012 solved this problem by introducing a new virtual hard disk format, VHDX for virtual machines; VHDX has a maximum permissible size of 64 TB.

NIC teaming for host and guest machines

Before the release of Windows Server 2012, in the early operating system version, administrators used to install third-party software for NIC teaming, which was only supported in the physical servers. Most of the time, these third-party NIC teaming and NIC management suites caused compatibility problems with the other installed Microsoft application on the servers, and were difficult to manage.

Windows Server 2012 addressed this problem, and provided a native feature in the operating system to set up the team for the NICs, which is not only supported for the physical boxes but also provides out-of-the-box support for the guest operating systems. This new feature provides both NIC failover and link aggregation (combining the bandwidths) of the NICs.

Hyper-V virtual switch improvements

The Hyper-V infrastructure based on Windows Server 2008 / 2008 R2 had limitations and issues with regards to Hyper-V vSwitch. Customers who were running virtual workloads in tenants and wanted to isolate their virtual machines' communications faced problems such as difficulty in performing QoS and network troubleshooting. Windows Server 2012 Hyper-V addressed all these problems, and came up with a series of new enhancements that catered to all of these requirements. Windows Server 2012 Hyper-V includes an extensible virtual switch feature, which is a layer-two virtual network switch and acts as a bridge between the virtual machine and the physical core network. This extensible virtual switch can also be used in enforcing policies for network-level security, network isolation, and multitenancy support.

This enhanced virtual network switch supports **Network Device Interface Specification (NDIS)** filter drivers and **Windows Filtering Platform (WFP)** callout drivers. This enhanced version of Hyper-V virtual network switch also provides the capabilities for non-Microsoft vendors to build and integrate APIs for rich-level integration with Hyper-V virtual network switches.

Scalable virtualization infrastructure

Hyper-V gained a lot of confidence from its customers after the first release in 2008. And with Dynamic Memory and CSV-based live migration, Hyper-V became a critical component in datacenters, and hypervisor administrators also started treating Hyper-V as a production virtual workload instead of keeping it only for testing virtual machines. But there were some caveats in Hyper-V Windows Server 2008 / 2008 R2 with regards to scaling up the virtual workloads, especially for virtual machines that require extensive amounts of processing and memory. These critical applications are usually **online transaction processing (OLTP)** databases and **online transaction analysis (OLTA)** applications. For another instance, you can take SQL Server as the best example of these resource-hungry applications, which requires a large number of processors and a large amount of RAM. For these types of applications, Hyper-V was failing because of the limits introduced: a maximum of four virtual processors and up to 64 GB of memory.

As a major feature of Windows Server 2012 Hyper-V, it provides support for up to 320 logical processors, and up to 4 TB or more of memory. This series of enhancements made Hyper-V significant in the market as a hypervisor among all other competitors.

Live storage migration

Windows Server 2008 R2 provided a handy way of migrating virtual machines from one Hyper-V host to another, while the virtual machine storage stayed in the same place. This feature helped administrators to migrate workloads in a planned migration window. But when it came to storage migration, no solution was available, except that we shut down the virtual machine and manually copy and paste the virtual machine storage to the target location.

Windows Server 2012 Hyper-V version 3.0 addressed these problems with the improved **Microsoft Cluster Service** (**MSCS**), where Windows Server 2012 supports a clustered virtual machine storage running on a clustered Hyper-V node, and can be migrated from one location to another while the virtual machine is up and running. This feature doesn't stop or save the virtual machine while the users are accessing the virtual machine.

Hyper-V support for SMB

Before the release of Windows Server 2012 Hyper-V version 3.0, virtual machine storage was not supported on a network share (SMB), which was the most awaited feature of Hyper-V. With the release of Windows Server 2012, Microsoft made this available, and now customers can use SMB file sharing for hosting their virtual machine storage files.

We will learn more about this in the coming chapters. So stay tuned.

Hardware requirements

In this section of Hyper-V prerequisites, we will go through the hardware requirements; and some of these requirements are hardcore requirements, meaning you have to have these elements available before you start virtualizing your workload on Hyper-V.

Processor

The difference between the earlier Microsoft virtualization products and Hyper-V is mainly the processor requirements: where the earlier Microsoft virtualization products, such as Virtual PC and Virtual Server, could run on the 32-bit operating system, Hyper-V only works with 64-bit compatible processor hardware. Along with the 64-bit processor available, there are two other elements that are required by Hyper-V in order for the processor to operate; they are as follows:

- **Hardware-assisted virtualization**: The processors that support hardware-assisted virtualization provide an additional privilege mode above Ring 0 (referred to as Ring -1) in which the hypervisor can operate, essentially leaving Ring 0 available for guest operating systems to run. In the market, each processor maker has given different names to its own hardware-assisted virtualization platform, for example, Intel calls it VT, and AMD uses the term AMD-V for it.

- **Hardware-based Data Execution Prevention**: The second requirement of Hyper-V from the processor side is Data Executive Prevention. Hardware-based **Data Execution Prevention (DEP)** allows the processor to mark sections of memory as nonexecutable. This feature is available in processors with AMD NX and Intel XD support.

We can summarize the processor requirements as follows:

- The following are the requirements when working with an Intel processor:
    - x64 processor architecture
    - Support for Execute Disabled Bit
    - Intel® VT hardware virtualization

- The following are the AMD processor's requirements:
    - x64 processor architecture
    - Support for Execute Disable Bit
    - AMD-V® hardware virtualization

Storage

All those storage designs that are supported and workable with Microsoft Windows Server for a particular operating system version are applicable for Hyper-V. But there is a catch—since usage of disk storage changes when it comes to Hyper-V, there are some recommendations that you should consider before you plan and buy hardware for your Hyper-V server.

There will be multiple concurrent sessions on the storage—where a number of virtual machines' virtual storage (VHD, VHDX) will be located—so disk storage with fewer disk spindles will provide poor disk I/O, which will eventually cause poor virtual machine performance. So it is always recommended to use storage with more disk spindles for Hyper-V, which provides better disk I/O, and thus better virtual machine performance.

Let me elaborate this: having more disk spindles means that on your storage side, either your local server storage or SAN storage, you would have more than one disk, and based on your performance and failover requirements you might want to choose an appropriate RAID model for this. So, in this type of setup, more disks would be added to your storage pool and the disk I/O for read/write would be spread across all these disks, which will provide a better resiliency and performance.

Disk types

The type of hard drive added to the host server or to the storage array for the host server, should have significant impact on the overall storage performance. The differential performance factor for the hard disks is the interface architecture (for example, U320 SCSI, SAS, or SATA). The two elements, which are the rotational speed of a hard disk (7200, 10k, or 15k RPM) and the average latency in milliseconds, play a vital part in the overall performance and availability of storage for a hypervisor server. Additional factors, such as the hard disk cache and the support for advanced features, for example, **Native Command Queuing** (**NCQ**), can also be considered as performance improvement factors.

For sound storage planning of the hypervisor and virtual machines, there are a few important elements that should always be carefully evaluated before choosing the right storage for your virtualization stack. These elements are the type of storage, storage IOPs, accepted storage latency, and of course storage size. Mostly, for the virtual machine, storage performance is not the first requirement but the storage size is. From a practical standpoint, I have seen many small, medium, and even large organizations where the hypervisor server has a good number of processors and a large RAM, but due to the unavailability of storage these hardware boxes remain underutilized. Therefore, it is always recommended to go for a bigger size of hard disk instead of finding an expensive one for good performance. Not all the virtual machines need to be placed on a high-speed disk; their OS virtual hard disk (VHD/VHDX) can be placed on a high-speed SATA, and their page file or application/data VHD/VHDX can be placed on a high-speed disk. Utilizing 15k RPM drives instead of 10k RPM drives can result in up to 35 percent more IOPS per drive.

Use the information given next to evaluate the cost/performance tradeoffs.

SATA disks

SATA could be your first choice when considering the Hyper-V storage. Among all other storage types, SATA is the cheapest option, and provides average read/write speed for the data. It is always recommended to go for a higher speed disk if your intended data or workload needs higher performance. SATA disks primarily come with the speed of 1.5 GB/s and 3.0 GB/s.

SAS disks

SAS disks are the next fastest type of disks. If you want fast disks for your highly touched data or accessed virtual machine, then SAS disks would be a standard choice. These disks provide faster I/O response from the read/write activities. Usually, SAS disks come with the rotational speed of 10k to 15k with an average latency speed of 2 to 3 milliseconds.

Fibre Channel disks

Fibre Channel disks perform in a similar way to SAS disks, but have a different interface for connectivity. Since they contain the word "Fibre", their connectivity medium is a fiber cable, which usually connects to the server HBA card on one end, and to the SAN switch on the other. Fibre Channel disks come in both variations of 10k and 15k RPM.

Recommendation
Instead of going to SATA disk, I would recommend going for SAS 15k RPM to 10k RPM disk, which provides better performance.

All of the previously specified storages can be used in the following ways for Hyper-V virtual workloads:

- Pass-through disk
- Fixed disk
- Dynamic disk
- Differential disk

We will discuss all of the preceding storage types in more detail in *Chapter 6, Insight into Hyper-V Storage*.

Memory

When it comes to memory planning, it is always recommended to go for server hardware that provides enough memory expansion and may accommodate your future memory needs. The Dynamic Memory Optimization feature of Windows Server 2008 R2 SP1 took Hyper-V to a new era, where Hyper-V changed the face of how Hyper-V memory assignment was done in VM workloads as compared to how it was done in the legacy Hyper-V versions. Dynamic memory gave a new way for administrators to set dynamic thresholds for VM workloads to start from an initial memory assignment and burst to a certain limit. It is always recommended to go for a larger number of filled memory slot banks for the Hyper-V boxes, because when it comes to the Hyper-V server memory planning, RAM legacy and speed is not much more important than the size. In addition to this, we should also pay attention while buying the server hardware for the Hyper-V role; we should focus on the server boxes that support more memory in terms of quantity, because this is your one-time investment, and buying a server with less support for RAM may end up with your investment having less ROI.

Networking

This is another crucial part: while considering hardware components for Hyper-V implementation, as we discussed previously, disk storage with more spindles is preferred. Due to high I/O utilization, it may provide better and fast response. In the preferred networking selection for Hyper-V, similar recommendations come to those that we saw for storage, where it is recommended to have multiple NICs available to the Hyper-V host.

Here we will see an example. We have an HY-SVR-0001 server, which has one NIC card with 1 Gbps of speed, installed on it. After installing Hyper-V role, we select this NIC and create an external virtual network on Hyper-V from the network manager. Now, this physical NIC is being used for all the virtual machines created on this server. In the initial days, when fewer virtual machines used to be created on Hyper-V, network performance while accessing virtual machines didn't suffer. But with the passage of time, and increasing demand for virtualization and support from the vendors and applications, more virtual machines are being created as compared to earlier. This increasing number of virtual machines need more bandwidth and better network planning for the Hyper-V role. After finding the root cause, the administrator found that the same physical NIC was being used for all the VMs, and on top of it the file server virtual machine's backup along with all virtual machines' backups were also configured on the same physical NIC.

Hence, it is highly recommended to carefully plan your Hyper-V physical network connectivity to the server farm. Depending on your Hyper-V server configuration, you may need to have more than one network configured, among the following network options:

- Cluster private network
- Live migration network
- Hyper-V replica traffic network
- Hyper-V management network
- iSCSI SAN connectivity network

As you can see in the example that we discussed previously, there is plenty of network traffic that our Hyper-V server will be part of; therefore, it is highly recommended to have multiple NICs available in your Hyper-V server so that it can individually cater to these different patterns of traffic. In addition to this, it would also be necessary for you to have teamed Hyper-V NICs for the client connectivity network, where the hosted application or VM may require more bandwidth due to the number of concurrent network connections from the client side.

Software requirements

After discussing the hardware requirements for Hyper-V implementation, we will now go through the software requirements and best practices for Hyper-V.

From Windows Server 2008 to Windows Server 2012, Microsoft changed its licensing scheme; Windows Server 2012 doesn't come as an enterprise edition. There are only two editions of Windows Server 2012 available—Standard and Datacenter. These two editions provide equal features, the only difference is that the Standard edition is for virtualization environments that are not mature, and the Datacenter edition is for highly virtualized environments.

Windows Server 2012 Standard edition gives only one virtual machine license free, while Windows Server 2012 Datacenter edition provides unlimited virtual machine licenses.

Operating system version

The following table shows the list of Microsoft Windows Server operating systems and their versions that can run Hyper-V:

Operating system	Version
Windows Server 2008	Standard, Enterprise, Datacenter, x64 bit
Windows Server 2008 R2	Standard, Enterprise, Datacenter, x64 bit
Windows Server 2012	Standard, Datacenter, x64 bit

Memory

The following are the memory requirements for the Hyper-V host and guest machines:

- Hyper-V host machine
    - ○ For Hyper-V to work properly, we need to have the same amount of minimum memory available as for Windows Server. A minimum of 2 GB memory is required for Hyper-V.
    - ○ Maximum memory per system for Windows Server 2008 R2/R2 SP1 is 1 TB, and for Windows Server 2012 it is 4 TB.
- Hyper-V guest machine:
    - ○ The minimum memory for a guest would be the same as for the Hyper-V server from the operating system perspective, but depending on the workload you can upgrade the memory of the guest machine,
    - ○ The maximum virtual RAM supported on the guest in Windows Server 2008 R2/R2 SP1 is 64 GB, and for Windows Server 2012 it is 1 TB per VM.

Disk space

Installing Microsoft Hyper-V requires 10 GB of disk space on the Server.

A couple of times, I have seen bad Hyper-V designs. In these, after upgrading the server memory or in the initial phase when the server was being sized, people ignored the importance of correctly sizing the hard disk. This would require adding a large amount of RAM afterwards.

We will now discuss the two major factors that may require sizing of disk storage with respect to paging file requirements.

Physical server's paging file requirements

It is a general recommendation and best practice for sizing to have a sufficient amount of server hard disk space for creating the page file for the server operating system. From my experience, I have seen people managing virtual memory (page file) divided into two parts or sometimes more, between various partitions because they didn't have sufficient of disk space in the system partition. Microsoft recommends keeping the paging file in the system partition for better performance. So make sure that if you have 32 GB of physical RAM in your server, you should allow that much free disk space on your server's local disk as well.

In addition to the page file requirement for the page file, we should also consider the free space requirement for each virtual machine that will be running on the same Hyper-V server, because when you give 10 GB of memory to a virtual machine and you turn on this virtual machine, it takes that 10 GB of memory from the same storage where the virtual machine configuration files are created. This is also true for the virtual machine backup requirements; if you are taking a virtual machine's backups using any third-party VSS software solution, there is a certain percentage of disk space that needs to be free for creating a snapshot of the data.

Guest virtual machine's paging file requirements

We saw the paging file's impact on the host server for hard disk space requirement; in the same way, when a guest operating system runs on the Hyper-V server, it takes the same amount of hard disk space as per the virtual memory assigned to the VM. This is the second big mistake I have seen people make in their Hyper-V environment—virtual machine disk storage requirements never included the physical disk space that the VM takes from the Hyper-V to reserve as a virtual memory.

Hyper-V version comparison

Everyone has been witnessing the ongoing improvements seen around Microsoft Server System's products, but when it came to Hyper-V (a new product a few years back), with each release of the product we saw a tremendous amount of improvements and new features to make the product fully equipped with all the features and functionalities required for enterprise-level virtualization management.

To see a complete comparison between Hyper-V version 3.0 and all the previous releases, visit the following URL:

```
http://blogs.technet.com/b/matthts/archive/2012/03/02/installing-
configuring-and-managing-hyper-v-server-8-beta.aspx
```

Hyper-V Windows Server 2012 guest VM support

In this section, we will cover the guest operating systems supported by Windows Server 2012. We will also divide these supported operating systems into two major categories in the server and the client operating systems.

Guest server operating systems

All the following listed server operating systems are supported to be virtualized on Windows Server 2012:

- Windows Server 2012
- Windows Server 2008 R2 with Service Pack 1
- Windows Server 2008 R2
- Windows Server 2008 with Service Pack 2
- Windows Server 2008
- Windows Home Server 2011
- Windows Small Business Server 2011
- Windows Server 2003 R2 with Service Pack 2
- Windows Server 2003 with Service Pack 2
- CentOS 6.0 to 6.2
- Red Hat Enterprise Linux 6.0 to 6.2
- SUSE Linux Enterprise Server 11 Service Pack 2

Guest client operating systems

All the following client operating systems are compatible and supported to be virtualized on Windows Server 2012 Hyper-V:

- Windows 8
- Windows 7 with Service Pack 1

- Windows 7
- Windows Vista with Service Pack 2
- Windows XP with Service Pack 3
- Windows XP x64 Edition with Service Pack 2

Licensing

As we mentioned, Microsoft changed the Windows Server licensing with the release of Windows Server 2012, where now only two editions, Standard and Datacenter, are available for Windows Server 2012. As you have read, Microsoft removed the enterprise edition from the Windows Server licensing catalog. These two available editions are exactly the same in the features provided. The only difference between these two editions is the scope for virtualization.

Windows Server 2012 Standard Edition gives customers only one free license for a virtual machine. Standard edition would be the best choice for companies that are not yet very well matured with respect to their virtualization, and are small in size. On the other side, the Datacenter edition gives customers unlimited virtual machine licenses. This edition is a good choice for enterprises where virtualization is the main infrastructure requirement, and most of their servers and applications are virtualized.

For more information about the Windows Server 2012 licensing, visit the following URL:

```
http://www.microsoft.com/en-us/server-cloud/buy/pricing-licensing.aspx
```

Summary

In this first chapter, we covered the Hyper-V deployment scenario first to get some hot information about where and why to use Hyper-V. This section also provided a great deal of information on how organizations can take advantage of the native hypervisor available in Windows Server, to fulfill their virtualization needs, and how it can also be helpful to set up the disaster recovery and business continuity environments.

In the next section, we moved straight to the Hyper-V architecture to get ourselves familiar with the different types of hypervisors, and see the difference between parent and child partition.

Then, after covering the Hyper-V architecture, we looked closely at the Hyper-V virtual machine service, which is the core engine of Hyper-V, for the management of both parent and child partitions. After discussing VMMS, we discussed the Hyper-V features, where we also compared the features of Windows Server 2012 Hyper-V with its older versions. And finally, we closed this chapter by discussing a few last topics, including Hyper-V hardware, software, and licensing information. With all of these important topics, we made ourselves fully familiar with what Hyper-V offers and we made ourselves ready to take this journey to the next level, where we will examine each Hyper-V pillar and its major service parts individually in the upcoming chapters.

In the next chapter, we will cover the topics of Hyper-V planning, designing, and implementation. These topics will provide all the information needed for us to plan and design our Hyper-V environment. Once the planning and designing part is done, we will also see how to implement Hyper-V in our organization and take care of its basic configuration.

2
Planning, Designing, and Implementing Microsoft Hyper-V

In *Chapter 1, Getting to Know Microsoft Hyper-V*, we covered the fundamental concepts of Hyper-V, where we discussed Hyper-V as a hypervisor for your server virtualization needs. Then we moved on with the discussion of Hyper-V deployment scenarios, for example server consolidation, **physical-to-virtual** (P2V) migration, research and development, business continuity planning and disaster recovery, and cloud computing. With this information, we became familiar with the usage of Hyper-V as a product, and then we moved forward with discussing Hyper-V architecture.

After going through the long journey of introducing Hyper-V as a hypervisor, now in this chapter, we will move forward with the step-by-step phase of planning and designing best practices for a Hyper-V infrastructure. This section will cover all the areas of Hyper-V core components, and will help you plan and design the Hyper-V environment that will best cater to your server virtualization needs. In this chapter we will first start with planning and designing best practices, and then install our first Hyper-V server in both fully GUI-based Windows Server 2012 and Windows Server 2012 Server Core Edition. After the installation of Hyper-V, we will finish this chapter by configuring and discussing the basic options of Hyper-V Server.

Planning and designing Hyper-V infrastructure

If you are referring to this book for starting your first server virtualization and consolidation project, then this section of the book is the important one for the success of your project. Good planning involves taking all infrastructure portions into consideration and ensuring that all project teams have carefully assessed them.

From a real-world standpoint, I have seen many organizations failing to get most out of their virtualization infrastructure because of poor planning at the early stages of their virtualization project. A sound planning process for a virtualization project not only involves sizing and designing your hypervisor server operating system or hardware, but also involves assessing the required infrastructure, for example, storage, server hardware, hypervisor selection, and many more.

Microsoft Solution Accelerators

Good news! If you are not an expert in planning and designing Microsoft-based infrastructure products, or don't want to hire an expensive consultancy firm, then there are guided materials available, which you can follow to make sure that your Hyper-V environment is built upon the best practices and recommendations. Microsoft invested a lot of efforts in developing the planning and designing frameworks for its products. These frameworks are called Microsoft Solution Accelerators. Microsoft worked with several customers, partners, and its own technology experts when developing these solution accelerators. These solution accelerators provide best practices and recommendations for solution planning and designing of different Microsoft products.

There are six distinct types of solution accelerators available, as follows:

- **MAP**: Microsoft Assessment and Planning Toolkit
- **MDT**: Microsoft Deployment Toolkit
- **SCM**: Security Compliance Manager
- **IPD**: Infrastructure Planning and Design Guide
- **MOF**: Microsoft Operations Framework
- **GRC**: Government, Risk, and Compliance Solution Accelerators

All these solution accelerators can be found online at `http://technet.microsoft.com/en-us/solutionaccelerators/bb819696`.

Hyper-V infrastructure planning and designing solution accelerators

As we saw there are various types of Microsoft Solution Accelerators available for the planning and designing best practices for Microsoft products. Now the question is which one should we consider for planning and designing a solution for Microsoft Hyper-V infrastructure? Let's summarize and also provide the links to the solution accelerators available online, which provide out-of-the-box planning and designing best practices for Hyper-V and all the related infrastructure portions, which plays a vital part in the overall solution delivery.

Solution accelerator name	Solution accelerator type	URL Source
Server Consolidation with Hyper-V	**Microsoft Assessment and Planning (MAP)**	`http://technet.microsoft.com/en-us/solutionaccelerators/dd537570`
Microsoft Private Cloud Fast Track	**Microsoft Assessment and Planning (MAP)**	`http://technet.microsoft.com/en-us/solutionaccelerators/hh324976`
Virtualization	**Infrastructure Planning and Design Guide (IPD)**	`http://technet.microsoft.com/en-us/solutionaccelerators/ee395429`

Upgrading legacy Hyper-V servers to Windows Server 2012

In this section we will be covering the upgrading path of the existing legacy Hyper-V server operating system to the latest Windows Server 2012. Let's say in your organization you have two sets of Hyper-V servers. In the first set you have five standalone Windows Server 2008 R2 based Hyper-V hosts, and in the other set of servers, you have a five node Windows Server 2008 R2 Hyper-V failover cluster hosts.

Now your company is planning to move forward with Windows Server 2012 Hyper-V servers, to take advantage of numerous new features added into the Windows Server 2012 Hyper-V version. To continue this section, we have divided this into two parts; in the first part we will see how we can upgrade the standalone Hyper-V hosts to Windows Server 2012 operating system, and in the second part we will see how to upgrade the Hyper-V cluster servers.

Upgrading Hyper-V standalone server

We will see the steps for performing the in-place upgrade of the existing Hyper-V servers to Windows Server 2012. Performing a Hyper-V upgrade is not like Microsoft Exchange or Microsoft SQL Server, because Hyper-V comes as precompiled binaries in the Windows Server operating system. And therefore to upgrade the pre-Windows Server 2012 Hyper-V server hosts, all we have to do is perform the in-place upgrade of the existing Hyper-V server host operating system to the latest Windows Server 2012.

Let me summarize the steps you need to perform in order to upgrade your existing Hyper-V server to Windows Server 2012. The following are the steps for in-place upgrade of Windows Server 2008 / 2008 R2 standalone Hyper-V server:

1. In the case of Hyper-V standalone servers, we recommend performing the backup of the virtual machine, either with the Windows Server backup feature or System Center Data Protection Manager.

> We will discuss backing up Hyper-V virtual machines with Windows Server backup feature and System Center Data Protection Manager in *Chapter 10, Performing Hyper-V Backup and Recovery*.

2. Now we will insert the Windows Server 2012 installation media to the Hyper-V server and start the operating system installation by running the `setup.exe` file from the explorer.

3. Once the setup starts, click on **Next** and continue till you reach the **Select the operating system you want to install** screen; from there you can select either **Windows Server 2012 Server Core** or **Windows Server 2012 Full Installation**.

4. After selecting the operating system, the setup will now ask you whether you want to go for a fresh (new) installation, which means formatting the existing operating system from the system partition, or you want to upgrade the existing operating system. Since we have an existing operating system, we will choose to upgrade.

5. After clicking on the **Upgrade** button, setup will go through a compatibility check of the server and scan for any issues associated with the current server operating system to be upgraded to the newer version.

6. Once the setup completes the compatibility check and finds that the existing operating system and hardware are compatible with Windows Server 2012, the upgrading process will start, which will take some time depending on the server hardware resources.

7. After successful completion of the setup, your existing Hyper-V server will be upgraded to Windows Server 2012 Hyper-V.

Upgrading Hyper-V cluster servers

In the previous section we looked at upgrading the Hyper-V host severs to Windows Server 2012, by performing the in-place upgrade of the operating system to the latest Windows Server 2012. Now, in this section, we will be looking at the upgrading of Hyper-V failover cluster servers. These Hyper-V failover cluster servers could be Windows Server 2008 / 2008 R2.

The recommended way of upgrading the Hyper-V failover cluster servers is not to perform in-place upgrade, but instead of this Microsoft recommends its customers to use Windows Server Migration Tools in Windows Server. Windows Server Migration Tools is part of the Windows Server operating system, and it's been there within various Windows Server operating system releases. We will be migrating Hyper-V server and newer Windows Server 2012 Hyper-V servers, so we will use Windows Server Migration Tool on both source and destination servers.

For a step-by-step guide to upgrade a Windows Server 2008 based Hyper-V cluster server and its data (virtual machines) to Windows Server 2012 Hyper-V, visit the TechNet library at `http://technet.microsoft.com/en-us/library/jj574113.aspx`, which shows the article *Migrate Hyper-V to Windows Server 2012*.

Installing Hyper-V server role

Since we have gone through the planning and designing recommendations and best practices, we will now install our first Hyper-V server. In this section, I will show you various methods of installing Hyper-V server, including installing a fresh Hyper-V server, while considering that you are absolutely new to Hyper-V world, and before that you have never ever installed Hyper-V server. Later on, we will touch the other types of Hyper-V installations, such as upgrading existing Hyper-V server to Windows Server 2012 Hyper-V role. We will also go deeper into the Windows Server Core concepts and see how to install and manage a Windows Server Core installation for Hyper-V server, by adding a Hyper-V role to a Windows Server Core.

Installing Hyper-V Server is not difficult, and can be done in a few steps; but before we install Hyper-V server in our environment, make sure that we have gone through the proper planning and designing exercises to better cater our server virtualization needs.

Hyper-V server role installation requirements

Before we move forward, let's remind ourselves that we have covered Hyper-V Server role based software and hardware requirements in *Chapter 1*, *Getting to Know Microsoft Hyper-V*. So if you would like to refresh your memory, or want to make sure that the necessary software and hardware requirements have already been put in place, and are correct, then revisit *Chapter 1*, *Getting to Know Microsoft Hyper-V*, and assess your host for the Hyper-V server role installation.

Installing a fresh Hyper-V server

Okay, now let's start our journey with some real stuff. We will now go through the steps for installing Hyper-V server role on a Windows Server 2012 machine. We will also see some of the screenshots for the step-by-step installation of Hyper-V server role.

For installing a fresh instance of Hyper-V server on a Windows Server 2012 machine, we first have to install the base operating system, which should meet the system and hardware prerequisites.

Let's see the following steps for installing a fresh copy of Windows Server 2012 operating system for server hardware supported by Hyper-V role. In this example, we will see the steps for installing Hyper-V server role on a GUI-installed instance of Windows Server 2012:

1. Insert the Windows Server 2012 installation media DVD into the server DVD drive.

2. Restart the server. When the server boots up with the DVD, press any key to boot the server with the Windows Server 2012 installation DVD media.

3. Once the server has run the Windows Server 2012 setup, click on **Next** and install the operating system.

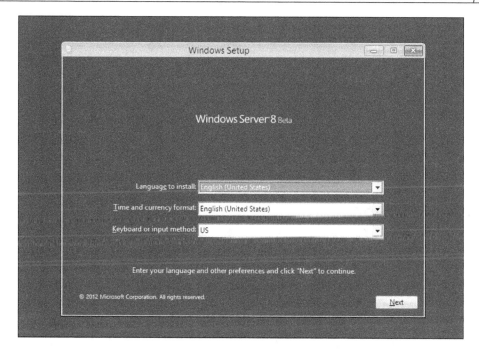

4. In the next step, we have to choose the operating system mode. As we said previously in this example, we will install a GUI mode-based Windows Server 2012 copy.

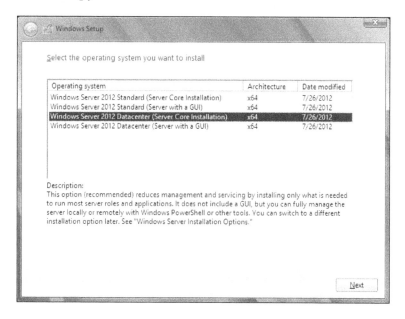

Once the operating system installation is complete, you can give the IP address to the machine and join it to your corporate Active Directory domain. Also note here that it is highly recommended to patch up the newly installed operating system, which fixes a series of known issues and other bugs in the operating system. Upon completion of all other formal server-setup-related activities, we will now go ahead and install the Hyper-V server role.

Before we go and see the steps required to install Hyper-V server role using Server Manager, let's first discuss a little bit about what Server Manager in Windows Server 2012 is.

Server Manager

Server Manager was introduced as a GUI utility for installing server roles and features on Windows Server 2008. So the form of Server Manager utility always existed in Windows Server operating system, but it was never given enough attention. If you remember the days of Windows Server 2003, where if we had to install the web server, we used to go to the **Add or Remove Programs** wizard in **Control Panel**, and from there we could select the IIS features to be added.

To make it handy for the administrators to assign server roles and install various Windows Server features on the Windows Server operating system, Microsoft introduced the Server Manager utility in Windows Server 2008, which divided server roles and operating system features into two parts. The same legacy is now followed in Windows Server 2012, but with more intelligence and automation. This newer version of Server Manager gives new ways to the administrator to manage and assign roles and services to the Windows Server operating system. The difference between these two different versions of Server Manager in the previous edition and the new Windows Server 2012 edition is that this new Server Manager provides more features and functionalities for managing server roles and feature installations in the bulk of servers.

While using Server Manager for installing Hyper-V role on Windows Server 2012 in the example ahead, we will show you how we can use Server Manager for installing server roles.

 To learn more about Server Manager, visit
http://technet.microsoft.com/en-us/library/hh831456.aspx.

Installing Hyper-V role using Server Manager

In the following steps, we will install the Microsoft Hyper-V server role on a
Windows Server 2012 GUI installation:

1. After logging in to the Windows Server 2012 box, Open **Server Manager** by
    clicking on the **Server Manager** icon in the upper-left corner:

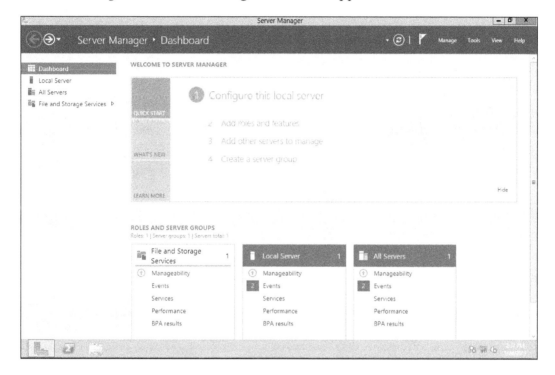

2. Now click on **Add roles and features** from the quick start ribbon of
    Server Manager.

3. On the **Add Roles and Features Wizard** window, click on **Next** and select
    Role-based installation or **Feature-based installation**, and click on **Next**.

4. From the list of servers, select the one on which you want to install the Hyper-V role; since we are doing this on the local server, you will find it already listed there.

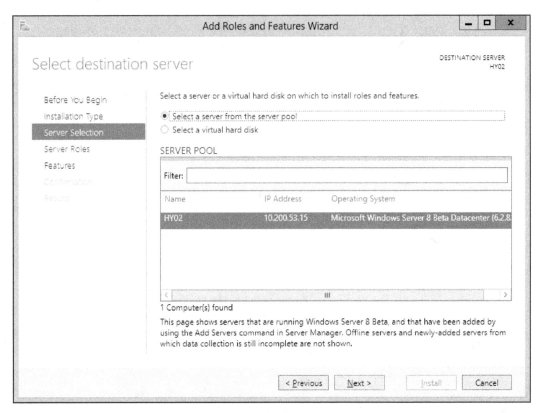

5. After selecting the server and upon clicking on **Next**, you will be presented with the list of server roles, and from there you can choose the Hyper-V role. Once you select the Hyper-V role, **Server Manager** will present you with all the related Hyper-V features, which are needed and are pending, before the installation of Hyper-V role. Click on the **Add Features** button to agree to the installation of these required features.

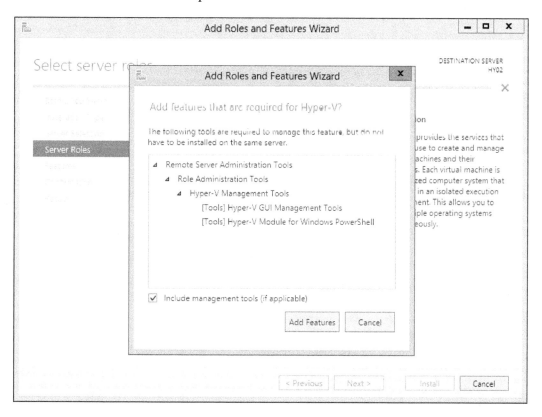

6. Once you click on the **Add Features** button and then on **Next, Server Manager** will present you with the **Create Virtual Switches** screen that (virtual switches are also called virtual networks). This area of the Hyper-V server role will allow you to create virtual switches, and bind them with the physical NIC of the server.

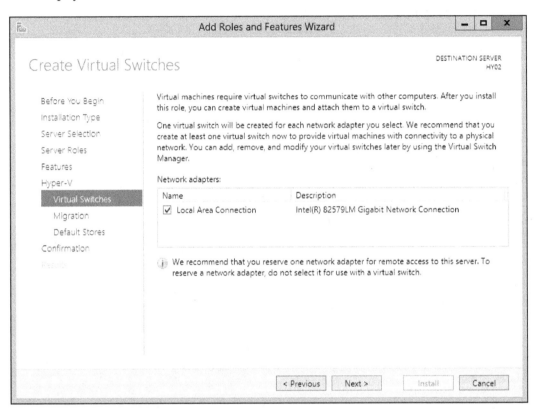

Windows Server 2012 provides an out-of-the-box NIC teaming feature, which provides link aggregation and fault tolerance for Hyper-V networking. To read more about NIC teaming feature, see the details in *Chapter 3, Setting Up Hyper-V Replication*.

7. Upon clicking on the **Next** button to create or ignore virtual switch creation, **Server Manager** will take you to the next subcategory, that is, configuration of the virtual switch, that lets you configure the **Virtual Machine Migration** settings, which means you can configure the Hyper-V server to allow it to send and receive live migration requests. At this moment, we will ignore the settings and configure it later.

8. The next step will ask you to set the default store for **Virtual Machine Configuration** and **Virtual Machine Hard Disk** location on the server, which you can either keep as default or change it if you want.

9. Finally, **Server Manager** will ask you to confirm the installation selection you made, and also provide you with a feature to be selected, which will automatically restart the server after the successful installation of the Hyper-V role.

After completing all the steps for adding Hyper-V role, Server Manager will take some time to complete the installation and restart the server. Once the server comes online, you can go and open the **Hyper-V** snap-in from **Administrative Tools**.

With the completion of this task, we have successfully installed the Hyper-V role on a newly installed Windows Server 2012 operating system.

Installing Hyper-V with Windows Server Core

In this section of installing Hyper-V with Windows Server Core, we will see the steps required for installing Hyper-V role on a Windows Server 2012 Server Core Edition. There are two methods and styles of installation available for Windows Server 2012. In the first type of installation, which is a traditional type, we get a **graphical user interface (GUI)** for managing the server roles and various installed applications on the server. In the second type of installation, we install Windows Server 2012 in a command-line style. This command-line style installation doesn't provide a GUI, but allows the administrator to manage the server using the command line or can be managed through remote management utilities. We will discuss more about Server Core Edition in the next section.

Introducing Windows Server Core

Before Windows Server 2008, all Microsoft Windows Server edition products, such as Windows NT Server, Windows Server 2000, and Windows Server 2003, came with full installation mode. This means when you install these operating systems, you get a GUI mode when the server starts. Just like Linux, that gives you the option to select whether you want to install the operating system with the **command-line interface (CLI)** or along with the **graphical user interface (GUI)**. The main purpose of having an operating system with only the CLI mode installed is to have minimal services running on the operating system, and to minimize the attack surface of the system. The earlier versions of Windows Server, as we specified, didn't have this feature, where users had to install Windows Server with full installation.

Microsoft has always been involved in bringing new enhancements to its server operating system, and securing the operating system platform by reducing the attack surface. With Windows Server 2008, Microsoft introduced a new Windows Server running mode, which was **Server Core**. Server Core has a similar concept to Linux Server running in CLI mode only, where Server Core allows a Windows Server installation to run only the minimal required services on it, and we can only administer the server using the command shell. Among all the benefits of selecting Server Core installation for Hyper-V server role, the most important benefit is that Windows Server Core Edition helps us minimize the attack surface by only installing the necessary components for running the required server role and features. While on the other side, using a traditional GUI or full installation of Windows Server makes it easier for the attacks to take place due to the wide variety of services running on the system.

For example, if you select to install the Hyper-V server role on Server Core, you will install only the services that are required to run the Hyper-V server on the operating system. Once you have installed the Hyper-V role, you can remotely manage the Hyper-V role and virtual machines using the **Hyper-V Manager** snap-in.

Another way of managing a Windows Server Core based Hyper-V server is using **Remote Server Administration Tools** (**RSAT**) for Windows 7 that is SP1 enabled and Windows 8. RSAT provides all the Windows Server management snap-ins on the Windows client operating system. Using Windows 7 RSAT we cannot manage Windows Server 2012 based server roles, and therefore we need to have Windows 8 based RSAT. Managing Hyper-V Server Core Edition and full installation of Hyper-V with RSAT is a good choice for small-to-medium size organizations. But in enterprise-level organizations, where we talk about hundreds of Hyper-V servers with thousands of virtual machines, we have considered managing Hyper-V infrastructure with an enterprise virtualization management platform, such as System Center Virtual Machine Manager (**SCVMM**). SCVMM is a part of the System Center 2012 suite, and provides awesome capabilities for managing not only Hyper-V but also VMware and Citrix Xen hypervisors. We will get to know more about SCVMM in *Chapter 7, Managing Hyper-V with System Center Virtual Machine Manager*.

 You can download Remote Server Administration Tools for Windows 8 from http://www.microsoft.com/en-gb/download/details. aspx?id=28972.

Now since we have understood the definition of Windows Server Core Edition, let's ask ourselves this question: Why should we choose Windows Server Core Edition instead of Windows Server full installation for Hyper-V server role, or any other Windows Server role service?

Benefits of using Windows Server Core Edition

The question why we should choose Windows Server Core over Windows Server full installation for Hyper-V or other server roles offered by Windows Server 2012, can be answered by seeing the following benefits of using Windows Server Core Edition:

- **Reduced total cost of ownership**: Fewer applications and services are installed on a server running the Server Core Edition, which leads to decrease in total cost of ownership for server administrators.

- **Less physical disk space required on server**: A Server Core installation requires only about 3.5 GB of disk space to install and approximately 3 GB for operations after the installation, which is low compared to the full installation of Windows Server.

- **Decrease in maintenance**: Server Core Edition installation option installs only what is required to have a manageable server for the supported roles, and therefore less maintenance is required than on a full installation of Windows Server 2008.

- **Better protection and decrease in the attack surface**: As Windows Server Core Edition runs only the minimal number of services on the server, the attack surface of the operating system decreases.

- **Less hardware resources utilization**: As mentioned before, Windows Server Core Edition takes less hard disk space for storing the binaries of the operating system. In the same way, Server Core Edition also consumes less physical memory from the available memory for its core operations. It also helps the operating system to request less processor cycles, because the smaller number of applications, services, and especially the unavailability of the GUI doesn't require an extensive number of processor cycles.

Installing and managing Windows Server Core

Okay, now let's install Windows Server 2012 Server Core operating system for our Hyper-V server role installation; the following steps will describe the method of installing Windows Server 2012 Server Core Edition:

1. Insert the Windows Server 2012 installation media DVD.

2. Start the server and let the server boot with Windows Server 2012 installation DVD.

3. Once the server is booted with Windows Server 2012 installation DVD, click on **Next** and go to the **Select the operating system you want to install** screen, and then select **Windows Server 2012 Datacenter (Server Core Installation)**, as shown in the following screenshot:

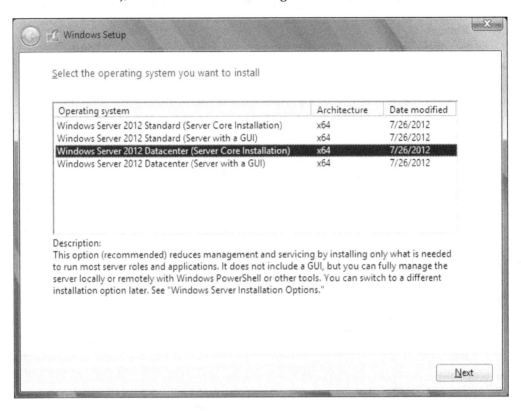

4. When the installation is complete, it will ask you to change the administrator password, and right after that, instead of having GUI loading, you will see a Windows command prompt opening for you.

Configuring and managing Windows Server 2012 Server Core

Now what shall we do next to give an IP address to our newly installed Windows Server 2012 Server Core instance? How do we change the server name, how do we join the server to the domain, and most importantly how do we enable remote administration capabilities?

Well, to answer all the preceding questions, let me show you a utility available in Windows Server Core, which helps you configure all these initial settings for your Windows Server and allows you to manage the Server Core instance remotely.

We are talking about SCONFIG. **SCONFIG** allows you to quickly set up the initial settings for the server, including setting IP address, changing server name, joining the server to the domain, and allowing remote administration capabilities. You can run SCONFIG by typing `sconfig` in the command prompt of Windows Server – Server Core, as shown in the following screenshot:

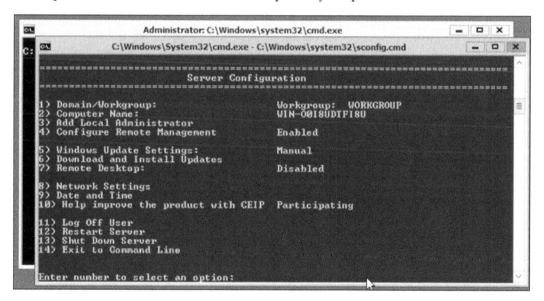

Upon opening SCONFIG from the Server Core command shell, we can set all the initial parameters for the server to become part of your production network.

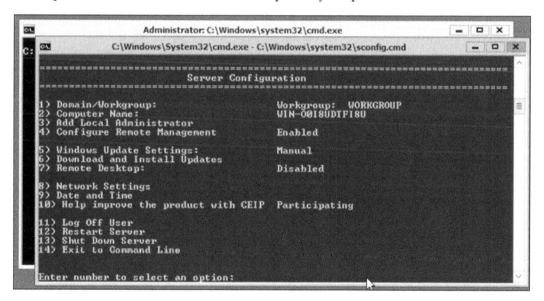

With the provided settings from the SCONFIG, you can configure the following settings in order to bring the server up, join it to the domain, and allow remote administration:

- **Date and Time**: Making correction to the server time and date
- **Network Settings**: For giving an IP address to the server
- **Computer Name**: For changing the default server name

- **Configure Remote Management**: For allowing remote administration
- **Domain/Workgroup**: For joining the server to your Active Directory domain

 It is highly recommended to install the Windows updates to the server after the operating system installation, whether it's Server Core or full installation. This practice of installing updates right after Windows installation saves a lot of your time from being hit later, after making this newly installed server part of your production network environment.

Adding Hyper-V server role for Windows Server Core

In the previous step, we gave an IP address to our newly installed Windows Server 2012 – Server Core Edition server, and also joined it to our corporate Active Directory domain. We also allowed the server to be remotely administered.

Now the next step is to add the Hyper-V role to this server, which can be done from any other GUI-based Windows Server. The following steps can be followed to add the Hyper-V role to our newly installed Windows Server 2012 – Server Core instance:

1. Open **Server Manager** on any other Windows Server 2012 GUI full installation instance. It could be physical or virtual.

2. From **Server Manager**, you can right-click on the local server name, and connect it to the remote server.

3. In the **Remote server name** box, you can either enter the IP address or the FQDN of your newly installed Windows Server 2012 Server Core Edition.

4. Once **Server Manager** successfully gets connected to the Server Core Edition instance, you can click on **Roles** and add the Hyper-V role.

5. This will take some time and also restart the server to complete the installation of the role.

Configuring basic settings for Hyper-V server role

Since we have now learned how to install a Hyper-V server, let's go and configure a few basic settings of Hyper-V, such as creating our first virtual machine. To do this, let's open our **Hyper-V Manager** for first time. Locate the **Hyper-V Manager** snap-in by navigating to **Control Panel | Administrative Tools**.

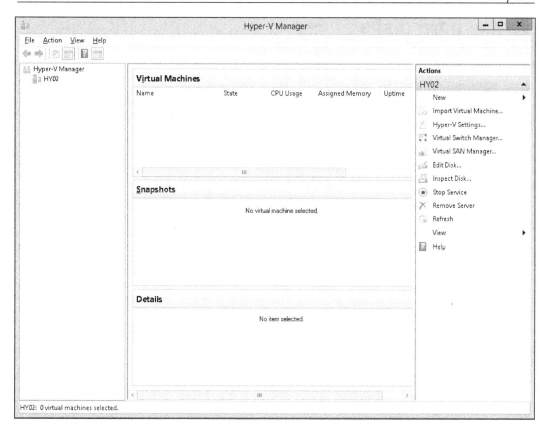

We will now move ahead with configuring a few of the basic settings of our Hyper-V server.

Hyper-V settings

As the first step, I always recommend to configure the settings of the newly installed Hyper-V server. The **Hyper-V settings configuration** window allows you to configure all the basic environmental settings for your Hyper-V server. Especially with Windows Server 2012 Hyper-V, most of the newly added features first need to be configured on the Hyper-V server as a server configuration, and only then can you use them.

Now we will go through all the basic Hyper-V server configuration settings available via the **Hyper-V Manager** console.

Virtual hard disks

This setting allows you to specify a default storage location for the virtual hard disk (VHD/VHDX) files. If you don't change the default path, the Hyper-V Manager on this server will present the default path, which is `C:\Users\Public\Document\Hyper-V\Virtual Hard Disks`, whenever you create a new VHD/VHDX file,. For details about the virtual hard disk see *Chapter 6, Insight into Hyper-V Storage*.

> As a best practice and recommendation, virtual hard disk (VHD/VHDX) files should always be placed on the different partition or hard disk than the system partition or operating system hard disk. Placing VHD/VHDX file on the OS partition/hard disk can cause performance issues for the operating system of the Hyper-V server. In the case of OS corruption and reinstallation of Hyper-V server, keeping virtual hard disk files on the Hyper-V server's OS disk can cause issues of these virtual hard disk files getting deleted, while reinstalling the operating system.

Virtual machines

Just like we saw the possibility of changing the default path for the virtual hard disk files, Hyper-V allows you to change and specify the default location for creating the virtual machine configuration file. It is also a good practice to change the default path for better manageability.

Physical GPUs

Let's first see what a GPU is **GPU** stands for **graphics processing unit**. Like the **CPU** (**central processing unit**), it is a single-chip processor. However, the GPU is used primarily for computing 3D functions. This includes things such as lighting effects, object transformations, and 3D motion. Because these types of calculations are rather taxing on the CPU, the GPU can help the computer run more efficiently.

We can allocate these types of extra features to a virtual machine, when there is such need for extra processing, which might not be provided in the default configurations. If your Hyper-V server hardware does support GPU, then you can leverage the RemoteFX feature. RemoteFX was introduced in Windows Server 2008 R2 SP1. It introduces a set of end-user experience enhancements for **Remote Desktop Protocol (RDP)** that create a rich desktop environment within your corporate network.

NUMA spanning

Non-Uniform Memory Access (NUMA) is a computer memory design used in multiprocessing, where the memory access time depends on the memory location relative to a processor. Under NUMA, a processor can access its own local memory faster than nonlocal memory, that is, memory local to another processor or memory shared between the processors.

Before you select the server hardware that you are going to use for your Hyper-V environment, you should first always check whether it supports NUMA architecture. NUMA adds a considerable amount of server hardware optimization for a virtualization stack. If it is enabled, it allows Hyper-V server to run more virtual machines at the same time. It can also provide a virtual machine with more memory than is available on the single NUMA node.

Live migrations

We will see in the upcoming chapter how the Hyper-V Windows Server 2012 live migration feature changes the face of Hyper-V live migration, as compared to the early versions of Hyper-V. Live migration is a feature, where an administrator can migrate a running virtual machine from one Hyper-V server to another, without affecting the virtual machine availability. With Hyper-V Windows Server 2012, Microsoft removed the dependency of having a shared storage between two Hyper-V nodes to leverage the functionality of live migration. Removing this dependency has allowed Hyper-V customers to perform live migration of their production workload at any time to any Hyper-V Windows Server 2012 Server.

Live migration settings allow you to enable or disable live migration functionality on the particular Hyper-V server. In addition to this, they also allow you to configure the preferred authentication protocol for live migration, set the allowed number of concurrent live migrations, and the dedicated IP address/interface for live migration. We will discuss live migration in detail in *Chapter 8, Building Hyper-V High Availability and Virtual Machine Mobility*.

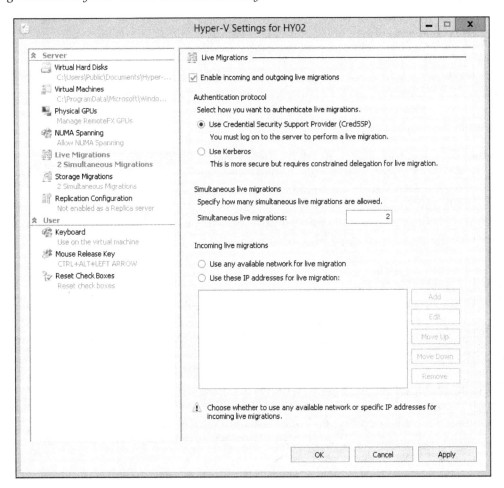

Storage migrations

Storage migration settings are the same as live migration settings that allow you to configure the allowed number of simultaneous storage migrations you can perform on the Hyper-V server. We will cover storage migration and related configuration in *Chapter 8, Building Hyper-V High Availability and Virtual Machine Mobility*.

Replication configuration

This setting allows you to configure the Hyper-V virtual machine replication. By default replication is not enabled on the Hyper-V server, so if you want to enable certain Hyper-V servers to have replication functionality, you may enable it explicitly on the specific Hyper-V servers.

This setting also lets you customize your Hyper-V replication configuration by allowing you to set the ports for Hyper-V replication for better replication functionality management. It also gives you the flexibility to manually allow certain Hyper-V servers to send their replication stream to particular Hyper-V servers, or alternatively you can configure your Hyper-V server to receive replication stream from any Hyper-V server.

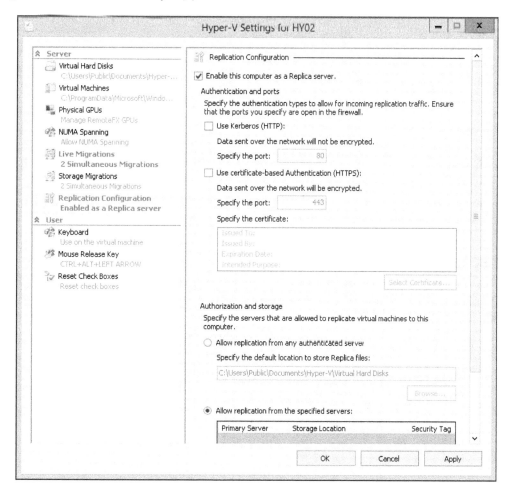

Once you set all these preceding important settings for your Hyper-V server, there are few other settings for customizing your Hyper-V Manager experience, which you may configure as per your requirement. The settings are as follows:

- **Keyboard**
- **Mouse Release Key**
- **Reset Check Boxes**

Virtual Switch Manager

After completing the initial settings for Hyper-V server, we will now configure Hyper-V virtual switch configuration, to allow the virtual machines to be created on the particular Hyper-V server to communicate with other virtual machines and network entities.

You can start configuring Hyper-V virtual switch by opening Virtual Switch Manager from **Hyper-V Manager**.

 We will not be able to cover everything related to Hyper-V virtual network switch, because it is a big topic. We will cover it separately in *Chapter 4, Understanding Hyper-V Networking*.

Since we have completed the initial configuration of our Hyper-V server, we will now go and create a virtual machine.

Creating a virtual machine

In the following steps we will see how to create a virtual machine on a Windows Server 2012 Hyper-V server. To create a virtual machine you can use either Hyper-V Manager or Windows PowerShell. But here we will only see the GUI-based creation of a virtual machine. The PowerShell method of creating a virtual machine is explained in *Chapter 5, A New World of Hyper-V Automation with PowerShell*.

1. Open **Hyper-V Manager** from Windows by navigating to **Start | Administrative Tools**.

2. From the right-hand side action pane, click on **New** and select **New virtual machine**.

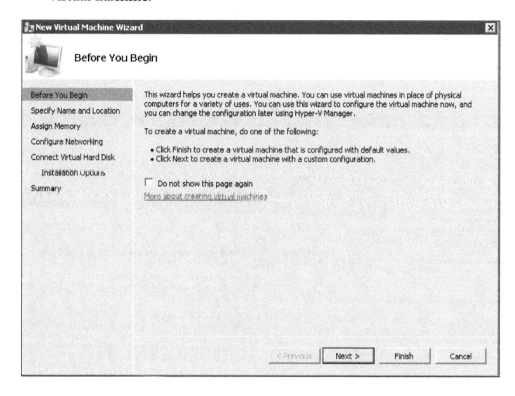

3. On the **New Virtual Machine Wizard** window, click on **Next**.

4. Now we have to specify the name of the virtual machine and the location for the virtual machine configuration files.

5. Assign static memory to the virtual machine.

This initial wizard for creating a virtual machine doesn't allow you to configure the dynamic memory for the virtual machine. So if you have a plan to assign dynamic memory to a virtual machine, initially you can set the static RAM, and later on from the virtual machine settings you can change it to dynamic RAM.

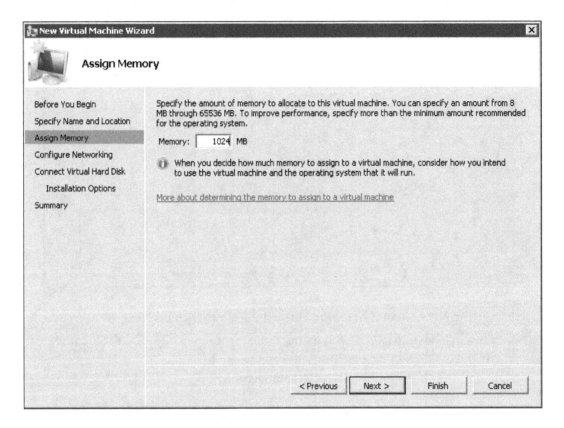

6. On the **Configure Networking** page, Hyper-V will allow you to select one of the precreated virtual network switches to connect your VM NIC.

 If you have a plan to add multiple NICs to your virtual machine, you can add them from the virtual machine settings later on after creating the virtual machine using this wizard.

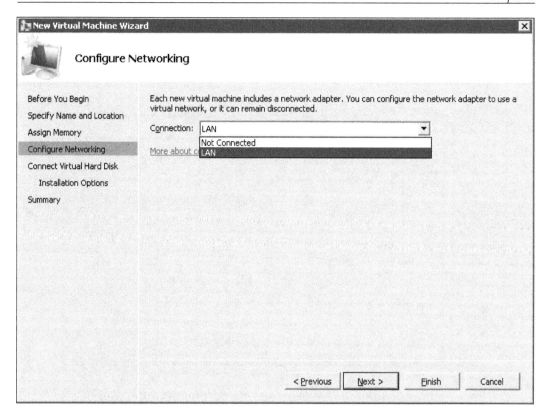

7. **New Virtual Machine Wizard** gives us the three following ways of connecting a virtual hard disk to a virtual machine:

   ° **Create a virtual hard disk**: This option only allows you to create dynamic virtual hard disk. A dynamic virtual hard disk initially gets created with a small size, and over time it grows upon adding more data to the virtual hard disk.

   ° **Use an existing virtual hard disk**: Using an existing virtual hard disk allows you to assign a precreated virtual hard disk to a virtual machine, or assign a virtual hard disk of a virtual machine that was created and set up earlier.

   ° **Attach a virtual hard disk later**: Use this case, if you wish to select and assign a VHD to a virtual machine later and go forward now.

The following screenshot shows the preceding options:

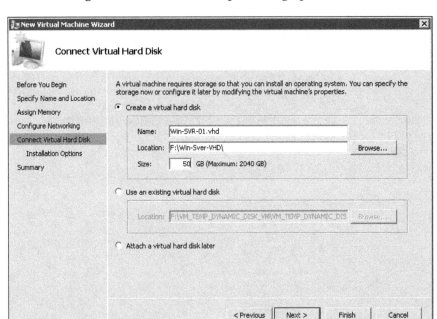

8. For installing an operating system on your virtual machine, you may select various available options, as follows:

    ○ **Install an operating system later**

    ○ **Install an operating system from a boot CD/DVD-ROM using physical DVD ROM of a Hyper-V box, or you can specify a ISO image file**

    ○ **Install an operating system from a boot floppy disk**

    ○ **Install an operating system from a network-based installation server**

9. On completing the **New Virtual Machine Wizard** page, you will get the summary of all the configurations you have set for creating new virtual machines.

Now since we have created a new virtual machine, let's go to the virtual machine settings to customize the configuration for the virtual machine. You can use virtual machine settings to customize the configuration of virtual machines, where the virtual machine settings customizing wizard allows you to add and remove hardware resources, which the initial **New Virtual Machine Wizard** doesn't provide.

To open virtual machine settings, you can either right-click on the virtual machine and click on **Settings**, or you can highlight the virtual machine in **Hyper-V Manager** and from the action pane on the right-hand side click on **Settings**.

Anytime after creation of the virtual machine, we can go to **Hyper-V Manager**, select the specific virtual machine and right-click on the virtual machine, and then click on the **Settings** tab for modifying the virtual machine settings.

There are several settings we can set from the virtual machine settings page, but here we will discuss only those that are not available in **New Virtual Machine Wizard**.

Memory

A Hyper-V virtual machine can have either static memory or dynamic memory configured for it. While creating a virtual machine using Hyper-V Manager, earlier we were not allowed to configure dynamic memory for a virtual machine. This problem got addressed in Windows Server 2012. Now while creating the virtual machine, we saw in the previous screenshot that we were able to set a virtual machine for dynamic memory during the creation wizard.

Dynamic memory for a virtual machine can be tweaked by taking the virtual machine properties and changing the required parameters from the virtual machine settings.

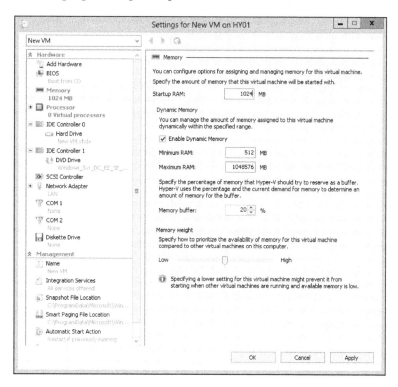

Processor

By default when you create a new virtual machine, it gets a single virtual processor from Hyper-V; but using virtual machine settings, we can specify multiple processors for a virtual machine.

Hard drive

As we saw in the new virtual machine configuration wizard, it gives us the ability to create only a dynamic disk and other options are included to either select an existing virtual hard disk or you can create a virtual hard disk later.

So using virtual machine settings, we can now create a new virtual hard disk, which will allow us to create more types of disks, especially the fixed disk. Fixed disks provide better performance, while dynamic disks are not known for good performance.

Summary

This chapter mainly focused on two areas, first on the planning and designing steps of Hyper-V implementation, and secondly we discussed the different types of Hyper-V installation. In the planning and designing section, we discussed the various steps, which are highly critical to Hyper-V infrastructure and are also the key factors that measure the success of the project.

In these steps of planning and designing Hyper-V infrastructure, we saw the benefits of Microsoft Solution Accelerators series for Windows Server 2012 and Hyper-V. These solution accelerators provide precooked information on all levels of Hyper-V and Windows Server for providing an effective and efficient virtualization platform. Later on in this chapter, we discussed the various types of installation of Hyper-V Windows Server 2012, where we first saw how we can perform a clean installation of Hyper-V on Windows Server 2012 in GUI mode. We then moved to a scenario where we upgraded a pre-Windows Server 2012 Hyper-V version to Windows Server 2012 Hyper-V server. Finally, we saw what Windows Server 2012 Server Core Edition is, and then we installed Hyper-V role on a Windows Server 2012 Server Core instance. At the end of the chapter, we saw how to create a new virtual machine, and also discussed briefly how we can tweak the virtual machine settings.

In the next chapter we will cover one of the hottest features of Windows Server 2012 Hyper-V, which is Hyper-V Replica. Hyper-V Replica provides a method of replicating one Hyper-V virtual machine and its data to other Hyper-V Replica servers.

3
Setting Up Hyper-V Replication

In this chapter we will introduce Hyper-V replication, which is also called Hyper-V Replica. Hyper-V Replica was first introduced within Windows Server 2012 Hyper-V. This new feature allows an administrator to replicate a production virtual machine from one Hyper-V server to another Hyper-V Replica server in the same site or any other site. The Hyper-V Replica feature provides a great level of disaster recovery and business continuity capabilities, where critical workload can be set to replicate to any Hyper-V server based on Windows Server 2012, regardless of its location and administrative boundary. Once the virtual machine is being replicated to the Hyper-V Replica server, an administrator can anytime perform a planned or unplanned failover, in which the replicated instance of the virtual machine is mounted on the Hyper-V Replica server. We will go deeper into the Hyper-V Replica architecture, and also see all its related components in the upcoming sections of this chapter.

In this chapter, after introducing Hyper-V Replica, we will go through the configuration steps for setting up Hyper-V Replica after first discussing the network best practices for virtual machine replication. Network best practices for deploying virtual machine replication using Hyper-V Replica are a critical component of your Hyper-V Replica planning phase, since you will be replicating your virtual machine workload data over an IP network. So the network availability and optimization are two of the highly critical factors for your planning consideration, and they should be addressed carefully. After seeing the network best practices for Hyper-V Replica deployment, we will see the steps for configuring Hyper-V Replication for a standalone Hyper-V server. We will also see how we can configure Hyper-V Replication for Hyper-V failover clustered servers. Once our Hyper-V servers are configured to the Hyper-V Replica feature's prerequisites, we will move ahead and set the virtual machine to start replicating from a Hyper-V server to the Hyper-V Replica server.

Maintaining the sound availability of information systems, or any other type of electronic or mechanical systems, requires proactive monitoring and checking. Therefore, after we complete the configuration part of Hyper-V Replica for the virtual machines, we will move to the next topic where we will discuss the monitoring of a Hyper-V Replica environment.

Introducing Hyper-V replication

In the first section of this chapter, we will go through an introduction to Hyper-V Replica. This section will provide an in-depth knowledge about Hyper-V Replica and all its related components. We will discuss the Hyper-V Replica architecture to understand the logic behind the scenes. Once we are familiar with the core architecture of Hyper-V, we will move forward with a discussion of the deployment scenarios of Hyper-V Replica in today's server-virtualized environments. We will also understand the hardware and software requirements for running the Hyper-V replication feature. And last but not least, we will see the security considerations of running Hyper-V Replica in our virtualized environments.

Hyper-V Replica uses an asynchronous replication mode to transfer VM-related changes from one Hyper-V server to the Hyper-V Replica server over a normal TCP/IP network. This approach of replicating your production workload VM-related data to another Hyper-V server gives an efficient disaster recovery and business continuity protection to the virtualized infrastructure.

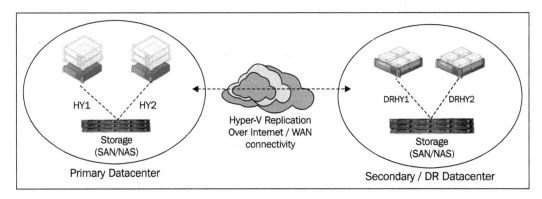

An organization can take advantage of the Hyper-V Replica feature without purchasing any expensive hardware appliance or software for providing VM-level disaster recovery. An organization doesn't need to have the same identical hardware for both the Hyper-V servers for replicating the virtualized workload data from one Hyper-V server to another. All we need to have is Windows Server 2012 as the operating system, because the earlier version of Hyper-V Windows Server doesn't support the Hyper-V Replica feature. Hyper-V Replica is a global feature, which you enable on the Hyper-V server by allowing the Hyper-V server to receive the replication stream from any Hyper-V server. Or, you can specify a selected Hyper-V server, which can replicate its virtual machine data to your Hyper-V server.

In the event of a disaster at a primary site, an administrator can restore a virtual machine from the replicated data on the Hyper-V Replica server to a point in time depending on the recovery history selection for the virtual machine.

One of the great features that Hyper-V Replica provides to its customers is to build enterprise-level disaster recovery and business continuity for critical workloads. Another benefit is that Hyper-V Replica provides a handy way to move a virtual machine, where an administrator can perform a planned or unplanned failover of a replicated instance of the virtual machine regardless of the Hyper-V Replica server's location of a part as the network.

Hyper-V Replica terminologies

As we are going forward with learning the architecture of Hyper-V Replica, it is imperative for us to first familiarize ourselves with the various terminologies related to Hyper-V Replica. We also need to understand the architecture of the different components associated with the virtual machine replication technology.

The following table explains some of the terms related to Hyper-V Replica:

Term	Definition
Recovery time objective (RTO)	The recovery time objective is the duration of time within which a business process must be restored after a disaster (or disruption) in order to avoid unacceptable consequences associated with a break in business continuity. This can also be referred to in business terms as a **service-level agreement (SLA)**.
Recovery point objective (RPO)	The recovery point objective describes the acceptable amount of data loss measured in time.

Term	Definition
Application-consistent replica	This is recovery to a point in time that is consistent from the application's perspective. To accomplish this, the **Volume Shadow Copy Service** (**VSS**) is used.
Standard replica	This is a crash-consistent replica of the primary virtual machine.
Primary server	This is the Hyper-V machine (Hyper-V failover cluster) that hosts virtualized production workloads.
Replica server	This is the Hyper-V machine (Hyper-V failover cluster) that hosts the replica virtual machines for a primary server.
Planned failover	A planned failover is a controlled event where an administrator gracefully moves a virtual machine from a primary site to a replica site.
Failover	A failover is an unplanned event where the primary site experiences a problem and the replica virtual machines have to be brought online at a replica site.
Test failover	This is a process that an administrator executes on a replica virtual machine to verify its functionality.

Software requirements

There is no special software requirement for installing and running Hyper-V Replica; all you need to have is a Windows Server 2012 Hyper-V role installed. If you want to use SSL certificate based authentication for encrypting the replicated data between two Hyper-V servers for your virtual machine replication traffic, you are required to have a certificate. You can either use your internal Microsoft **certification authority** (**CA**) certificate or you can purchase a third-party CA certificate. The latter one is preferred if you are planning to replicate your virtual machine data over a public medium such as the Internet.

Hardware requirements

We mentioned about the software requirements in the preceding section. Similarly, there are no special requirements for the hardware section, as the Hyper-V Replica feature can work with any hardware topology where Hyper-V is running and supported.

Deployment scenario for Hyper-V Replica

After taking a look at the introduction to Hyper-V Replica and understanding the basic definition of what Hyper-V Replica is, let's now take a look at the deployment scenario for the Hyper-V Replica feature.

There are four major deployment scenarios, which we will discuss next.

Head office and branch office

This is one of the most common usages of the Hyper-V Replica feature, where small-to-medium size organizations have a central datacenter located in their head offices, and also have one or more in branch offices. Due to their small- to medium-sized business scale, these types of organizations cannot afford expensive, high-availability solutions. While implementing the Hyper-V Replica feature, they can easily build a disaster recovery instance of their critical services by running in either the primary or secondary datacenter.

Due to the flexible architectural requirement of Hyper-V Replica, it takes less effort and time to start replicating critical workloads to the remote Hyper-V server. It is always recommended to have a primary failover of a service or virtual machine in the primary datacenter, but what if the entire datacenter goes down? In such a case where your primary datacenter is completely down, you might take some time to think. Let's build such an environment where a virtual machine can be mounted and resume from the disaster recovery site. In this case, the Hyper-V Replica feature works very well to help organizations to set up their disaster recovery in the remote branch office, where a single or a group of virtual machines can be set to replicate to a disaster recovery site. And in case of a complete disaster at a primary site, the same replicated virtual machines can be brought up online from the disaster recovery site.

In terms of the actual steps that an administrator executes to implement disaster recovery using Hyper-V Replica, the enterprise datacenter scenario is very similar to the head office and branch office scenario. The main difference would be scale. Enterprise environments typically include one or more large, geographically dispersed datacenters supporting a greater number of virtualized workloads running on more servers. Enterprise environments may also implement third-party or "home-grown" applications. These applications take advantage of Hyper-V Replica's **application programming interfaces** (**APIs**) in an effort to streamline the internal management processes.

Geographically dispersed datacenters

The geographically dispersed datacenters and the head office and branch office scenario for deploying the Hyper-V Replica feature are quite similar in nature. The only differentiating factor is the number of datacenters involved, where in the head office and branch office structures, there is usually one hot site, and the others are cold sites.

On the other hand, in the geographically dispersed datacenter type of organizations, multiple datacenters are being operated by the organization to provide better resiliency and multitenancy for the IT services. In this type of environment, an organization can implement the Hyper-V Replica feature to replicate the virtualized workload data in between the datacenters. So in case one Hyper-V server fails or the completed datacenter goes down, the same virtual machine that earlier got replicated to another datacenter—which could be at a different location, in a different country, or even in a different region—can restore the virtualized workload to any point in time from the replica Hyper-V server located in the other datacenters.

Managed services and hosting provider

The managed services and hosting provider scenario is similar to the geographically dispersed datacenters scenario in terms of the actual steps that an administrator executes to implement disaster recovery using Hyper-V Replica. The difference is that the managed services companies have additional concerns, such as dealing with multiple customers (tenants) on a shared internal infrastructure. This needs implementing stricter isolation policies within the datacenter and a billing system that can accurately track resource usage.

Cloud service provider

Infrastructure as a Service (IaaS) is a part of cloud services, in which a cloud service provider provides the computing infrastructure, also known as a virtual machine. The customers of this service utilize these virtual machines as the disaster recovery computing units for their own production services, running in their own datacenters. While on the one hand, the cloud service providers have to take these machines as their operational workload, which should be carefully planned for disaster recovery. So on the other hand, the cloud providers can take advantage of the Hyper-V Replica feature, where they can replicate their clients' virtual machine from one Hyper-V cluster of servers to another disaster recovery or secondary datacenter.

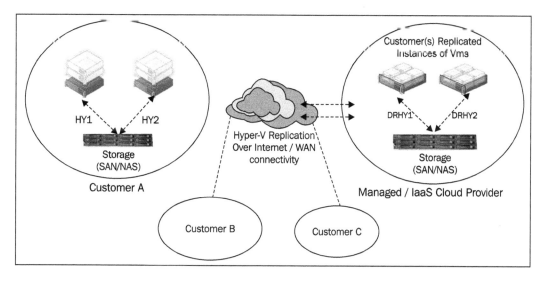

Looking at this from the client side, these small-to-medium size organizations utilize the cloud-hosted Hyper-V servers for replicating their virtual machine data. So in \the event of a failure of their primary instance of Hyper-V, they can resume their cloud-hosted instance.

Technical overview of the Hyper-V Replica feature

An organization can deploy Hyper-V Replica as a virtual machine replication solution for replicating all the VM-related data and changes to its secondary computing site or a disaster recovery site. Hyper-V Replica can use the normal LAN or WAN medium for transmitting this replication data from one site to another. A functional Hyper-V Replica solution between two different sites will look like the following diagram:

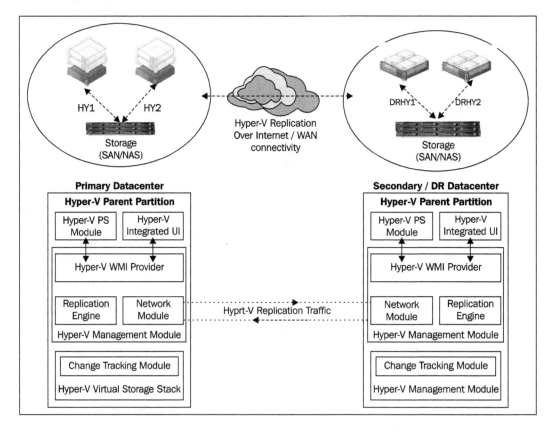

In this section we will cover the core components of Hyper-V Replica, such as the Hyper-V Replica "Replication Engine", change tracking, and network module. All these components work together to make Hyper-V virtual machine replication happen, with all the luxuries and facilities that Hyper-V Replica provides.

Replication Engine

Replication Engine is the heart of the Hyper-V Replica feature. Among the many other responsibilities of Replication Engine, its main responsibility is to ensure that the configured virtual machines and their data get replicated to the Hyper-V Replica server. Replication Engine also holds the configuration store for all the settings related to the Hyper-V Replica feature, including both server specific and virtual machine specific settings. Replication Engine handles the initial replication, delta replication, failover, and test-failover operations between two Hyper-V Replica servers. It also tracks virtual machines and storage mobility events, and takes appropriate actions as required, that is, it pauses the replication events until the migration events complete and then resumes them from where they left off.

Change tracking

The Hyper-V Replica change-tracking component tracks the VM-level changes for the primary Hyper-V server by keeping track of the write operations that happen in the virtual machine. This component is designed in such a way that it doesn't care where the virtual machine hard disk is stored.

Network module

The Hyper-V network module performs the Hyper-V virtual machine data replication between the Hyper-V servers. The default networking module performs data compression before it transfers the replica traffic from the primary Hyper-V server to the replica Hyper-V server. It uses the HTTP/HTTPS protocol for network communication, and also supports integrated and certificate-based authentication.

Hyper-V Replica broker

The Hyper-V Replica broker is a component used in the Windows Server 2012 failover cluster scenario. In the event of a migration of a replica virtual machine from one cluster node to another, this feature provides seamless data replication. This goal is achieved by interacting with the **Windows Server Failover Clustering (WSFC)** service and the Hyper-V network module. The Hyper-V Replica broker redirects all VM-specific events to the appropriate node in the replica cluster. Then to decide which Hyper-V node should receive which events, the Hyper-V broker module queries the Hyper-V cluster database. This operation ensures that all the events are passed on to the correct Hyper-V cluster node in the event of live migration and quick migration, or even in storage migration scenarios.

Hyper-V Replica best practices

Before we go to the next section of this chapter for configuring Hyper-V Replica, it is essential for us to understand the best practices for Hyper-V Replica implementation. You can apply these best practices in the early stages of planning and sizing of your Hyper-V Replica implementation project. These best practices will strengthen your Hyper-V Replica environment and will allow you to make the most of this feature. The following are the three major pillars of the Hyper-V Replica architecture, which will be discussed along with their best practices:

- Security
- Networking
- Storage

Security

Windows Server 2012 strongly focuses on cloud computing, and therefore, security becomes more critical in nature when it comes to Windows Server 2012 core infrastructure. Especially when we talk about cloud computing or multitenancy, where a single cloud service provider hosts services for multiple customers, it is highly imperative for the cloud service provider to maintain a high level of security for its core infrastructure like the hypervisor layer and other dependent elements.

Hyper-V, like other Microsoft products, doesn't really need to be part of Microsoft Active Directory Domain unless you are running a Hyper-V failover cluster. If you are running your Hyper-V servers as standalone servers, your server security and server hardening approach gets divided in a decentralized fashion. On the other hand, if your Hyper-V servers are part of your Active Directory Domain, it becomes a centralized approach for hardening and securing your Hyper-V servers.

Hyper-V security best practices can be explained as follows:

- For securing the incoming replication traffic to your Hyper-V server, you can either use HTTP (port 80) or HTTPS (443). HTTP—where the data transition is not secure—is not a good option if you are concerned about your Hyper-V virtual machine replication traffic; especially when you are using a shared medium, such as Internet.

- Using HTTPS (443) is a recommended approach, where you are requested to provide an SSL-based certificate. This certificate could be provided from your internal Microsoft certification authority, or you can get one from any public certification authority. Choosing the right certificate for your Hyper-V Replica deployment depends on your topology. If all your Hyper-V servers, including the Hyper-V Replica instances, are located in your Active Directory Domain, going for an internal Microsoft CA could be an advisable approach. But if your destination Hyper-V Replica servers do not belong to your Active Directory sites, or in some cases, if you are replicating to a cloud or hosted Hyper-V Replica server, going for a third-party CA certificate should be your primary choice.

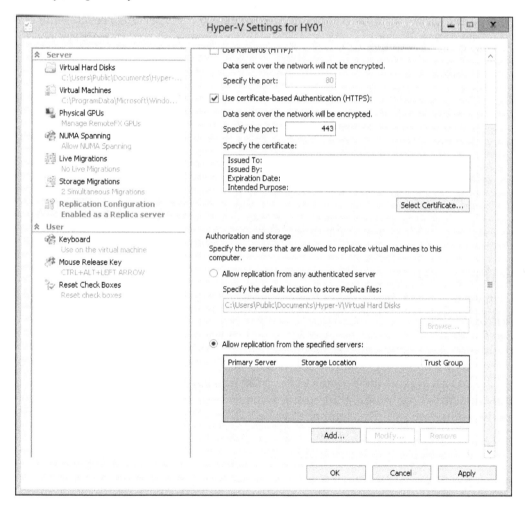

The preceding screenshot shows the configuration settings for the Hyper-V Replica feature, in which we can select the certificate. We want to go for certificate-based authentication over the HTTPS protocol.

- Now let's look at more settings for securing the Hyper-V Replica environment. After seeing the authentication part of the Hyper-V Replica feature in the previous point, we will cover the Hyper-V Replica Authorization settings in this point. The Hyper-V Replica Authorization settings give you two types of choices. In the first choice you can trust any authenticated server, which is the weakest approach because you are telling your Hyper-V server to accept replication from any Hyper-V server. The recommended approach is to allow replication from the specified servers. This second approach of specifying the selected Hyper-V server to replicate its data with your Hyper-V Replica server gives you a set of features to customize your Hyper-V Replica Authorization settings, as explained in the next bullet.

- You can specify the primary server that you want to allow to send virtual machine replication traffic to your Hyper-V Replica server. Hyper-V also gives you the flexibility to use wildcard characters in connection to the fully qualified domain name <FQDN>. So, let's say you want to add an authorization entry for all the servers in the Contoso domain. You might use *.contoso.com, and in there specify the location for the trust group files. Hyper-V will automatically create a group for your configuration set with the name contsoso_com, to differentiate this configuration set of servers from the other allowed authorization sets.

Networking

When we discussed the Hyper-V Replica deployment scenario, we saw that one of the highly used scenarios for Hyper-V Replica deployment is to set up the disaster recovery site for critical virtual machines. Normally, disaster recovery sites have a different IP addressing scheme than their primary site instance of the application and services. In this type of situation, when a planned or unplanned failover of the services and application occurs at the primary site, and the replication-enabled virtual machines try bringing themselves up from the Hyper-V Replica server, they simply fail in doing so. This happens because of the IP addresses configured on these primary instances of the application and services.

To accommodate this requirement, there is a built-in functionality in Hyper-V Replica where the virtual machines' network settings can be modified to include configuration information for a different network at a disaster recovery site.

To take advantage of this, Hyper-V Replica instances of virtual machines should be configured on the replica server. Hyper-V allows an administrator to set both IPv4 and IPv6 configurations of these replica virtual machines. As you can see in the next screenshot, we have the flexibility to define the networking configuration for the virtual machine. These networking settings can also be called failover networking configuration. These settings will be injected into the virtual machine as hardcoded settings at the time of the virtual machine failover from the Hyper-V server to the Hyper-V Replica server.

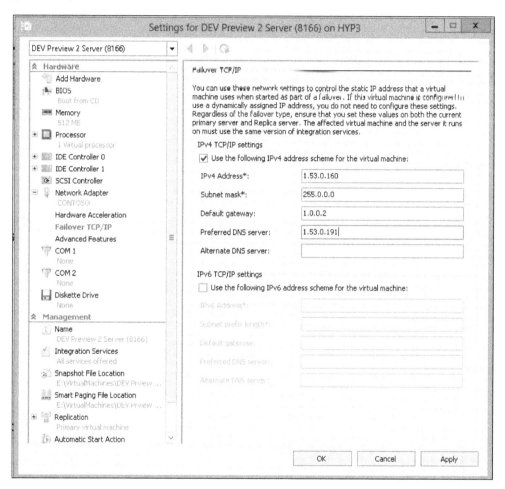

The **Failover TCP/IP** configuration section in the virtual machine configuration settings allows a virtual machine to have preassigned network configuration for a planned and unplanned failover to a Hyper-V Replica server.

For better understanding, let's say we have a SQL Server virtual machine running in our primary datacenter, and later on we decide to replicate this VM to our disaster recovery Hyper-V Replica servers. And to get a seamless failover to disaster recovery, we configure the network settings on the SQL Server replica VM instance to always have the SQL Server servicing IP address.

It should be noted here that these TCP/IP settings can only be configured on the synthetic network adapter, and cannot be configured on the legacy network adapter.

The operating system running on the guest virtual machine must be one of the following:

- Windows Server 2012
- Windows Server 2008 / 2008 R2
- Windows Server 2003 (or higher)
- Windows 8, Windows Vista SP2 (or higher), Windows X SP2 (or higher)
- Windows 7

Other network best practices may include dedicating a VLAN and an NIC for the Hyper-V Replica traffic. Since Hyper-V Replica uses the asynchronous replication traffic mode, ongoing traffic will always be there based on your configuration. It is also an imperative point to isolate traffic within your fabric. Keeping all the eggs in the same basket may end up with affecting other traffic and services going through the same subnet and NIC. Another best practice is to dedicate an NIC card on a Hyper-V server for making Hyper-V a member of the Hyper-V replication VLAN. If you use a single NIC for both Hyper-V virtual machine network and for replication communication in this type of approach, you will see performance bottlenecks for both the types of communications.

Storage

Storage is another main pillar for your Hyper-V Replica infrastructure. Storage planning for rolling out Hyper-V Replica is very critical, especially when you have a single site that is going to host all the replica instances of all your production virtualized workloads. Storage best practices for Hyper-V Replica are the same as for Hyper-V roles in general. And from a practical standpoint, I would like to emphasize the planning aspect of storage with regards to Hyper-V Replica adoption. Because, the more Hyper-V Replica will be used for protecting your critical virtual machine instances, the more storage amount will be required on your disaster recovery or any other site where your Hyper-V Replica servers are located. Organizations can also use cheaper and low-performance storage for their Hyper-V Replica instance.

Setting up Hyper-V Replica

So far we have been introduced to Hyper-V Replica and have seen the technical overview of the Hyper-V Replica feature. We also looked at the best practices section, where we discussed the various best practices and recommendations for implementing Hyper-V Replica in your environment.

Now that we have made ourselves familiar with Hyper-V Replica, we will move ahead with some real-world implementation, and will discuss how and where we can configure the Hyper-V server to replicate the virtual machine to a Hyper-V Replica server.

Enabling Hyper-V replication

Before we configure the replication settings for virtual machines, we are first required to enable the Hyper-V replication feature on the Hyper-V server. Hyper-V Replica is a built-in functionality added into the Windows Server 2012 Hyper-V role, and there is no need for you to install any other service or feature to enable its functionality. We know that Hyper-V works in two types of configurations. In the first configuration Hyper-V could be a standalone server, and in the second type of configuration a Hyper-V server can be a member of Windows Failover Cluster Service. So therefore, to better understand the process of enabling Hyper-V replication for these two types of Hyper-V configurations, let's divide this into two steps. In the following example, we will first see how to enable replication for standalone Hyper-V servers, and then we will move on to clustered Hyper-V servers.

Enabling Hyper-V replication for standalone Hyper-V servers

To enable the Hyper-V Replica feature on your Windows Server 2012 Hyper-V server's standalone member server, the following steps need to be carried out:

1. Open **Hyper-V Manager** from **Administrative Tools**.
2. On the right-hand action pane, click on **Hyper-V Settings**.
3. On the **Hyper-V settings** page, in the **Settings** tab on the left-hand side, locate **Replication Configuration** and open it.
4. In the upper-right corner, check on the checkbox for **Enable this computer as a Replica server**.

5. After checking the checkbox, under the **Authentication and ports** section either select **HTTP (port 80)** or **HTTPS (443)**. Once you select one of these, the **Select certificate** button becomes active, which allows you to select the appropriate certificate for your server.

6. The next step is to select the authorization and storage settings for your Hyper-V server. Under the authorization settings, you can select either **Allow replication from any authorized server** or **Allow replication from specified servers**. You may select any of the options that best suit your requirement and topology. We should not forget that we can select any of the authorization options for our Hyper-V Replica server, but we have to specify a default store (storage) for our VM's replica data to be stored.

7. After completing all the configuration settings, you can click on **Apply**, and then on **OK** to save the configuration.

8. When you click on **Apply**, Hyper-V will notify you in the background that the required Windows Firewall rules will get created for allowing replication traffic to pass between the Hyper-V servers.

 Make sure that your security team allows the required ports between the Hyper-V server and Hyper-V Replica server instances to replicate virtual machine data over either port 80 or port 443, depending on your configuration.

In the next screenshot, we will see the Hyper-V Replica sever-level configuration, where we specify whether this server can have Hyper-V Replica functionalities enabled or not. After the settings for either enabling or not enabling the Hyper-V Replica feature on the Hyper-V server as a global configuration, it's time for us to make the second major architectural choice. We have got two choices here; the first choice is to send data between the Hyper-V server and Hyper-V Replica server over port 80, which is not a secure choice to make. And the second choice is to go for port 443, which is the preferred way for sending data over the network.

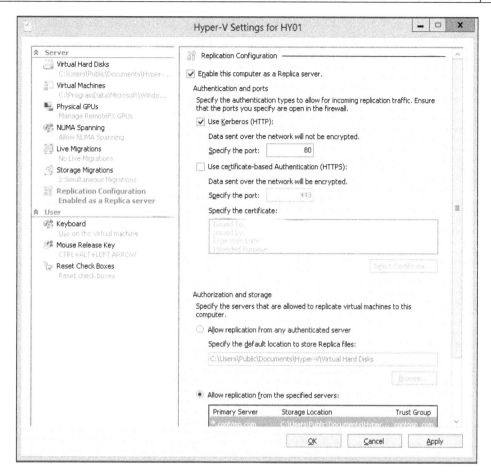

 It is recommended that on the Hyper-V Replica server, an administrator should not specify the system partition (`C:`) as the default store for the virtual machine replica store.

Enabling Hyper-V replication for clustered Hyper-V servers

To enable the Hyper-V Replica feature on your Windows Server 2012 Hyper-V failover cluster member nodes, we have to add the Hyper-V Replica broker cluster service to your Hyper-V failover cluster.

Adding the Hyper-V Replica broker to your Hyper-V failover cluster is described in detail in *Chapter 8, Building Hyper-V High Availability and Virtual Machine Mobility*. The following screenshot shows the **Hyper-V Replica Broker Configuration** window, where we can enable Hyper-V replication for clustered Hyper-V servers:

Configuring Hyper-V Replica

We will see the three scenarios for configuring Hyper-V Replica in this section.

Configuring Hyper-V Replica for standalone virtual machines

In the previous section we looked at how to enable the Hyper-V Replica feature on your Hyper-V server. In this section, we will see how to configure and enable the Hyper-V Replica for VMs.

Follow the steps outlined here for configuring virtual machine replication using Hyper-V Failover Manager for standalone Hyper-V servers, and Failover Cluster Manager for Hyper-V failover clustered nodes:

1. Open the **Hyper-V Manager** snap-in from **Administrative Tools** or from **Server Manager**.

2. Once **Hyper-V Manager** opens, right-click on the desired virtual machine that needs to be configured for replication, and click on **Enable Replication**.

   Upon clicking on the **Enable Replication** menu, the **Enable Replication for <VM-NAME>** box will open, in which the first configuration setting you have to provide is the **Specify Replica Server** details.

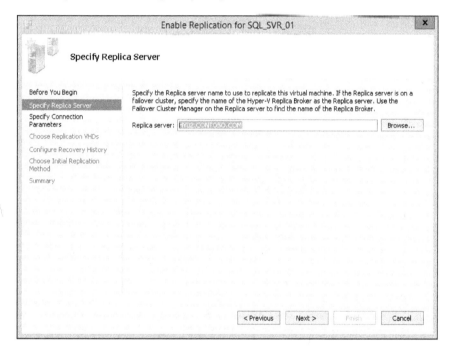

> If you are going to replicate this virtual machine to a standalone Hyper-V server, specify the FQDN of the replica Hyper-V server. If this virtual machine is going to be replicated to a Hyper-V failover cluster, make sure that you provide the Hyper-V Replica broker address.

3. After specifying the Replica Hyper-V server, click on **Next** and then Hyper-V Manager will verify that the destination, which is specified as being a replica server, does contain the Hyper-V role installed.

4. Upon verification, when the next window screen of **Specify Connection Parameters** comes up, you see that all the details are already set as shown in the following screenshot. This preconfiguration is a part of enabling your Hyper-V replication on the server.

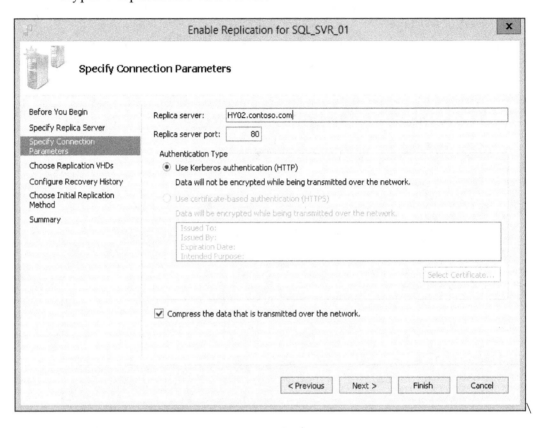

5. In the **Specify Connection Parameters** window, if you wish, you can change the authentication type from HTTP to HTTPS depending on your configuration, which you did on your Hyper-V server while enabling Hyper-V replication.

 In the previous example, we are using HTTP (80 port) for authentication, but in the real-world scenario, it is highly recommended that you use HTTPS (port 443) for authentication.

6. In the next step of the virtual machine replication settings, we have to choose **virtual hard disks (VHDs)**, which will be replicated to the Hyper-V Replica server. To conserve the bandwidth and storage on the disaster recovery site, let's not choose the extra VHD files, such as the paging file VHD to be moved. So in this case, while choosing replication VHDs, you may drop the unwanted VHD files from being part of the replication copy.

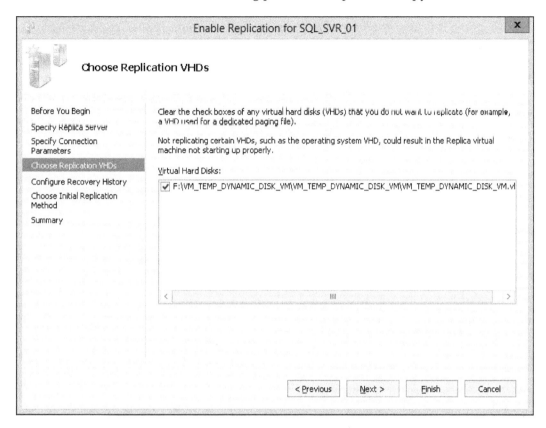

7. After specifying the required VHDs for replication, we have to configure the recovery history for the virtual machine replication in the next step. The Hyper-V Replica feature provides two levels of virtual machine recovery. In the first level of recovery, Hyper-V Replica lets the administrator configure the virtual machine to have only the latest recovery point. This means that if the virtual machine is configured to have only a single recovery point, in case of recovery, the administrator has to restore only the last single recovery point. It is also good for saving the storage on your Hyper-V Replica server. The dark side of having a single recovery option is that it doesn't provide you a point-in-time recovery option. The second option allows an administrator to create multiple recovery points for a given virtual machine. To further customize the need for recovery, an administrator can also select the number of recovery points that the virtual machine will be allowed to create. In addition to these, we can also set the frequency for the incremental replication VSS copy.

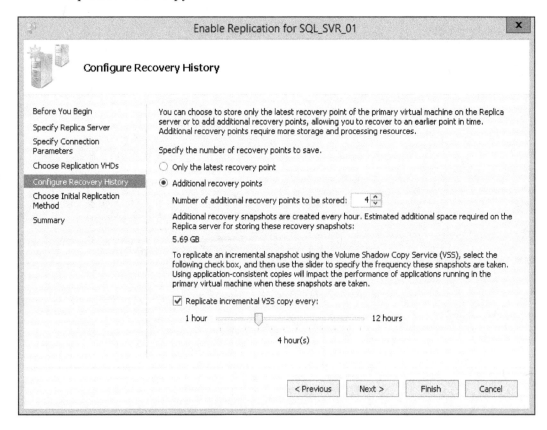

8. The last step of configuring the virtual machine replication settings is to configure the initial replication method. You can see these methods in the next screenshot. Let's take a look at each method in detail:

   ° **Send initial copy over the network**: Copying or sending the initial virtual machine hard disk over the network is a good option for all those environments where the replica Hyper-V server is not so far away from the primary Hyper-V server and the network latency is not very high. This option is also good for those environments where the WAN link between two sites has an affordable speed, which can be used to replicate the virtual machine hard disk.

   ° **Send initial copy using external media**: This option may help the administrator to set up the initial copy when the initial hard disk has been exported into an external media, such as an external hard disk or USB drive. In this option an administrator can specify the location where he/she wants to export the initial copy.

   ° **Use an existing virtual machine on the Replica server as the initial copy**: The last option is to set up the initial copy for the virtual machine hard disk by using the existing virtual machine on the replica server as an initial copy. Usually in this case, an earlier replicated copy on the replica server can be used as an initial copy.

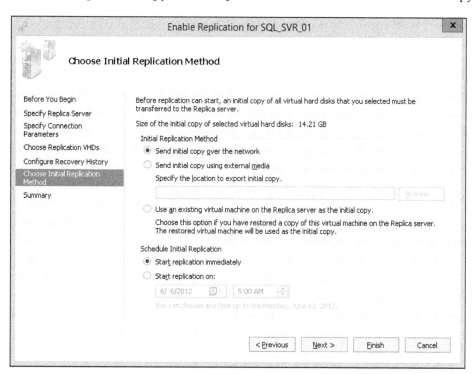

9. After configuring the initial copy for the virtual machine hard disk, we are done with the virtual machine replication settings. On the summary page, Hyper-V gives an overview of the whole configuration as shown in the following screenshot:

Replica server:	HY02.contoso.com
Replica server port:	80
Compress data:	Yes
Authentication type:	Kerberos authentication
VHDs not selected for replication:	None
Store additional recovery points:	Yes
Number of additional recovery points:	4
Use application-consistent snapshots:	Yes
Application-consistent replication frequency:	4 hour(s)
Initial replication method:	Using network, start immediately

In the preceding screenshot, as we can see, before we hit **Commit**, Hyper-V Manager gives us a handy summary of the configuration we have selected for the given virtual machine for its Hyper-V Replica parameter. Depending on your configuration selection, each part of the Hyper-V Replica settings for the virtual machine will be displayed on this summary page.

If you select **Start replication immediately** during the initial copy settings, when you finish the virtual machine replication settings, you will see in the Hyper-V Manager virtual machine dashboard that the virtual machine replication has started. It will also show you the percentage of the initial copy completed, as shown in the following screenshot:

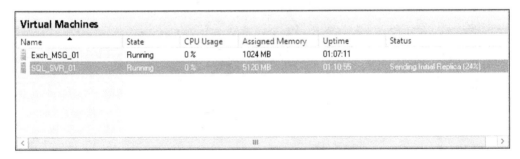

Upon completion of the initial copy of your virtual machine, you will see that a virtual machine with the same name gets created on the replica Hyper-V server, and the state of the virtual machine is set to offline. When you select the replica virtual machine on the Hyper-V Replica server, you will see that a snapshot has been created with the date and time at the bottom of the **Hyper-V Manager** window under the **Snapshots** section, as follows:

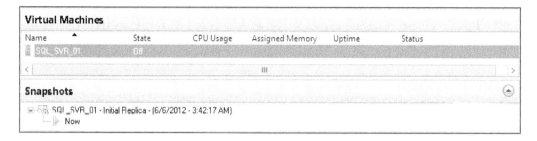

If we open the virtual machine replica store on the Hyper-V Replica server, we will find that the following folders have been created for the replicated virtual machine:

Configuring Hyper-V Replica for a highly available virtual machine using Failover Cluster Manager

In the earlier example of configuring Hyper-V Replica for virtual machine replication, we used a configured virtual machine on a standalone Hyper-V server. Since the overall concepts and steps are quite similar for both the types of virtual machines, we take an overview of configuring a highly available virtual machine resource in Failover Cluster Manager in this section.

Hyper-V Failover Replication broker architecture

The Hyper-V Replica broker (the Hyper-V Replica feature for clustered Hyper-V nodes) runs in a Replica cluster and provides a Replica server name (connection point also known as **Client Access Point (CAP)**) for the initial virtual machine placement when contacted by a primary server. Once the virtual machine is initially replicated to the Replica failover cluster, the Hyper-V Replica broker provides the virtual machine to the replica server (cluster node) for setting the virtual machine. This is done to ensure that the primary Hyper-V server can replicate data from the virtual machine to the correct cluster node in the cluster, and also to support mobility scenarios on the replica side.

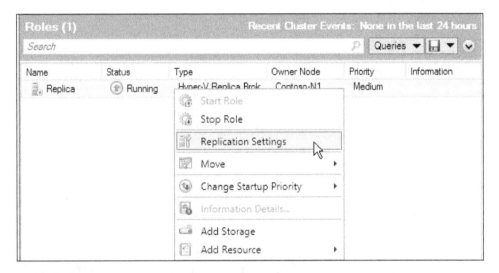

The Hyper-V Failover Replica broker is used to configure the virtual machine replication settings for all nodes in the cluster. In the case of Hyper-V standalone servers, we use Hyper-V Manager to configure all the VM-related replication settings.

Configuring Hyper-V Replica for reverse replication

This is an important setting, which should be configured on your Hyper-V Replica primary site's Hyper-V servers. It will act as the primary Hyper-V Replica instances in normal times. Let me first make clear what reverse replication means. For understanding what reverse replication is, let's see an example. Contoso Ltd. has two datacenters: one is the primary datacenter in Los Angeles and the other is the disaster recovery datacenter in Dubai. Contoso has all its servers running as virtual machines, and in the event of any problem with the SQL Server VM in the primary datacenter, the administrator carries out a failover of the VM to the Hyper-V Replica server. After the successful failover of the SQL Server VM from the disaster recovery datacenter, the Hyper-V Replica server starts sending the virtual machine and data changes to the primary datacenter SQL Server virtual machine. This functionality of sending the data changes from the Hyper-V Replica server to the Hyper-V server (primary instance) is called **reverse replication**. And later on, when your primary Hyper-V Replica servers and the site become active, you need to restore these virtual machine instances to these Hyper-V Replica primary servers in the primary site. If your primary Hyper-V Replica servers are not enabled for the Hyper-V Replica feature, or you say the replication is not enabled on them, you will not be allowed to fail back to these primary Hyper-V Replica servers.

It is important that you enable this feature on all the Hyper-V Windows Server 2012 instances at the time of configuring the Hyper-V Replica feature on your Hyper-V servers. This gives you the flexibility to fail over and fail back easily between the Hyper-V servers in your environment.

We have now completed the setting up virtual machine replication section of this chapter. In the next section of this chapter we will understand the management operations and virtual machine failover testing for virtual machines.

Monitoring Hyper-V Replica environment

In the previous section of this chapter, we discussed the steps for configuring Hyper-V replication for virtual machines for standalone and clustered Hyper-V instances. Configuration is always the first duty of any administrator; once configuration is done, it is imperative that the administrator monitor it and enhance it with the day-to-day management tasks.

In this section of the chapter, we will first understand the various methods of monitoring the Hyper-V Replica environment.

Monitoring the IT infrastructures is an essential part of information technology operations' management. Monitoring of applications and services gives you the ability to get the full picture of the health of your applications and servers, and how they are being served to the corporate users of your organization.

In particular, monitoring the Hyper-V Replica environment is critical, because being a disaster recovery and business continuity solution for an organization makes it necessary that the Hyper-V Replica instances are always available and consistently working without any problem. In this topic we will be discussing the following methods of monitoring the health of the Hyper-V Replica instances:

- Hyper-V virtual machine replication health checking
- Performance monitoring for Hyper-V Replica virtual machines
- Reviewing the Microsoft Hyper-V VMMS logs for Hyper-V Replica

Hyper-V virtual machine replication health checking

Once we enable the replication for a virtual machine on a Hyper-V Replica feature-enabled instance with whatsoever initial replication method you choose, the Hyper-V Replica feature starts replicating the virtual machine data from the Hyper-V primary server to the Hyper-V Replica server. Periodically checking the replication status of a virtual machine is crucial for your Hyper-V replicated virtual machine. If you have configured your highly critical virtual machine's recovery points to be created on the Hyper-V Replica server after every hour, monitoring the health of your virtual machine becomes more important for you to restore your virtual machine at any point in time.

You can check the replication health of your replicated virtual machine by performing the following steps:

1. Log in to either the Hyper-V primary server or the Hyper-V Replica server, and open the **Hyper-V Manager** snap-in from **Administrative Tools**.

2. Right-click on any of the virtual machines that is set up for the replication, and move your mouse cursor on the **Replication** tab and click on **View replication health....**

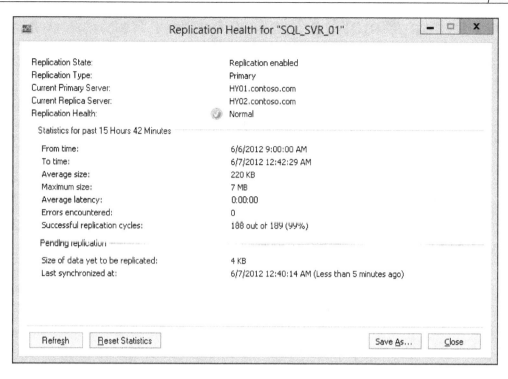

3. You will see that the **View replication health** window gives you all the information you need to know about your virtual machine's replication status. We can see from the preceding screenshot that there are a few other options available on this small status window. Let's discuss the following functions that this small window performs for us:

    ◦   **Refresh**: When you click on the **Refresh** button on the **View replication health** window, it refreshes the data statistics displayed for the related virtual machine replication.

    ◦   **Reset Statistics**: If you want to see a fresh view of your virtual machine's replication statistics, you can also reset the statistics. This will start collecting fresh statistics and resetting the statistics will not have any impact on your virtual machine availability.

    ◦   **Save As...**: If you want to save or export the statistics figures to a **Cluster Shared Volumes (CSV)** file, you can also do that by clicking on the **Save As...** button, which will let you export this data to a CSV file.

Performance monitoring for Hyper-V Replica virtual machines

Windows Server Performance Monitor utility is an out-of-the-box monitoring tool for any of the Windows components, and greatly helps in the event of any troubleshooting performance bottlenecks. Performance Monitor can be used to monitor any of the Hyper-V performance data counters. When we particularly talk about the performance monitor capabilities for the Hyper-V Replica instance, it provides the following list of data counters to be monitored:

- Average replication latency
- Average replication size
- Compression efficiency
- Last replication size
- Network bytes received
- Network bytes sent
- Replication count
- Replication latency
- Resynchronization bytes

To perform Hyper-V Replica virtual machine monitoring with Performance Monitor, you can execute the following steps:

1. Open **Performance Monitor** from **Control Panel | Administrative Tools**.
2. Expand **Monitoring Tools** on the left-hand side of the **Performance Monitor** window, and right-click on **Performance Monitor**. Then click on **Properties**.
3. In the **Properties** window, click on the third tab, which is **Data**, and click on the **Add** button.
4. Then from the available counters, select **Hyper-V Replica VM**, and select from the instances of the selected object list the virtual machine for which you want to monitor the Hyper-V Replica health.
5. To specifically choose the data counter for your Hyper-V Replica monitoring, you can expand the **Hyper-V Replica VM** data counter and select any of the previously listed data counters for your virtual machine, as shown in the following screenshot:

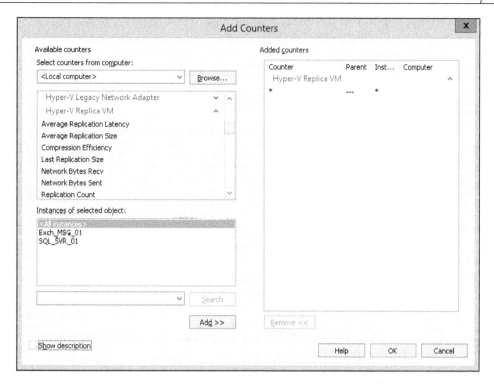

6. After making the selection, click on **OK** in the **Add Counters** window, and then click on **Apply** and **OK** in the **Performance Monitor** main window.

This will add all the data counters you selected for your virtual machine, and then runtime monitoring for the selected data counters will start. The performance graph will be created based on your Performance Monitor graph view settings.

Reviewing Microsoft Hyper-V VMMS logs for Hyper-V Replica

To see the Microsoft Hyper-V Replica server health status, you can also take a look at the event viewer for the **Virtual Machine Management Service (VMMS)** logs. Perform the following steps to review your VMMS logs for Hyper-V Replica on the local Hyper-V server:

1. Open **Event Viewer** from **Control Panel | Administrative Tools**.

2. Expand **Applications and Services Logs** on the left-hand side of the main **Event Viewer** window, and open **Microsoft | Windows | Hyper-V-VMMS | Admin**.

3. In the **Hyper-V-VMMS Admin** section of **Event Viewer**, all the logs are associated to the VMMS administrator for Hyper-V virtual machine replication.

Summary

It's been an interesting chapter that covered the advantages of the Hyper-V Replica feature. Hyper-V Replica is a functionality introduced in the Windows Server 2012 Hyper-V role, where an organization can set a virtual machine running on Windows Server 2012 Hyper-V to replicate its configuration and data files to another Hyper-V Replica server placed in a same or different part of the network.

Hyper-V Replica gives a handy way to organizations to build the disaster recovery of their critical virtual workload running in their primary datacenter. Hyper-V Replica can be set on an individual virtual machine or can also be set for all the virtual machines running on the same Hyper-V server. Hyper-V Replica is a free and default feature available in both Hyper-V standalone and clustered instances.

In this chapter we were first introduced to Hyper-V Replica, its technical overview, configuring Hyper-V Replica, and last but not the least, the monitoring aspect of Hyper-V Replica. All this information provided us great knowledge for implementing Hyper-V Replica as a kick-off for setting up a replica of our critical servicing VM, running in our head office / primary datacenters.

In the next chapter we will look at Hyper-V networking, and understand how we can virtualize the network fabric with the new features available in Windows Server 2012 and Hyper-V. We will also look at the best practices for network virtualization for virtual machines and Hyper-V.

4
Understanding Hyper-V Networking

In this chapter, we will cover the deeper side of Hyper-V networking while discussing both host and guest Hyper-V networking components. For starters, we will first take a look at an overview of the Hyper-V virtual networking switch, where we will see what Hyper-V network virtualization looks like and what it offers. After this, we will move ahead with going through the new features and functionalities added in Hyper-V Windows Server 2012. We will also see what benefits we will get by implementing these newly added features in our Hyper-V virtualization infrastructure.

After building the knowledge base platform for Hyper-V network virtualization, we will move ahead with understanding the configuration and management steps required for the Hyper-V virtual network switch. In this section, we will cover the different types of Hyper-V virtual network switches. In the second section, we will start discussing the hottest features of Windows Server 2012 and Hyper-V, which are load balancing and failover with NIC teaming. In this section, we will see how we can utilize the benefits of this feature for both host and guest virtual machines. Lastly, we will see a summary of what we covered in this chapter and we will move on to the next chapter.

Hyper-V virtual switch technical overview

To understand Hyper-V networking, it is essential to discuss the Hyper-V virtual switch, which provides networking capabilities to the virtualized workload created on Hyper-V. The Hyper-V virtual switch or virtual network has evolved over time with each different release of Hyper-V versions in Windows Server operating system releases.

The Hyper-V virtual switch functionality can be set up in three ways, either as an external virtual switch, an internal virtual switch, or a private virtual switch. A Hyper-V virtual switch can either connect to a single interface (**network interface card** or **NIC**) of the server or to multiple interfaces (NIC team). In the case of connecting to multiple network interface cards (NIC teaming), a Windows Hyper-V virtual switch can take full advantage of its network load balancing and failover capabilities. Depending on the type of communication needed for virtualized instances running on Hyper-V, an administrator can create multiple Hyper-V virtual switches, which may serve the virtual machines as per their need.

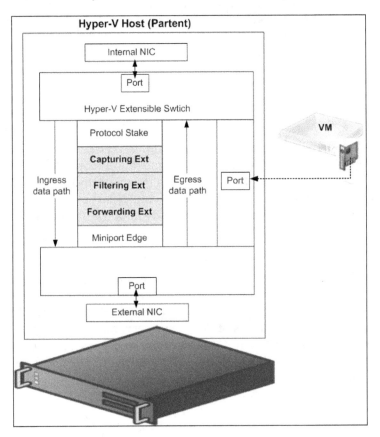

The Hyper-V virtual switch is a virtual layer of network subsystems that can also be called a layer-2 network switch. It is a part of the Hyper-V parent partition architecture and provides network connectivity between the child partition and the physical network. The Hyper-V virtual switch is the one that manages data transmission, implementing security for the virtualized network between parent-to-child and child-to-child communications.

After we saw a great evolution in server virtualization and datacenter consolidation practice, organizations are following virtualization as a technology regardless of their sizes, and the need for the IT department to implement it has taken on a great deal of importance. After realizing the importance and benefits of virtualization, we start with the server virtualization and datacenter consolidation approach, where we see another concept called cloud computing; here the server, networking, storage, and human resources come together and create a pool of resources that are used to provision computing units (VMs) and various services (for example IaaS, PaaS, SaaS). Cloud computing uses virtualization as a base platform on which it builds the service architecture for cloud-based offerings.

The Microsoft Windows Server 2008 platform initially provided Microsoft cloud-based offerings in combination with other Microsoft System Center families and cloud orchestration tools; this gained a lot of attention from the industry because they allowed Microsoft customers to integrate their existing platforms in such a way that they could take advantage of building public and private clouds. At that time, Microsoft Hyper-V played a vital role in helping these customers build a cloud-based setup, by providing a virtualization layer that to some extent provided features necessary for cloud-based offerings.

But still, with Windows Server 2008 Hyper-V, customers faced limitations on fully applying cloud computing concepts and building enterprise-level, private and public cloud environments, especially when it comes to the multitenancy and built-in security for sharing cloud resources between different businesses and organizations. Windows Server 2008 doesn't provide these features.

Windows Server 2012 – a cloud-ready platform

Windows Server 2012 introduced a huge number of new features and capabilities for features based on cloud computing, such as multitenancy, extensible Hyper-V virtual switch, traffic shaping, built-in protection against malicious networking behavior of VMs, network bandwidth management, and many more, which were needed for the purpose of offering an enterprise-level cloud solution based on Microsoft Windows Server platform.

The Microsoft virtual switch supports **Network Device Interface Specification (NDIS)** filter drivers and **Windows Filtering Platform (WFP)** drivers, and also enables third-party organizations to develop Hyper-V APIs for integration purposes.

Improved Hyper-V virtual network switch

Now that we have seen a brief overview of a few of the Hyper-V virtual switch enhancements made in Windows Server 2012, in this section we will discuss all these improvements in detail.

Before we go ahead and discuss the new and improved Hyper-V virtual switch, let's first see the comparison between the Hyper-V virtual switch capabilities of Windows Server 2008 and Windows Server 2012:

Feature	Windows Server 2008 (R2)	Windows Server 2012
NIC teaming	Yes; through external NIC teaming software provided by third-party hardware vendors	Yes; a built-in NIC teaming feature for both the host and guest
VLAN tagging	Yes, with R2 SP1	Yes
MAC spoofing protection	Yes, with R2 SP1	Yes
ARP spoofing protection	No	Yes
Single root I/O virtualization (SR-IOV)	No	Yes
Network QoS	No	Yes
Network metering	No	Yes
Network monitor extension	No	Yes
IPSEC task offload	No	Yes
VM trunk mode	No	Yes
Port mirroring	No	Yes

Now we will explore the new features that have been added into the Hyper-V virtual switch, and we will also discuss how these newly added features can help to build an enterprise class virtualized platform. So let's go for it.

Load balancing and failover (NIC teaming)

Earlier, configuring load balancing and failover for an NIC card on Windows Server was done by installing an NIC card management utility from an NIC manufacturer that allows the configuration of the NIC teaming feature on the server. What is NIC teaming? **NIC teaming** is a function where you virtually create a network connection by combining multiple NIC cards on the server. This gives the ability to aggregate the bandwidth of all these NICs and combine them for this virtually created network connection.

These NIC management utilities also allow an administrator to configure the NIC failover feature; this means that if one NIC fails among all these combined NICs, this virtually created network connection will not stop functioning. These third-party NIC management utilities provide help to load balance the traffic between the servers, the NIC failover, and the redundancy feature. But at the same time, there are a few caveats associated with this practice, among which the most critical one is updating the NIC utility. As being a third-party application for the NIC management and failover capabilities, it has been seen that most of the time this third-party interface and these APIs have compatibility issues with operating systems and other server-based applications.

Windows Server 2012 covered this gap by providing the built-in NIC load balancing and failover (NIC teaming) feature, which allows the server administrators to configure load-balancing and failover capabilities for the server's NICs. This built-in feature makes administration and manageability for the NIC teaming feature easy and covers all the shortfalls of having external NIC teaming utilities. However, it should be noted here that this doesn't mean that Windows Server 2012 doesn't support external NIC management utilities for the NIC load balancing and failover feature.

So this was for the physical host server; now what about the virtual machine? Well, Windows Server 2012 Hyper-V allows administrators to configure the NIC teaming settings for virtual machines, where an administrator can configure the advanced settings of a virtual machine NIC card to be set as the NIC teaming functionality is enabled.

Soon, we will see more benefits of the native NIC teaming feature available with Windows Server 2012 in the *Implementing NIC teaming for Hyper-V host and guest* section.

Quality of service and bandwidth management

Windows Server 2012 introduced the new functionality of **quality of service (QoS)** bandwidth management that allows an administrator to configure multiple types of network traffic to be transmitted from a single NIC with a predictable level of service. This new feature allows the setting of bandwidth throttle for a virtual machine, which can be set from virtual machine settings in Hyper-V Manager or from Windows PowerShell cmdlets.

This bandwidth management functionality allows you to configure the minimum and maximum network bandwidth utilization allowed for a virtual machine. You can set the network's bandwidth as per your need for each virtual NIC of a virtual machine for a specific type of network traffic, for example, you may have multiple NICs on the virtual machine for server farm VLAN, SCSi SAN, and backup VLAN, and for each virtual NIC we may configure the minimum and maximum network bandwidths.

Single root I/O

Single root I/O virtualization allows a Hyper-V server to utilize the standard PCI Express devices that are to be shared among multiple VMs, by allowing them to have direct access to a hardware path for providing input and receiving output. For us to be able to benefit from this feature, Hyper-V server should support single root I/O virtualization capable NICs. SR-IOV reduces network latency, reduces CPU utilization for processing network traffic, and increases network throughput.

Extensible Hyper-V virtual switch

Windows Server 2012 Hyper-V made changes to the Hyper-V virtualized stack by making the Hyper-V virtual switch extensible. What this means is that the Windows Server 2012 Hyper-V virtual switch allows new capabilities to view and manage the traffic on your server that is running Hyper-V.

Extensible Hyper-V virtual switch architecture allows external third-party Microsoft partners to create APIs for monitoring, filtering, and forwarding extensions. The Hyper-V virtual switch supports any extensions that are created and implemented using **Network Device Interface Specification** (**NDIS**) filter drivers or **Windows Filtering Platform** (**WFP**) callout drivers.

ARP/ND poisoning (spoofing) protection

ARP/ND poisoning (spoofing) protection provides protection against malicious VMs using **Address Resolution Protocol** (**ARP**) spoofing to steal IP addresses from other virtual machines running on Hyper-V Windows Server 2012. It also helps prevent attacks that are launched against IPv6 using **Neighbor Discovery Protocol** (**NDP**) spoofing.

DHCP guard

The **Dynamic Host Configuration Protocol (DHCP)** guard setting has been introduced as a safety shield for your virtualized environment, where a DHCP guard prevents DHCP server messages from unauthorized virtual machines pretending to be the DHCP server.

Port access control lists (ACLs)

This functionality allows an administrator to configure traffic filtering based on **Media Access Control (MAC)** or **Internet Protocol (IP)** addresses/ranges on a virtual machine, which will set up virtual network isolation, and this feature can benefit a lot in cloud- and multitenant-based environments.

Trunk mode to a VM

This feature can especially be used for today's virtual-appliance-based deployment, for example, if you have a network load balancer or a web application firewall that is running as a virtual machine, this feature would be your favorite one. We are seeing a great development in cloud-based services, especially for **Infrastructure as a Service (IaaS)**, where computing, networking, and storage are provided as a service. In this type of business, having such advanced virtualization and multitenancy capabilities is the utmost requirement, to allow the service provider to utilize the same hardware for providing isolated services to different customers, while allowing the customers to extend their internal network to the cloud-based services. The trunk mode to a VM is one of the features that allows customers to extend their internal network to cloud-based workloads using the improved virtual network switch of Windows Server 2012.

Network traffic monitoring

Hyper-V Windows Server 2012 virtual switch capturing extensions allow an administrator to capture the network traffic coming into and going from a virtual machine through the Hyper-V virtual switch. Hyper-V also allows external third-party vendors to build Hyper-V capturing and other network-based extensions, which can be integrated with a Hyper-V virtual stack to better perform network-related operations.

Configuring the Hyper-V extensible virtual network switch

So far in this chapter, we have covered the technical overview of the Hyper-V virtual switch, and the improvements introduced in Windows Server 2012 Hyper-V, so that the required platform is ready to take this journey to the next level. This section has been divided into two subparts. In the first part we will cover the host section, and in the second part we will see the available VM-related networking settings.

In this section of configuring and managing Hyper-V networking, we will discuss the steps for setting up the Hyper-V virtual switch, where we will discuss the different types of Hyper-V virtual switches and their different types of working domains and deployment scenarios. Hyper-V Windows Server 2012 introduced tons of new features, and in this section, we will cover the set of advanced virtual machine features available for both synthetic and legacy network adapters of a virtual machine.

Configuring the Hyper-V host virtual network switch

In this section, we will first get a detailed understanding of the various types of Hyper-V virtual switches, and then we will go through the configuration steps for our virtual machines, to make our Hyper-V infrastructure ready to benefit from these different, out-of-the-box virtualized networking features.

Types of Hyper-V virtual network switches

Understanding the various types of Hyper-V virtual switches is essential, because these different types of Hyper-V virtual network switches provide different levels of accessibility to your virtual machines. A single Hyper-V host can have all these multiple sets of virtual network switches, and a single virtual machine can be connected to multiple virtual switches at the same time.

In Hyper-V, you can create the following types of virtual networks that are now called Hyper-Virtual switches. This virtualized network layer provides different types of network connectivity to your virtual machines based on your requirements. Creating and configuring Hyper-V virtual switches is a global configuration that you perform on the host level, and all the virtual machines can use them whenever they need it.

- External
- Internal
- Private

External

External Hyper-V virtual switches are created to build a bridge between Hyper-V virtual networks and external networks. An external virtual network gets bound to this entire virtual network with external NICs of the Hyper-V server to directly communicate with the rest of the network. We can create as many external virtual network switches as we want for our virtual machines.

> In *Chapter 2, Planning, Designing, and Implementing Microsoft Hyper-V*, we discussed the various best practices for designing the physical networking infrastructure; this is quite essential for your Hyper-V host server to perform and provide better virtualized networking capabilities to your virtual machines. In addition to these best practices, in this chapter we will also discuss the best practices for Hyper-V virtual switches that will help you size and configure them to get the most out of your virtual network stack for the better performance and availability of your virtual machine network.

Now let's configure our Hyper-V server for external virtual network, which will be used by our virtual machine to communicate with the other networks (VLANs) and servers, based on the network configuration on the physical network switches.

> Hyper-V external virtual switch entirely relies on the physical connection / NIC / switch port configuration, which means Hyper-V external network switch will simply transmit the packet to the network switch, and now it is the responsibility of a physical network admin how he/she configures his/her networking protocols and switching infrastructure for the entire Hyper-V server to communicate with other parts of the network.

To create an external virtual switch, perform the following steps:

1. Open **Hyper-V Manager** from **Administrative Tools (Control Panel)**.
2. From the action pane on the right-hand side, click on **Virtual Switch**.

3. On the left-hand side, click on **New virtual network switch** under the **Virtual Switches** section, and on the right-hand side under the **Create virtual switch** section, select **External** as the type of switch; then, click on **Create Virtual Switch** as shown in the following screenshot:

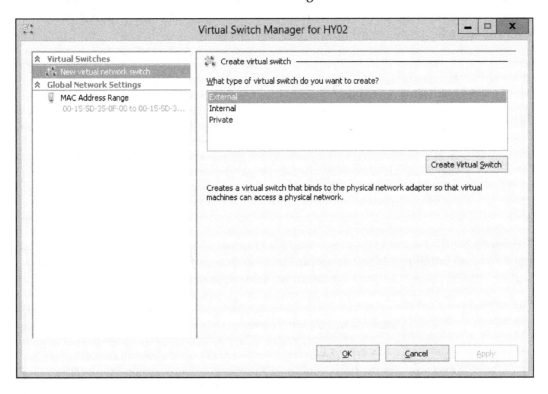

4. In the **Name** field, insert any name that reminds you of the functionality of the switch.

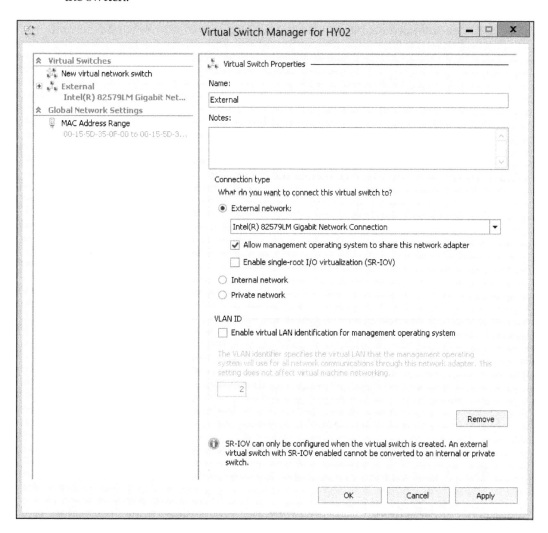

5. Make sure that the **Connection type** field is set to **External network**, and select the external network card on which you want to send traffic.

6. Depending on your choice, you may check the **Allow management operating system to share this network adapter** checkbox. If you have a server that has a single NIC, not checking this box means that you or any other administrator has to visit the server room to remotely take control of the server. Or if you have multiple interfaces, you may select this option, so you will be allowing the Hyper-V server to receive remote access only on the management interface of the server.

7. You can also check **Enable single-root I/O virtualization (SR-IOV)** for this virtual switch, depending on your need. We will cover single root I/O virtualization in a later section of this chapter.

8. If your virtual network switch wants you to select VLAN tagging for this virtual network, you may select the **VLAN ID** option. This will allow your virtual network switch to specify the virtual LAN that the management operating system will use for all the network communication through this network adapter.

9. After selecting all the configuration parameters, click on **Apply** and then on **OK**.

Internal

An internal virtual switch allows communication to happen only between the virtual machine and the hypervisor host. This type of virtual switch allows the virtual machine to access other internally hosted virtual machines and offered services and applications. This type of virtual switch also provides a great level of network isolation for any research and development product; you may not want to have any outer network interaction with this instance. To create an internal virtual network switch, you may perform the following steps:

1. Open **Hyper-V Manager** from **Administrative Tools (Control Panel)**.

2. From the action pane on the right-hand side, click on **Virtual Switch**.

3. On the left-hand side, click on **New virtual network switch** under the **Virtual Switches** section, and on the right-hand side under the **Create virtual switch** section, select **Internal** as the type of switch and click on **Create Virtual Switch**.

4. In the **Name** field, insert any name that reminds you of the functionality of the switch.

5. Make sure that the **Connection type** field is set to **Internal network**.

6. If your virtual network switch wants you to select VLAN tagging for this virtual network, you may select the **VLAN ID** option. This will allow your virtual network switch to specify the virtual LAN that the management operating system will use for all the network communication through this network adapter.

7. After selecting all the configuration parameters, click on **Apply** and then on **OK**.

Private

The key differentiator between the internal virtual switch and private switch is that the internal virtual network allows the virtual machine to interact with the hypervisor in such a way that network hosted services and resources can be accessed by the virtual machine; but when virtual machines use a private virtual network, they are not allowed to access these network resources hosted by the hypervisor. As it sounds, it is an exclusive connection between the virtual machines.

To create a private virtual switch, perform the following steps:

1. Open **Hyper-V Manager** from **Administrative Tools (Control Panel)**.

2. From the action pane on the right-hand side, click on **Virtual Switch**.

3. On the left-hand side, click on **New virtual network switch** under the **Virtual Switches** section, and on the right-hand side under the **Create virtual switch** section, select **Private** as the type of the switch and click on **Create Virtual Switch**.

4. In the **Name** field, insert any name that reminds you of the functionality of the switch.

5. Make sure that the **Connection type** field is set to **Private network**.

6. After selecting the connection type, click on **Apply** and then on the **OK** button to apply the changes.

Configuring Hyper-V virtual machine network settings

After discussing configuring and managing Hyper-V networking in the previous section of this chapter, let's now discover how we can configure the virtual machine network settings for Hyper-V. Configuring the Hyper-V virtual switch is one part of Hyper-V networking, and the second part is configuring the virtual machine for virtual networking. When you create a virtual machine, Hyper-V Manager only gives you the option of selecting a single NIC to connect to the available virtual switches, but once you have finished creating it, you can change the virtual machine's network settings. A single virtual machine can have multiple networks connected to it by means of multiple virtual network adapters. In a single virtual machine, you can add up to eight synthetic (high speed) network adapters and four legacy network adapters. We will explore more about these network adapter types in the next section.

We will divide the discussion on virtual machine network settings into two domains, as follows:

- Virtual network adapter types
- Advanced network configuration

Virtual network adapter types

Hyper-V provides two types of virtual network adapters that you can add as network adapters (hardware resource) into the virtual machine; they are:

- The synthetic network adapter (network adapter)
- The legacy network adapter

Now we will discuss each of the preceding network adapters in detail, so that you get a better idea of which type of network adapter (virtual) you need to add into your virtual machine to achieve a required type of network connectivity and the features related to it.

Synthetic network adapter

The synthetic network adapter or high-speed network adapter provides high-speed connection to the virtual machine. Usually, this is the preferred choice for any of the virtual machines we create on the Hyper-V server, unless and until there is a specific need to choose the legacy network adapter. By default, when we create a virtual machine on Hyper-V, a synthetic network adapter gets added automatically and connects to the virtual switch that we selected in the new virtual machine creation wizard.

To take full advantage of the synthetic network adapter, you need to install Hyper-V integration services in the guest operating system. If the Hyper-V integration services have not been installed on the guest operating system, you will see that the synthetic network adapter will be listed in the device manager as an "unknown" device. You can see in the following screenshot that the Hyper-V synthetic network adapter also provides you with a bandwidth management feature, which is a new feature that has been introduced in Hyper-V Windows Server 2012:

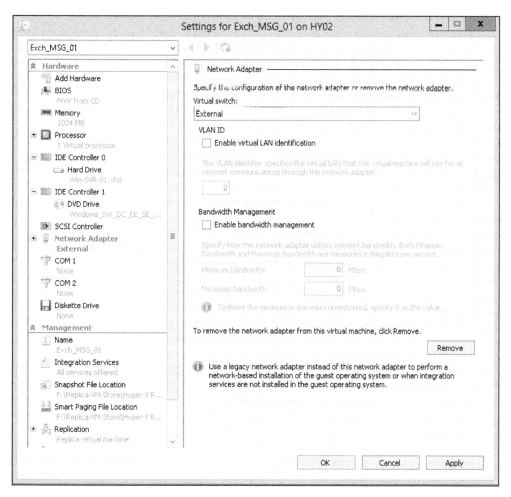

Legacy network adapter

A legacy network adapter, as it sounds, allows legacy operating systems and non-Microsoft operating systems to have networking capabilities. Other network adapters require you to install Hyper-V integration services, but the legacy network adapter works directly on the host network driver, which is why it works with all types of operating systems. One disadvantage of the legacy network adapter is that it gives you a 100 MB connection, so it has a slow network bandwidth. In a single virtual machine, you can only add up to four legacy network connections.

The legacy network adapter uses Intel 21140-based PCI Fast Ethernet Adapter. It also supports the **Preboot Execution Environment** (**PXE**). If you have a look at the following screenshot of the legacy network adapter, you will realize that the legacy network adapter doesn't provide the bandwidth management feature, which was introduced in the Windows Server 2012 Hyper-V release; there are few other features that don't come with the legacy network adapter.

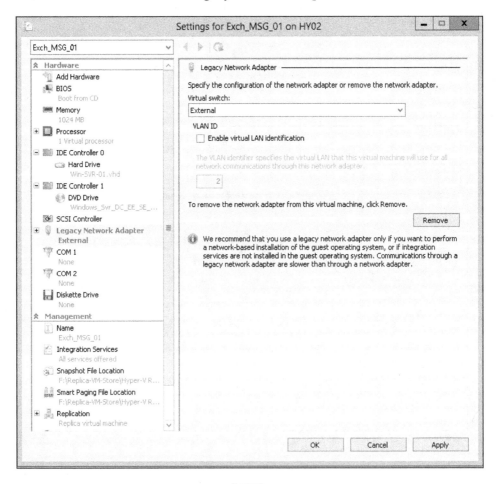

Configuring advanced network settings

In the preceding section about the virtual machine network settings, we discussed setting the basic network for a virtual machine, to allow the virtual machine to communicate over the network. Hyper-V Windows Server 2012 has introduced a series of new features related to virtual machine networking capabilities. These new features allow an organization to better slice up its physical network infrastructure between the virtualized workload to better allocate resources where they are needed the most. Especially when we talk about dynamic data centers and cloud computing, these new, out-of-the-box enhancements help us optimize our use of the physical infrastructure, allowing IT organizations to scale in during peak times and and scale out during non-peak times. These enhancements have become the topmost requirement for any small to medium size companies.

Now let's discuss these new, advanced network settings for a virtual machine that allow us to wisely utilize physical resources where we think they are most needed and improve the performance of our core virtualized platform.

Windows Server 2012 Hyper-V introduced the following list of new features; most of these features are part of Windows Server 2012 and a few of them are part of the Hyper-V role:

- Bandwidth management
- Hardware acceleration
    - Virtual machine queue
    - IPSEC task offloading
    - Single root I/O virtualization
- Failover TCP/IP
- Advanced features of a virtual machine network adapter
    - MAC address spoofing
    - DHCP guard
    - Router guard
    - Port mirroring
    - NIC teaming

Now we will go through each of these features and discuss how we can enable these features in a virtual machine, and how we can take advantage to optimize the network utilization and enhance the performance of our virtual machine.

Bandwidth management

With Hyper-V Windows Server 2012, it is now possible to set a bandwidth throttle for a virtual machine, where an administrator can set the bandwidth utilization limit for a particular virtual machine. This setting comprises two parts, namely minimum bandwidth and maximum bandwidth. Both of these minimum and maximum bandwidth limits are measured in megabits per second. In the following screenshot, we have tried to set a bandwidth limit for a virtual machine on SQL Server where we set **Minimum bandwidth** to **100 Mbps** and allow it burst up to 1000 Mbps (1 Gbps).

This new feature allows you to optimize the network unitization and enhance the performance of your critical virtual machine, by allowing it to have a better network bandwidth available.

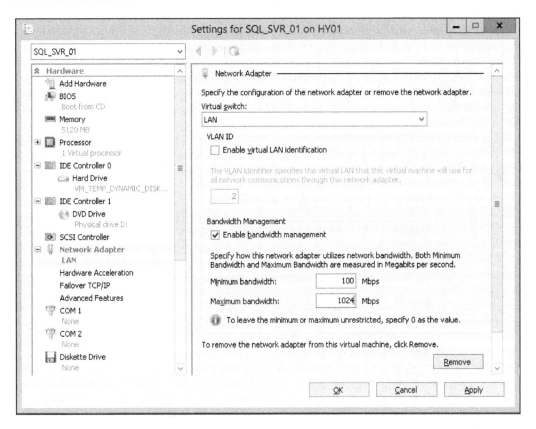

Hardware acceleration

Hardware acceleration settings for a virtual machine allow you to offload the physical host network adapter by configuring the various settings available for a virtual machine. These settings are the standard components of a virtual machine, and tweaking them allows an administrator to offload the excessive usage of the physical resources on the host server.

The hardware acceleration settings available for optimizing host network utilization are given as follows.

Virtual machine queue

The **virtual machine queue** (**VMQ**) feature was introduced in Windows Server 2008 for the first time for the Hyper-V server role, which has a VMQ-supported network adapter installed. The VMQ technology uses a hardware, packet-filtering mechanism to deliver the IP packet data from an external virtual machine network directly to virtual machines, which helps the virtualized network to reduce its load by copying routing packets from the Hyper-V management host OS to the VM itself.

With Hyper-V Windows Server 2012, we can enable the VMQ feature directly from the virtual machine settings, which will enable our physical server network adapter to get free from the excessive load of the VM-oriented data by making it directly accessible to the virtual machine itself.

IPSEC task offloading

The IPSEC task offloading feature was introduced for the first time in Windows Server 2012 Hyper-V. This feature requires that the physical network adapter of the host Hyper-V server and virtual machine be configured to take advantage of the IPSEC offloading feature. In cases where sufficient hardware resources are not available, security associations are not offloaded and they are handled in the operating system of the virtual machine.

We can set the maximum number of offloaded security associations in the range from 1 to 4096.

Single root I/O virtualization

SR-IOV is a standard that allows PCI Express devices to be shared among multiple virtual machines by providing them with a direct hardware path for the I/O. Hyper-V provides support to SR-IOV capable network adapters. SR-IOV reduces network latency, reduces CPU utilization to process network traffic, and increases network throughput. SR-IOV requires specific hardware. It may also require drivers to be installed in the guest operating system. When sufficient hardware resources are not available, network connectivity is provided through the virtual machine.

Enabling the SR-IOV feature for a virtual machine requires that the Hyper-V host's hardware support the SR-IOV feature. Enabling this feature on the supported hardware allows significant amount of hardware optimization and improves the virtual machine's network performance.

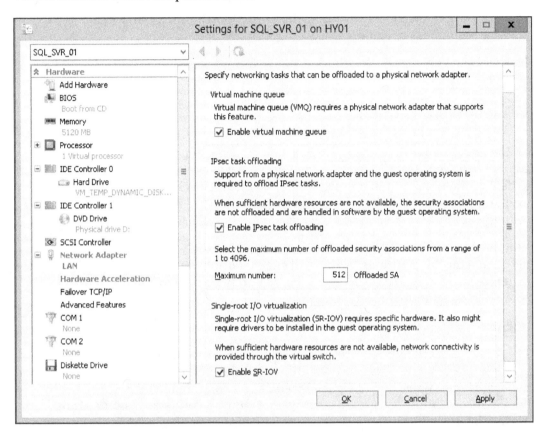

Failover TCP/IP

We discussed the failover TCP/IP setting for a virtual machine in *Chapter 3, Setting Up Hyper-V Replication*, when we discussed the Hyper-V Replica deployment scenario. We saw that one of the most highly used scenarios of the Hyper-V Replica feature is the **disaster recovery (DR)** site building scenario. DR sites usually have different IP addressing schemes and everything related to the physical network all together. With the help of this feature, we preconfigure the IP addressing configuration on the virtual machine, so when the virtual machine tries to come up at the DR site from the Hyper-V Replica server, it gets this IP addressing configuration inserted.

To take advantage of this, Hyper-V Replica instances of virtual machines should be configured on each VM wherever we want to take advantage of this feature. Hyper-V allows administrators to set both IPv4 and IPv6 configurations of these replica virtual machines.

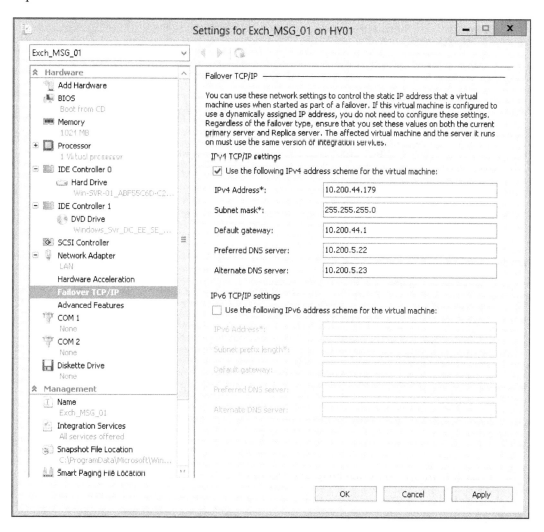

The preceding failover TCP/IP information provided in the advanced virtual machine network adapter settings of the Hyper-V Replica server VM instance allows it to seamlessly fail over while running on the Hyper-V Replica server. These failover TCP/IP settings can only be configured on the synthetic network adapter and not on the legacy network adapter. The operating system running in the guest virtual machine must be either Windows Server 2012, Windows Server 2008 R2, Windows Server 2008, Windows Server 2003 SP2 (or higher), Windows 7, Windows Vista SP2 (or higher), or Windows XP SP2 (or higher). The latest Windows Server 2012 Integration Services must be installed on the virtual machine.

Advanced features of the virtual machine network adapter

In this section, to configure the virtual machine network adapter's advanced features, we will see the series of new features that have been added to the Hyper-V legacy. All these new features have been introduced in Windows Server 2012 Hyper-V, except the MAC address spoofing feature.

Now let's have a look at each of these features to customize your virtual machine network's usage experience one by one.

MAC address spoofing

MAC address spoofing usually comes into play when a virtual machine is configured to change the MAC address. The best real-world example would be to set up **Microsoft Network Load Balancing (NLB)**. When you create a **Windows Network Load Balancing (WNLB)** cluster on Windows Server, WNLB changes the MAC address on the NIC used for NLB creation and puts the WNLB MAC address. If you create a WNLB cluster on virtual machines without enabling MAC address spoofing, the outgoing packets won't be able to bind the WNLB MAC address on the packet, so your WNLB cluster will not work as expected. This is why WNLB is required to configure the virtual network adapter of the virtual machine with the MAC address spoofing feature.

DHCP guard

The DHCP guard setting was introduced as a safety shield for your virtualized environment, where the DHCP guard prevents DHCP server messages from unauthorized virtual machines pretending to be the DHCP server. When you enable this feature on a virtual machine, you actually tell Hyper-V that this virtual machine is not a DHCP server, and so you tell it to not forward the DHCP server message over to the network.

Router guard

The router guard setting is another security feature that has been introduced in Hyper-V Windows Server 2012. The concept of a router guard is the same as a DHCP guard, where the router guard prevents router advertisement packets and redirection messages from unauthorized virtual machines pretending to be routers, where the routing and remote access service is configured for IP routing protocols.

Port mirroring

This is another great feature that makes network troubleshooting handy and allows an administrator to have full control of the virtualized networking stack. Port mirroring allows an administrator to configure another virtual machine to receive the network communication (both incoming and outgoing packets) destined for a particular virtual machine. In this way, another machine is able to perform analysis on the second machine that is receiving the network communication, to get an insight into network-layer issues. This makes network-based troubleshooting handier and fixes the problem in less time, saving both time and money.

NIC teaming

We will explore the benefits of NIC teaming for both the virtual machine and host later on in this chapter. Although we usually set up NIC teaming for the Hyper-V host servers, if needed, we can utilize the NIC teaming functionality for the virtual machine as well. If you don't configure this setting, the virtual machine will set it up by default; so in this case if any of the physical NICs stop working, NIC teaming inside the virtual machine will experience network connectivity failures.

Implementing NIC teaming for Hyper-V host and guest

We were introduced to load balancing and failover with NIC teaming at the beginning of this chapter, in the *Load balancing and failover (NIC teaming)* section. This is an important feature, so let's take a look at it in detail in this section.

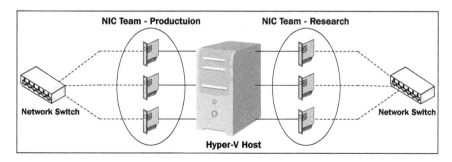

Various NIC manufacturers refer to the NIC teaming solution as **Load Balancing and Failover (LBFO)**. These manufactures have been in the market for a long time, providing NIC teaming software for their NICs. Customers buying servers have to install this NIC teaming software after setting up an operating system to create a team consisting of multiple physical NICs. This functionality has been around in the industry for some time now, and most of our critical applications and database servers are configured for NIC teaming.

NIC manufacturers provided this great functionality of making the server network capable of load balancing and failover on multiple NICs available inside the server; but on the other end, it has also been noticed that most of the time, while troubleshooting most network- and performance-related issues, NIC teaming is the cause of the problem. This is because sometimes an old software release of the NIC teaming software has compatibility issues with the application or service. And sometimes it is the physical network components' misconfiguration that causes the system administrator to break the NIC teaming on the application or database server.

NIC manufacturers provide NIC teaming software separately, which has always been difficult for patching up, because this software is not a part of the Windows operating system, and so always gets neglected when the routine maintenance and patch management of servers is being carried out.

Native OS NIC teaming feature – the most awaited feature

With the advantages and disadvantages of the hardware manufacturer NIC teaming feature, we have all been waiting for native NIC teaming functionality in the Windows Server operating system.

And here comes the good news; Microsoft has introduced a series of new features in the Windows Server 2012 operating system. Among all these awesome features, Microsoft has also introduced the NIC teaming feature that allows an administrator to create an NIC team by combining multiple physical NIC cards for server network load balancing and NIC failover capabilities. This new feature allows companies to configure NIC teaming on the server without installing any additional software; they can create an NIC team using their native Windows features with easy configuration steps. Microsoft NIC teaming is available in all Windows Server 2012 releases, including the Server Core edition of Windows Server.

NIC teaming requirements

To create an NIC team, we must have at least one NIC available on the server. The Windows Server 2012 NIC teaming functionality allows an administrator to make changes to add and remove NIC team members at any time. Adding at least one NIC into a team is the minimum requirement for creating a team, but having a single NIC added to the team will not provide the network with load-balancing and failover capabilities. All modes that provide fault protection through failover require a minimum of two Ethernet NICs in the team. The Windows Server 2012 implementation supports up to 32 NICs in a team.

 Before you go and buy your server hardware, make sure to check the Windows Hardware Qualification list for the tested and compatible NICs available in the server hardware. Visit `http://www.windowsservercatalog.com/results.aspx?bCatId=1283&avc=10` for Windows Server Catalog to check for server hardware compatibility.

NIC teaming architectural consideration

It is highly advisable to visit the NIC teaming supportability consideration before you start your physical Hyper-V host for creating and hosting production-virtualized workloads. This is because when your environment is hosting production virtual machines, or especially in the case of setting up a Hyper-V cluster, changing the setup of base NICs becomes very difficult and sometimes breaks the configuration.

We will mention all the NIC teaming setup considerations here, which should be included in any type of server or application hosting:

- Constructing an NIC team consisting of NICs capable of operating at different speeds but presently operating at the same speed is supported by the Microsoft NIC teaming feature.

- Setting up NIC teaming on Windows Server 2012, where member NICs have different speeds, is not supported. Having different speeds of network connections will not stop you from creating a team or adding an NIC to the team, but the actual functionality of a teaming mode or load-balancing feature may not work as designed.

- As we said previously, having different NIC speeds is not supported by the NIC team, but still if you want to form a team of members with different NIC speeds, then creating an NIC team where active/standby configuration is used would work. The NIC with the lower speed will always be used as the standby for the sake of maintaining connectivity. Active/Active Configuration is not supported.

- Mixing of the Microsoft NIC teaming solution with other third-party NIC teaming software is not supported, and it should not be done, because it may make the system unstable and can cause network disconnection.

- The Microsoft NIC teaming solution allows you to add a maximum of 32 NICs into a single NIC team.

- NIC teams should contain homogenous NICs, for example, an NIC team "Server Farm" should contain 1 GB of NICs; it should not have 10 GB of NICs. And when you create another NIC team "Research Farm" of 10 GB of NICs, you should not add 1 GB of NICs into this.

- The Microsoft NIC teaming solution allows you to add a maximum of 32 NICs into a single NIC team.

Configuring NIC teaming for the Hyper-V host

Perform the following steps to configure the NIC teaming feature on the Hyper-V host server:

1. Open **Server Manager**; click on the **Hyper-V** role and right-click on the local server name, and click on **Configure NIC Teaming** as shown in the following screenshot:

2. Now from the **ADAPTERS AND INTERFACES** section in the lower-right corner, select both the available NICs, that is, **Ethernet 1** and **Ethernet 2**, right-click on them, and click on **Add to New Team** as shown in the following screenshot:

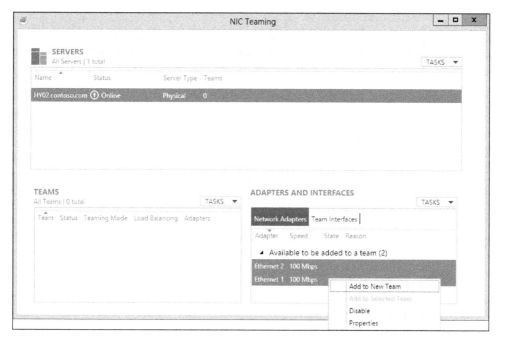

3. In the **New team** creation window, give a name to your NIC team that you want to create. If you are creating multiple teams on the server for different applications and services, it is recommended that you give a name that will help you to differentiate between the purposes of these teams.

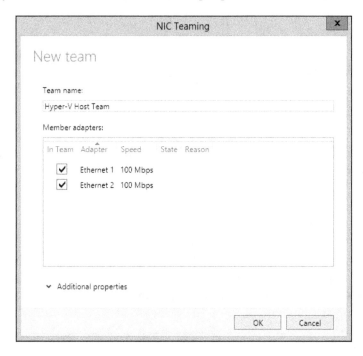

4. After entering the name for your team, click on the **OK** button. This will save your settings and provision a team NIC interface with the same name that you gave to your team in step 3.

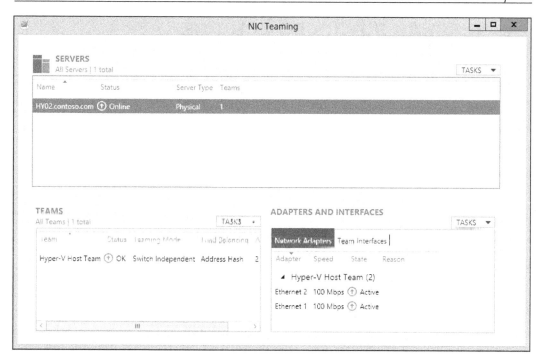

Since we are now provisioning an NIC team consisting of two physical network adapters, if you go to **Network and Sharing Center**, you will see a new NIC adapter shown there with the name of your NIC team. The Windows NIC teaming software is not like other NIC teaming software that we used to configure in our servers in the past, where after creating a team, the server management IP address automatically moves from one of the NICs to the team interface. Once you have created the NIC teaming feature within Windows Server 2012, you have to set up the IP addressing related information, and we can then use this interface for the intended types of communication.

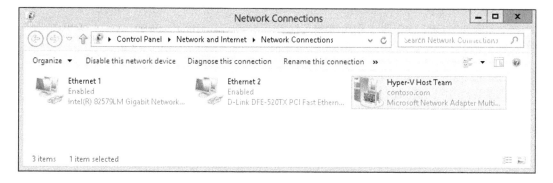

In the next section, we will discuss the various available NIC teaming modes.

NIC teaming advanced settings

As we said previously, after creating an NIC team, we can go to the NIC properties section at any time and customize the team functionality as per our need. This gives us the flexibility to have multiple NIC teams on the interface with different sets of functionality for different services and applications hosted by the host server.

The NIC teaming feature's advanced settings allow you to change or configure three major settings, which are as follows:

- Teaming mode
- Load-balancing mode
- Standby adapter

Now let's discuss each of the NIC teaming feature's advanced settings.

NIC teaming mode

Windows Server 2012 supports three modes for NIC teaming that allow an administrator to customize the NIC teaming functionality as per the need of the network load balancing and failover capabilities. And before we explore the NIC teaming modes, let's first understand the two available flavors of Windows Server 2012 NIC teaming, which are as follows:

- Switch independent (default)
- Switch dependent

Let's explain both of these NIC teaming configuration concepts so as to get a better idea of choosing the correct NIC team mode for our Hyper-V environment.

Switch independent

When we create an NIC team on Windows Server 2012, the switch independent mode gets selected for the team by default, which can later be changed. The switch independent mode, as it sounds, is totally independent from the physical network switch(es) that your server is connected to. Network switches don't participate in the switch independent mode and hence don't know whether the server has configured the NIC teaming software or not. So it is very much possible that the Hyper-V host containing multiple NICs for multiple NIC teams and configured as the switch independent NIC teaming mode can be connected to multiple physical network switches.

Switch dependent

Another type of Windows Server 2012 NIC configuration is the switch dependent mode. In this type of NIC teaming configuration, the NIC teaming functionality depends on the physical network layer, where the network switches should be configured and support the NIC teaming configuration. With a switch dependent NIC teaming environment, you are required to connect all the NICs of the server to the same switch, which comprises a single NIC team.

Since we have understood the two types of NIC teaming modes, we will now discover the submodes of the previously explained NIC teaming modes. We can also call them functionality sets for NIC teaming modes.

Static teaming

Static teaming or generic teaming is covered in IEEE 802.3ad draft v1. With static teaming configuration, we are required to configure both switch and host NICs that take part in the NIC teaming. And since it's a manual or static solution, we do not have the luxury of identifying if a network cable has been disconnected or any other fault in the communication channel with static teaming.

Dynamic teaming

Dynamic teaming is the second mode of Windows Server 2012 NIC teaming; this is covered in IEEE 802.1ax, LACP. This standard is most widely known as IEEE 802.3ad as it was developed in the IEEE 802.3ad committee before being published as IEEE 802.1ax. IEEE 802.1ax uses **Link Aggregation Control Protocol (LACP)** to dynamically determine the NICs that are connected with the host and physical network switch. Dynamic teaming enables the automatic creation of a team, in theory but rarely in practice, and it enables the expansion and reduction of a team simply by the transmission or receipt of LACP from the peer entity. Typical server-class switches support IEEE 802.1ax, but most of them require administration to enable LACP on the port.

Load-balancing mechanisms

Now we will understand the load-balancing mechanisms that Windows NIC teaming uses to distribute the load among the NIC members of the team. There are basically two load-balancing algorithms that Windows Server 2012 uses for load balancing the traffic between NIC team members. These algorithms are as follows:

- Address hash
- Hyper-V port

Address hash

By default, the address hash gets chosen as a load-balancing mode for your NIC team created in Windows Server 2012. The address hash algorithm generates a hash value based on the address components of an IP packet and then assigns packets on the basis of the hash value assigned to them to one of NIC team members' interface cards. This method load balances the traffic across all interfaces of the team.

The components that take part in the hashing mechanism are as follows:

- Source and destination MAC addresses
- Source and destination IP addresses (2-tuple hash)
- Source and destination TCP ports, usually used along with the IP addresses (4-tuple hash)

The most granular distribution of traffic streams is created by 4-tuple hash, resulting in smaller streams that can be moved independently between interfaces. But it cannot be used for traffic, such as IPSEC-protected traffic, that is not TCP or UDP based, or where the TCP and UDP ports are hidden from the stack. So in this case, the hash falls back to the 2-tuple hash, or remains as the MAC address hash as the traffic is not IP traffic.

Hyper-V port

The Hyper-V port load balancing mode is recommended for hypervisors, where each virtual machine has its own independent MAC address or could be connected to the dedicated port through the Hyper-V virtual switch. Using this scheme in virtualization comes with an advantage. As the connected switch sees a particular MAC address on one and only one connected interface, the switch will load balance the ingress load (the traffic from the switch to the host) on multiple links based on the destination MAC (VM MAC) address.

We said previously that the Hyper-V port load balancing mode is a more relevant and recommended approach to load balance traffic for a hypervisor, but when the Hyper-V environment along with the physical hardware is configured for the VMQ feature, the usage of the Hyper-V port becomes brighter and adds value to improve the quality of load balancing between the multiple hypervisors with the same Hyper-V virtual switch. However, this mode may not be granular enough to get a well-balanced distribution if the host has only a few VMs. This mode will also always limit a single VM (that is, the traffic from a single switch port) to the bandwidth available on a single interface. Windows Server uses the Hyper-V switch port as the identifier rather than the source MAC address as, in some instances, a VM may be using more than one MAC address on a switch port.

Configuring NIC teaming for Hyper-V guest virtual machines

In the preceding section, we discussed how NIC teaming can help you load balance the network traffic for your Hyper-V server and how the failover feature of the NIC teaming tool lets you configure the server NICs' failover capability.

Now what about the virtual machine? Well, Hyper-V also allows you to configure the NIC teaming functionality for virtual machines running on Hyper-V Windows Server 2012. While configuring VM-level NIC teaming, you are required to set the NIC teaming feature on the virtual machine's NICs, which enables the virtual machine's NICs to perform the same NIC team functionality inside the virtual machine, as if they are physically teamed NICs.

Now we will see the steps you need to take to configure the NIC teaming feature on a virtual machine running on Windows Server 2012 Hyper-V:

1. Open **Hyper-V Manager** from **Administrative Tools**.
2. Select the virtual machine properties for which you want to configure the NIC teaming.
3. Just as with the physical server, we can create an NIC team containing a single NIC—but a single NIC doesn't offer load-balancing and failover capabilities—and this is the same scenario that applies to the virtual machine's NIC teaming feature as well, where you would always want to enable the NIC teaming feature for a virtual machine that will have more than one virtual NIC configured.
4. Now expand each virtual NIC in the virtual machine settings and click on **Advance Features**. In the **Advanced Features** list, you will find the **NIC Teaming** feature at the bottom, where you are required to check the **Enable this network adapter to be part of a team in the guest operating system** checkbox.

5. Now perform the same operation for other virtual NICs that have been added to the same virtual machine.

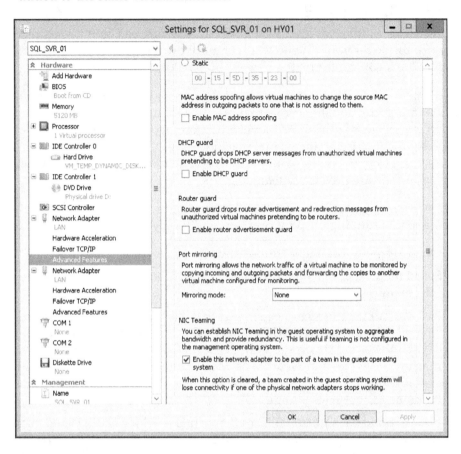

Summary

Within this chapter, we first saw a technical overview of the Hyper-V virtual switch, and then we went through a number of newly added features in the Windows Server 2012 Hyper-V virtual switch. While discussing all these newly added features in Hyper-V Windows Server 2012, we also saw how these new features can help us build an enterprise-level virtualized platform for server virtualization and cloud-based virtualized environments.

After completing the Hyper-V virtual switch overview and discovering the newly added features of Hyper-V with Windows Server 2012, we discussed the configuration and management of the Hyper-V virtual switch. We saw the step-by-step configuration of the Hyper-V virtual switch for different sets of network communication, for example, for the external virtual switch, the internal virtual switch, and, last but not least, the private virtual switch for a virtual machine running on a single box. After understanding the configuration of the Hyper-V virtual switch, we discussed the virtual machine network settings, where we discussed a number of newly added virtual machine network capabilities and their benefits.

Lastly, we discussed the load-balancing and failover capabilities of Windows Server 2012 for a physical Hyper-V host and virtual machine. In this section of the chapter, we discussed the NIC teaming functionality of the Hyper-V host and virtual machine in depth, which allows configuring the NIC load balancing and failover settings. We also discussed the importance of NIC teaming, which can also be considered the best practice for teaming within Windows Server 2012, in general, and Hyper-V too.

In the next chapter, we will see how we can benefit from Windows Server 2012 PowerShell for the purpose of Hyper-V automation and scripting.

5
A New World of Hyper-V Automation with PowerShell

In this chapter we will discover the capabilities of Windows Server 2012 PowerShell for the Hyper-V role. The earlier version of Windows Server PowerShell didn't provide full support for Hyper-V and we were able to execute only the basic level of server management tasks, especially in a Hyper-V environment. But with the release of Windows Server 2012, Windows Server PowerShell 3.0 now provides a great level of Hyper-V management and automation functionalities.

We will start this chapter by discovering Windows PowerShell as a command-line and scripting platform for scripting and automating tasks. Then we will go deeper into the Windows PowerShell technology, and will understand the various core components of PowerShell, such as cmdlets, pipelining, scripting, and versions.

To take our journey further to the next level, after finishing the Windows PowerShell overview, we will see what new features and capabilities Windows Server 2012 PowerShell has brought to us for server task scripting and automation. In that section of the chapter we will also discover the enhancements made to Windows PowerShell Version 3.0.

At the end of the chapter we will witness the capabilities of Windows PowerShell 3.0 for Hyper-V Windows Server 2012, where we will see some of the important PowerShell cmdlets for management- and maintenance-related operations. We will also see how we can use these cmdlets and arrange them in an order for scripting the task to be automatically be carried out for Hyper-V. Before finishing this chapter, we will see a reference to all the available cmdlets for Windows Server 2012 Hyper-V.

Introduction to PowerShell

PowerShell, as a scripting and automation framework from Microsoft, has been around for quite a long time now. System engineers and server administrators realized its importance and credibility after the launch of Windows Server 2008, where PowerShell integrated inside Windows Server 2008 as a management and task automation utility. Afterwards, we all saw a turning point when all the Microsoft products were heavily integrated with PowerShell, and most of their custom configuration was made available only through the command-line interface (PowerShell), especially Microsoft Exchange Server, Forefront Family Products, System Center Family Products, and Lync Server. This change allowed an extreme level of flexibility for customer configuration and command-level automation. On one hand, it provided great flexibility and automation capabilities, but on the other hand, in the beginning, it required all the system and server administrators to upgrade their skills. This was because the Microsoft products had never worked this closely with any command-shell utility, and most of the configuration capabilities were present in the GUI fashion.

Being a shell-scripting and automation framework tightly integrated with .NET Framework, PowerShell introduced a new world of scripting. PowerShell provides full system access to COM and WMI scripting and automation. Also, it is not bound to the local instance, can perform remote server management, and has scripting capabilities.

Windows Server PowerShell provides hosting capabilities, where an administrator can host another application inside the PowerShell runtime. This other application uses PowerShell as a platform for carrying out tasks and operations, either while running on GUI or command-shell interface. PowerShell's remote capabilities allow these hosted applications running inside PowerShell to perform the management and operating for similar or different instances running on the remote server. Right after integrating PowerShell as a .NET Framework integrated command-shell and scripting platform, Microsoft, as a product vendor, now helps in building applications that are completely manageable and scripted with PowerShell. PowerShell enables the application to leverage the base platform of Windows Server and frees up the application processes to have more memory and process free time to provide fast and reliable application computing functionalities.

Technical overview

PowerShell is an installable feature available in Windows Server 2008, which can later be installed and removed from the server as needed by the server administrator. PowerShell is nowadays the basic requirement of the Microsoft server systems products. PowerShell utilizes .NET Framework as a platform and uses cmdlets or commandlets to perform its operations. We may use a single cmdlet to perform a single task, or we can combine multiple cmdlets in one PS1 script (PowerShell scripting extension) and perform multiple tasks.

The following screenshot shows the PowerShell cmdlet command-line interface:

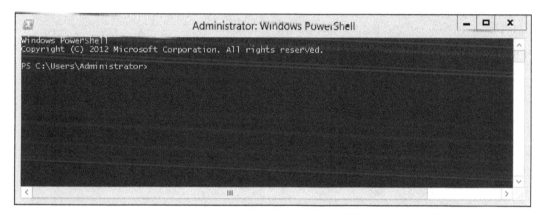

Let's move further ahead, and describe PowerShell and its related components in detail, this This will later on help us to understand the PowerShell's power for Hyper-V.

Cmdlets

Cmdlets or commandlets are the functional drivers of PowerShell. An administrator can use a cmdlet to invoke any runtime operation, or can combine multiple cmdlets together to complete a series of steps to take full advantage of automation. A cmdlet can be executed against the local or a remote system. Each cmdlet has certain attributes and functionality assigned, which can only be executed in the correct fashion and in order. The beauty of PowerShell is that you can very easily combine several PowerShell cmdlets to work with each other for carrying out the intended operation. For example, in the first part of the PowerShell command, we can call a cmdlet (Get-*) for selecting all the objects for the same attributes, and then in the second portion of the command, we will use another cmdlet (Set-*) for performing the required attribute changes on all the selected objects.

There are hundreds of cmdlets available in Windows Server 2012, which provides the best-of-breed scripting and task automation capabilities. We can see all the commandlets by running `Get-Command` from PowerShell, as shown in the following screenshot:

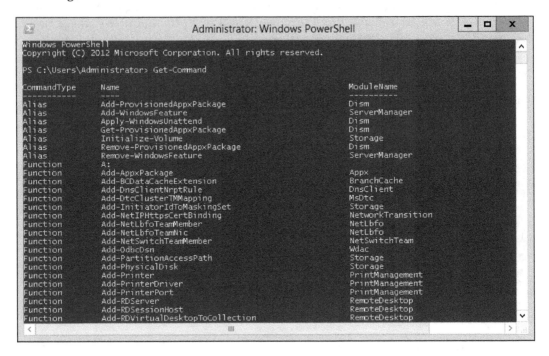

To get more familiar with cmdlets, let's see how the normal Windows command prompt commandlets and PowerShell commandlets are different:

- Commandlets are constructed instances of the .NET Framework classes, and just like Windows command prompt's commands, they are not standalone binary executables.

- Commandlets can be constructed from as few as a dozen lines of code.

- Commandlets do not perform error presentation or commandlet output formatting, they get all these functionalities from the base platform of PowerShell.

- Windows commands are usually less compatible with the piping mode, whereas cmdlets are fully compatible with it. A single cmdlet can be piped with another command, and this combination can perform a complex task as easily as possible.

Cmdlets pipelining

A single cmdlet can perform an operation such as `Get-Command`, which will bring all the PowerShell cmdlets available in the operating system for the installed PowerShell version. Cmdlets pipelining comes into the picture when you want to perform an operation that will take input from the output of the first cmdlet operation and then perform the second operation, which will complete the desired job.

Pipelining is extremely useful in any **command-line interface** (CLI)-based management and multitasking automation utilities. This allows an administrator to take an efficient decision, where he/she can minimize the errors introduced due to the manual process of providing inputs, using pipelining, where we take system data to perform various tasks.

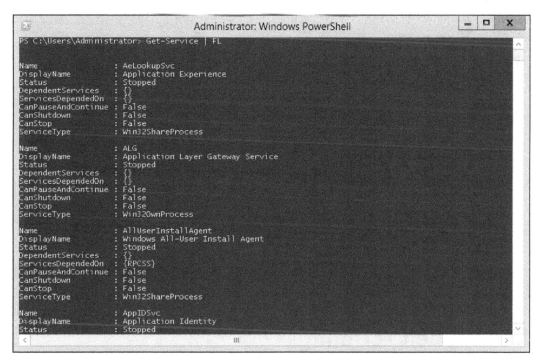

Microsoft's PowerShell implementation is similar to Linux/UNIX, where PowerShell uses a pipeline. But the PowerShell pipeline structure is different from the one that the Linux and UNIX pipeline uses. Among other differences, the main difference of pipeline usage here is that the Linux/Unix pipe structure contains unstructured data, while with Windows PowerShell, due to the presence of .Net Framework, uses structured data.

Now let's take an example of pipelining for Hyper-V related operations. In this example, we will see how we can benefit from the PowerShell cmdlet pipelining feature. So we have a Windows Server 2012 Hyper-V server, on which we have five VMs created. Our objective is to quickly see which ISO files are mounted on these virtual machines. To do this we will first import the Hyper-V module into PowerShell by executing **Import-Module Hyper-V**. Once the Hyper-V module is imported into PowerShell, we will execute the `Get-VM | Get-VMDvdDrive | fl` command. This will provide us with a list of the virtual machines configured with the ISO file mounted, as shown in the following screenshot:

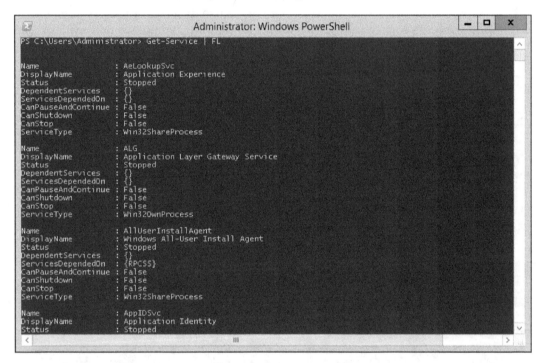

PowerShell scripting

PowerShell provides a much more powerful scripting platform as compared to the other traditional scripting formats, which we have used in the past. Other scripting technologies use the WMI and COM objects to perform various tasks. But no other language has the level of integration that PowerShell has with .Net Framework, and with the COM and WMI objects. This makes PowerShell very simple yet strong enough to automate even a complex task, by making it easy to understand and alter it as needed.

PowerShell also provides a security feature, which none of the other scripting languages provides. PowerShell by default prevents any PowerShell-based script (`.ps1`) from executing on the server. PowerShell prevents these security threats by implementing various security practices, such as a default path for the scripts to execute and a script execution policy. If you try to execute a script that doesn't fulfill the requirements and goes against these two securities and other PowerShell built-in security features, you will be restricted and the script will not be executed. All these types of built-in security features that defend your application and server from possible threats are not available in any other scripting language, which makes PowerShell different from the others.

PowerShell Version 3.0 overview

Microsoft PowerShell Version 3.0 hit the surface with Windows Server 2012. At the time of writing this book, PowerShell 3.0 is the latest version of PowerShell, which contains all the great features from the previous versions. There are also some very cool new features added into this wave of the product, which we will discuss shortly in this section.

PowerShell 3.0 is designed in such a way as to cater to the need for a high level of automation, to better support the vision of Windows Server 2012, where Microsoft claims that Windows Server 2012 is a cloud-ready platform. It means that through datacenter dynamics and cloud computing, high-class automation capabilities have already been provided in the operations system in the name of the built-in PowerShell.

Windows Server 2012 added the following new features into the PowerShell legacy:

- Simplified language syntax that makes commands and scripts look a lot less like code and a lot more like natural language.
- Finding and running any of the cmdlets installed on your computer with ease, with improved cmdlet discovery and automatic module loading.
- `Show-Command` is a cmdlet and ISE add-on that helps users find the right cmdlet and view its parameters in a dialog box.
- Workflows that run long-running activities (in sequence or in parallel) to perform complex, larger management tasks, such as multimachine application provisioning. The Windows PowerShell workflows are repeatable, parallelizable, interruptible, and recoverable, using the Windows Workflow Foundation at the command line.
- Robust sessions that automatically recover from network failures and interruptions, and allow you to disconnect from the session, shut down the computer, and reconnect from a different computer without interrupting the task.

- Scheduled jobs that run regularly or in response to an event.
- Delegated administration that allows us to execute commands with a delegated set of credentials, so that users with limited permissions can run the critical jobs.

Since we have now completed the PowerShell introduction and understood its different components and features, let's move on to learn about PowerShell 3.0. We will be covering the detailed feature set of PowerShell 3.0, and will also see the step-by-step installation method of PowerShell 3.0 on a server based on the Windows Server 2012 operating system.

Insight into Windows Server 2012 PowerShell (3.0)

Before we hit the installation topic of this section, let's first go ahead and understand the requirements for installing and running PowerShell 3.0.

PowerShell OS support

PowerShell 3.0 is supported on the following listed operating systems as of now. All these supported operating systems provide the same level of functionality for local and remote PowerShell sessions.

- Windows 7 with Service Pack 1
- Windows Server 2008 R2 with Service Pack 1
- Windows Server 2008 with Service Pack
- Windows 8
- Windows Server 2012

System requirements

We already explained a bit about the system requirements of PowerShell in the *Introduction to PowerShell* section. PowerShell 3.0 has the following set of requirements, which should be met before you install PowerShell on any of the supported operating systems.

Windows Management Instrumentation 3.0

Windows PowerShell 3.0 requires **Windows Management Instrumentation (WMI)** 3.0. This program is included in Windows 8 Release Preview, Windows Server 2012, and Windows Management Framework 3.0 Beta. If this program is not installed on the computer, the features that require WMI, such as the CIM commands, do not run.

Common Language Runtime 4.0

Installing PowerShell 3.0 requires **Common Language Runtime (CLR)** 4.0 to be installed. PowerShell 3.0 is compiled in such a way that it requires the latest version of CLR to be installed.

.NET Framework

PowerShell 3.0 has different .Net Framework requirements, where PowerShell 3.0 requires an administrator to install Microsoft .Net Framework 4.0 before installing PowerShell 3.0. By default Windows Server 2012 and Windows 8 include .Net Framework 4.0, but for the other earlier versions, we have to download the latest .Net Framework and install it wherever we want.

WS-Management 3.0

Just like .Net Framework, PowerShell 3.0 requires the updated version of WS-Management, which is WS-Management 3.0. This updated version is made available in Windows 8 and Windows Server 2012 by default.

Since we now know the basic requirements for running PowerShell 3.0 on Windows Server 2012 and the earlier operating systems, let's go ahead and install PowerShell 3.0.

Installing PowerShell 3.0

When you install Windows Server 2008 and the later versions, PowerShell is installed on the system by default, because PowerShell is a native management utility for managing your Windows Server operating system. To encourage administrators, the PowerShell shortcut also appears in the menu bar of Windows Server 2008 and Windows Server 2012.

For the other supported operating systems, you first have to install the prerequisites for PowerShell 3.0 — as explained in the system requirements — and after that you may launch PowerShell 3.0 Redistributable, which can be downloaded from Microsoft Download Center.

PowerShell 3.0 Redistributable can be downloaded from Microsoft Download Center (`http://www.microsoft.com/en-us/download/details.aspx?id=29939`).

Managing Windows Server 2012 Hyper-V with PowerShell 3.0

Okay, now that we have gone through all the information about PowerShell and Windows Server 2012 enhancement for PowerShell, let's see how PowerShell can help us manage Hyper-V. Earlier, PowerShell's support for Hyper-V was not available in a direct way. What I mean by a direct way is that we didn't have PowerShell cmdlets for the Hyper-V role of Windows Server, but we had PowerShell support for **System Center Virtual Machine Manager (SCVMM)**. It let us perform a few Hyper-V related tasks, but it was an indirect method as you had to automate and perform management tasks for SCVMM, which actually performed jobs for Hyper-V.

With Windows Server 2012, Microsoft introduced Hyper-V specific cmdlets for managing and automating Hyper-V related simple and complex tasks. An organization can use these available cmdlets and create its custom scripts to get the most out of Hyper-V automation.

Power-Shell 3.0 provides the possibility of end-to-end configuration and change management of your Hyper-V infrastructure. Now let's discover the usage and benefits of PowerShell 3.0 for Hyper-V Windows Server 2012 to get a better idea of how we can leverage the most powerful scripting language made for the Windows Server platform till now.

PowerShell usage scenarios for Hyper-V management and automation

An administrator and organization can leverage PowerShell 3.0 for the end-to-end management of their Windows Server 2012 and Hyper-V 3.0. PowerShell 3.0 includes all the bits and pieces that are required to fully manage Windows Server 2012 as a base component of a hypervisor and the hypervisor as a base virtualization layer. PowerShell can be used by an administrator to manage the day-to-day routine tasks for the management of Hyper-V as a standalone instance, or a number of clustered Hyper-V servers. Let's go ahead and discuss the following different PowerShell usage scenarios for Hyper-V management and automation:

- Research and development environments
- Virtualized datacenter management
- Cloud management and automation

Research and development environments

PowerShell provides a great handy way to an administrator to build the research and development environments for product testing and POCs. An administrator can use PowerShell to manage the Hyper-V research and development environments, where hundreds of virtual machines have been created, and for building and simulating different test cases, each set of virtual machines contains a different set of properties. In this type of environments, using the GUI mode to manage the virtual machine becomes difficult and time consuming. At the same time, performing these reparative tasks again and again makes it time consuming and hectic to set up the research and development environments. Because of the nature of the research and development and testing environments, the administrators and developers require a fresh environment every time they perform testing for the given system.

With PowerShell 3.0, an administrator has all the cmdlets available, which allows him/her to build the research and development and testing environment over and over again with full automation. It means that he/she can script the creation and change-management tasks for hundreds of virtual machines with one simple PowerShell script. We will see examples of these types of script in the upcoming section. This is not all; PowerShell provides seamless integration with the other Hyper-V integrated products, such as the Microsoft System Center 2012 family products, which allows an administrator to have full control over the virtualized platform and its integrated components.

Virtualized datacenter management

With Hyper-V Windows Server 2008, we all managed the Hyper-V related operations and virtual machine configurations with Hyper-V Manager's GUI mode. But at some point of time, we all missed the luxury of CLI or a command-shell type of utility for the management purposes, although if you were using SCVMM for your Hyper-V management, you could have managed Hyper-V with PowerShell to some extent, but still with limited capabilities.

Windows Server 2012 PowerShell 3.0 gives you enough flexibility and agility to manage your local and remote datacenter from a normal Windows workstation. This flexibility opens new doors to automation and management capabilities for administrators. The administrators can manage their day-to-day routing tasks for Hyper-V using PowerShell; and at any point in time, making any bulk modification and configuration of virtual machines can be fully automated. PowerShell 3.0 seamlessly integrates with all the other datacenter management applications, such as System Center 2012 Management Suite, which makes the scripting and remote-shell connectivity with other servers and applications easy.

Cloud management and automation

As we initially took a look at an introduction to cloud computing, we discussed virtualization as the base component on which cloud computing builds its home, and provides services to all the guests coming to its party. As cloud computing uses the pool of resources for providing the shared services to its users, virtualization is used for the base computing platform. Thus, the management of this base platform—on which you provision services (virtual machines) for your customers—becomes critical and requires an extensive level of reliability and uptime.

Since cloud computing provisions the virtual machines and other services to hundreds of its customers, its infrastructure is also huge and may contain hundreds of hypervisors. Managing and maintaining these hypervisors could be a difficult task for the administrators, because most of the time these hypervisors are geographically dispersed across different datacenters. So this problem of managing and maintaining a sound infrastructure could get worse, if only the GUI-based administration was available, which we all faced with Hyper-V Windows Server 2008. Within Windows Server 2012 and Hyper-V 3.0, the cloud-computing providers—especially those who are running Hyper-V as the base hypervisor—can now take full advantage of PowerShell 3.0, which allows them to manage a single or hundreds of Hyper-V servers in less time with more automation. The PowerShell 3.0 cmdlets for Hyper-V 3.0 can be used to manage a local or a remote datacenter Hyper-V, where a cloud-computing provider provisions the services (VMs) and integrates with the other cloud-computing management suites, such as System Center 2012.

Windows PowerShell 3.0 capabilities for Hyper-V

Okay, since we have now gone through the technical overview of PowerShell, and the enhancements made to PowerShell 3.0 for Hyper-V management and automation, let's proceed to the last section of this chapter. Here we will discuss the PowerShell 3.0 cmdlets for Hyper-V, or in other words, the capabilities of PowerShell 3.0 for Hyper-V management and task automation.

Now let's see the capabilities that PowerShell 3.0 provides for the management and automation of Hyper-V. For this assessment, we will see the following examples of PowerShell cmdlet usage for Hyper-V management and operations.

> To take a look at the list of PowerShell cmdlets for Windows Server 2012 Hyper-V, please visit the following TechNet URL:
> http://technet.microsoft.com/en-us/library/hh848559.aspx

Example 1 – creating a new virtual machine

In this example we will create a new virtual machine on our Windows Server 2012 Hyper-V using PowerShell. We will first create a new virtual hard disk, and then create a new virtual machine by attaching the pre-created virtual hard disk.

Let's perform the following steps for creating the virtual hard disk and virtual machine:

1. Open the Windows Server 2012 PowerShell management console.
2. As we said, let's first create the new virtual hard disk by executing the `New-VHD -Path D:\sqltestvm\os_disk.vhdx -SizeBytes 15GB` cmdlet.

3. After creating the VHD for our new virtual machine, let's now create a new virtual machine by executing the `New-VM -Name "SQL Test VM" -MemoryStartupBytes 5GB -VHDPath "D:\sqltestvm\os_disk.vhdx"` cmdlet, as shown in the following screenshot:

```
                          Administrator: Windows PowerShell            _ □ X
PS C:\Users\Administrator> Import-Module Hyper-V
PS C:\Users\Administrator> New-VHD -Path D:\sqltestvm\os_disk.vhdx -SizeBytes 15GB

ComputerName          : HY01
Path                  : D:\sqltestvm\os_disk.vhdx
VhdFormat             : VHDX
VhdType               : Dynamic
FileSize              : 4194304
Size                  : 16106127360
MinimumSize           :
LogicalSectorSize     : 512
PhysicalSectorSize    : 4096
BlockSize             : 33554432
ParentPath            :
FragmentationPercentage : 0
Alignment             : 1
Attached              : False
DiskNumber            :
IsDeleted             : False
Number                :


PS C:\Users\Administrator> New-VM -Name "SQL Test VM" -MemoryStartupBytes 5GB -VHDPath "D:\sqltestvm\os_disk.vhdx"

Name        State CPUUsage(%) MemoryAssigned(M) Uptime   Status
----        ----- ----------- ----------------- ------   ------
SQL Test VM Off   0           0                 00:00:00 Operating normally

PS C:\Users\Administrator>
```

Example 2 – creating a new virtual network switch

In this example, we will see how we can use PowerShell for creating a new virtual network switch on the Hyper-V server. Now perform the following steps:

1. Open Windows Server 2012 PowerShell.

2. Let's first import the Hyper-V module into the PowerShell by running `Import-Module Hyper-V`.

3. Before we create a new virtual network switch, let's also list all the available network adapters installed on the Hyper-V host by executing the `Get-NetAdapter` cmdlet. This will provide a list of all the physical NICs installed on the server.

4. Since we now have all the required data to put into the cmdlet for creating a new virtual switch, let's run the `New-VMSwitch "External "-NetAdapterName "Ethernet"` cmdlet for creating a new switch with the name of `"External"`.

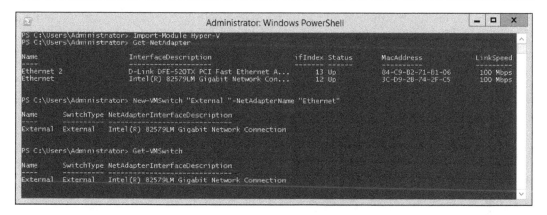

Example 3 – configuring and attaching a virtual network switch to a virtual machine

So far we have seen how to create a new virtual machine and a new virtual network switch using the Windows Server PowerShell management console. Now in this example, we will look at how to configure a virtual machine for attaching the Hyper-V virtual network switch that we created in the previous example.

Perform the following steps for configuring the virtual network switch for virtual machines pre-created on our Hyper-V server:

1. Open the Windows Server 2012 PowerShell management console.

2. Always remember to import the Hyper-V PowerShell module, before trying to use any Hyper-V specific cmdlet.

3. Now let's first try to see how many virtual machines have been created, and what are their current network adapter settings for the virtual switch configuration. To do this we will first try to execute the Get-VM cmdlet. This will return all the running VMs created on this server. Then we will run Get-VM | Get-VMNetworkAdapter, which will return all the VMs for their network adapter settings. Here we can see that all VMs do not have settings defined for the virtual switch configuration.

4. Since we have only one VM switch created on our Hyper-V server, we will execute `Get-VMSwitch | Connect\VMNetworkAdapter -VMName <VM-Name,VMName>`. This will configure all the VMs for the `External` switch, as we can see in the following PowerShell output:

```
Administrator: Windows PowerShell                                        _  □  X

PS C:\Users\Administrator> Import-Module Hyper-V
PS C:\Users\Administrator> Get-VM

Name          State   CPUUsage(%) MemoryAssigned(M) Uptime      Status
----          -----   ----------- ----------------- ------      ------
Exch13_CAS_VM_1 Running 0           4096              4.21:24:51  Operating normally
Exch13_CAS_VM_2 Running 0           4096              4.21:23:52  Operating normally
Exch13_MBX_VM_1 Running 0           4096              4.21:24:16  Operating normally


PS C:\Users\Administrator> Get-VM | Get-VMNetworkAdapter

Name            IsManagementOs VMName          SwitchName MacAddress    Status IPAddresses
----            -------------- ------          ---------- ----------    ------ -----------
Network Adapter False          Exch13_CAS_VM_1            00155D359500         {}
Network Adapter False          Exch13_CAS_VM_2            00155D359501         {}
Network Adapter False          Exch13_MBX_VM_1            00155D359502         {}


PS C:\Users\Administrator> Get-VMSwitch | Connect-VMNetworkAdapter -VMName Exch13_CAS_VM_1,Exch13_CAS_VM_2,Exch13_MBX_VM
_1
PS C:\Users\Administrator> Get-VM | Get-VMNetworkAdapter

Name            IsManagementOs VMName          SwitchName MacAddress    Status IPAddresses
----            -------------- ------          ---------- ----------    ------ -----------
Network Adapter False          Exch13_CAS_VM_1 External   00155D359500  {0k}   {10.200.53.135, fe80::44b2:ac94:26d2:1ff}
Network Adapter False          Exch13_CAS_VM_2 External   00155D359501  {0k}   {10.200.53.150, fe80::b8ac:9e1f:2c56:e...
Network Adapter False          Exch13_MBX_VM_1 External   00155D359502  {0k}   {10.200.53.137, fe80::28da:2f06:af2b:f...


PS C:\Users\Administrator> _
```

Example 4 – shutting down all virtual machines

There are times when, due to some emergency hazard, we have to shut down all the virtual machines at once. To deal with this type of situation, a Hyper-V administrator can run a single cmdlet to shut down all the virtual machines in one shot. Let's see how:

1. Open the Windows Server 2012 PowerShell management console.

2. Execute `Get-VM | Stop-VM`. This cmdlet will find all the VMs running on the local Hyper-V server, and will then turn them off.

```
Administrator: Windows PowerShell                               _  □  x

PS C:\Users\Administrator> Import-Module Hyper-V
PS C:\Users\Administrator> Get-VM

Name            State    CPUUsage(%) MemoryAssigned(M) Uptime        Status
----            -----    ----------- ----------------- ------        ------
Exch13_CAS_VM_1 Running  0           4096              00:02:53      Operating normally
Exch13_CAS_VM_2 Running  0           4096              00:02:42      Operating normally
Exch13_MBX_VM_1 Running  0           4096              4.22:01:55    Operating normally
SQL Test VM     Running  0           512               00:02:37      Operating normally

PS C:\Users\Administrator> Get-VM | Stop-VM

Confirm
Hyper-V cannot shut down virtual machine SQL Test VM because the Shutdown integration service is unavailable. To avoid
potential data loss, you can pause or save the state of the virtual machine. The other option is to turn off the
virtual machine, but data loss might occur.
[Y] Yes  [N] No  [S] Suspend  [?] Help (default is "Y"): Y
PS C:\Users\Administrator> Get-VM

Name            State CPUUsage(%) MemoryAssigned(M) Uptime        Status
----            ----- ----------- ----------------- ------        ------
Exch13_CAS_VM_1 Off   0           0                 00:00:00      Operating normally
Exch13_CAS_VM_2 Off   0           0                 00:00:00      Operating normally
Exch13_MBX_VM_1 Off   0           0                 00:00:00      Operating normally
SQL Test VM     Off   0           0                 00:00:00      Operating normally

PS C:\Users\Administrator>
```

Example 5 – starting all virtual machines in one step

This example is the second part of the previous example, where we saw how we can shut down all the virtual machines running on a local Hyper-V server with one PowerShell command.

In this example, we will look at the possibility of bringing up all the powered-off virtual machines on the local Hyper-V Server, with one PowerShell command. Perform the following steps:

1. Open the Windows Server 2012 PowerShell management console.

2. If you first want to see the current state of the VMs on your local Hyper-V Server, you can do this by executing the Get-VM cmdlet.

3. Since we now know which VMs are down, we will execute the
   `Get-VM | Start-VM` cmdlet. This piped cmdlet will first select
   all the down VMs and will then bring them up.

```
Administrator: Windows PowerShell                                    _  □  x

PS C:\Users\Administrator> Import-Module Hyper-V
PS C:\Users\Administrator> Get-VM | Start-VM
PS C:\Users\Administrator> Get-VM

Name            State    CPUUsage(%) MemoryAssigned(M) Uptime     Status
----            -----    ----------- ----------------- ------     ------
Exch13_CAS_VM_1 Running  0           4096              00:00:12   Operating normally
Exch13_CAS_VM_2 Running  0           4096              00:00:10   Operating normally
Exch13_MBX_VM_1 Running  0           4096              00:00:08   Operating normally
SQL Test VM     Running  0           512               00:00:08   Operating normally


PS C:\Users\Administrator>
```

Summary

In this chapter first we went through the introduction to PowerShell as the shell
scripting utility for management and automation of Windows Server, where we
also touched on the various core components of PowerShell, including the technical
overview, cmdlets, and different versions released. Then we went ahead with
Windows Server 2012 PowerShell 3.0, and discussed the PowerShell 3.0-specific
features and enhancements, including the system requirements and management
part of PowerShell.

Finally we looked at the PowerShell 3.0 capabilities for the Windows Server 2012
Hyper-V role, and laid out some examples of the PowerShell cmdlets for the
Hyper-V Windows Server 2012 role.

This chapter was relatively short but provided an insight into the shell
scripting capability and command-line utility of Windows Server 2012, which
can be used to manage and automate the various tasks related to the Hyper-V
virtualization infrastructure.

The next chapter will talk about the various types of Hyper-V storage that we can
use and configure for our Hyper-V infrastructure. In the next chapter we will also go
deeper into the storage design considerations and their different uses for Hyper-V
and virtual machine setup. After the completion of the next chapter, you will be able
to configure the different types of storage scenarios for Hyper-V deployment, and get
the most out of your Hyper-V storage architecture.

6
Insight into Hyper-V Storage

In this chapter, we will dive deeper into Hyper-V storage, where we will discuss the various types of storage options available with Microsoft Windows Server 2012 Hyper-V for a virtual machine in detail.

We will start this chapter by introducing what virtual storage is in a virtual machine, and then we will see the technical aspect of it. After this, we will move forward with the discussion of the different types of Hyper-V virtual storage. During this discussion, we will touch upon all types of virtual storage options offered by Hyper-V for a virtual machine. This will give a detailed overview of each type of storage. This section will help you plan the virtual storage for your server virtualization, so at any point you can come back to this and read it and refresh your memory, so you always choose the right type of storage for yourself.

After getting familiar with the various different storage options available for your virtual machine, we will then discuss a number of storage and virtual machine settings available in Hyper-V for virtual storage related operations, which include adding additional storage and removing storage from a virtual machine, and compacting, converting, and expanding the virtual hard disk for your virtual machine. Information about these advanced options for virtual storage within Hyper-V will make you a guru of Hyper-V storage.

Before finishing this chapter, we will also see the Hyper-V storage best practices, where we will sum up all the best practices for Hyper-V storage, which will help you choose the correct type of storage for your virtual machine, and also in the event of any disaster and mass migration, help you determine what series of steps you need to carry out to make sure your virtual machine and virtual storage always remain healthy and operate smoothly.

Understanding virtual storage

A virtual machine that simulates the same computing architecture as the physical machine holds the virtual storage for its operating system. This storage can be set up in many different ways, where a virtual machine can have the same or different sizes of storage at the same time. This virtual storage can be accessed by the guest operating system, and in the case of a file server or other content and application server based virtual workloads, it can also be made available to the users accessing the virtual machine, and the hosted and shared connections can be accessed from there.

A virtual machine can have different types of virtual storage, but from the early days of x86-based virtualization, file-based virtual storage or specifically the **virtual hard disk (VHD)** type of virtual machine storage is famous and the most widely used. There are other types of virtual storage such as pass-through disks, where the administrator attaches the physical or local disk of hypervisors to the virtual machine, so the virtual machine is not writing on a file-based virtual storage but a physical disk or SAN LUN attached to the hypervisor machine, which is then made available to the virtual machine as a pass-through disk.

Virtual machine storage requirements are based on the type of server role and application running and the workload. This emphasizes the need to configure the correct type of virtual storage required by the virtual machine. For example, let's say we have a requirement to install a database server application, for instance Microsoft SQL Server; in this case, SQL Server may require several types of storage, such as an OS disk, application disk, database files (MDF), and database logs (LDF). So for each of these types of storage, we may configure and provide the virtual storage for our SQL Server virtual machine as follows:

Virtual storage type	Purpose	VM disk
VHD – file-based virtual storage	OS installation	`C:`
VHD – file-based virtual storage	System page file (SWAP)	`D:`
VHD – file-based virtual storage	Application installation	`E:`
Physical disk – pass-through	Database files (MDF)	`M:`
Physical disk – pass-through	Database logs (LDF)	`L:`

The preceding table shows the recommended types of virtual storage needed for the Microsoft virtual machine. So in this case if an administrator chooses a wrong type of virtual storage, it will result in a low-performance disk with slow I/O allotted to the SQL Server database or transactional logs, which would then result in poor SQL Server database performance.

Later on in this chapter, we will discuss the best storage practices for a Hyper-V virtual machine, which will guide you to choose the correct type of virtual machine storage for your critical virtual machines; we will also discuss a few real-world scenarios where insufficient planning and inadequate virtual machine resources can affect virtualization projects negatively, after which we will address the solution to overcome these issues related to performance and virtual machine storage.

For a better understanding of virtual storage, let's first start by discussing the numerous new virtual machine storage features that have been introduced in Windows Server 2012 Hyper-V 3.0. Then we will discuss the various types of Hyper-V storage for virtual machines, which will provide you with end-to-end knowledge about the different types of virtual storage you can use for your virtual machine.

Improved Hyper-V storage

Windows Server 2012 Hyper-V has introduced a series of improvements for virtual machine storage. All these new storage features and improvements in the existing storage types for virtual machines have allowed Hyper-V to fully cater for the end-to-end needs of server virtualization.

In the earlier version of Hyper-V, there were a few caveats for virtual machine storage selection. These virtual machine storage caveats didn't allow customers to select relaxed and flexible virtual machine storage platforms. One of the examples of these types of rigid storage selections for virtual machines is that virtual machine storage cannot be placed on an SMB file share. There are other major problems with virtual machine storage selection that we saw in the previous Windows Server and Hyper-V releases. These problems are as follows:

- Inability to perform live storage migration
- Incapability of connecting the virtual machine to fibre channel storage
- Limited size of virtual hard disk, that is, 2 TB
- Difficulty in building a guest virtual machine cluster with only iSCSI SAN
- Incapability of performing a disk merge operation while the VM is running

Microsoft Windows Server 2012 addresses all these problems that customers were faced with in the earlier versions of Windows Server and Hyper-V. Now let's go ahead and discuss how Windows Server 2012 and Hyper-V address these problems related to virtual machine storage and provide flexible virtual machine storage selection for customers.

The following newly added features and enhancements of Windows Server 2012 Hyper-V now make it much easier for customers to select a wide variety of virtual machine storage options:

- Virtual Fibre Channel connectivity for a virtual machine
- Larger virtual hard disk support of up to 64 TB
- Virtual machine storage and live virtual storage migration based on **Server Message Block (SMB)**
- The possibility of relaxed virtual machine clustering with virtual Fibre Channel
- Native disk support of 4 KB sectors
- Live disk merging operations for a virtual machine hard disk
- Availability of secure offloading data transfer for virtual machine storage

Let's now discuss a few of the preceding new features added to Hyper-V storage in detail.

Virtual Fibre Channel connectivity for virtual machines

This is one of my favorite features within Windows Server 2012 Hyper-V. This feature allows Hyper-V based virtual machines to access external SAN storage based on the Fibre Channel. This will open a new door for building clustered virtual machines and making your critical workloads highly available with fully supported Fibre Channel SAN storage.

Working of Hyper-V Virtual Fibre Channel

Hyper-V Virtual Fibre Channel for virtual machines in Windows Server 2012 works in a manner similar to the physical connectivity that was established when you connected a physical server to the Fibre Channel SAN storage. For Hyper-V Fibre Channel connectivity for virtual machines in Windows Server 2012, we use **N_Port ID Virtualization (NPIV)** technology. As a process of virtualizing your Fibre Channel SAN, an NPIV port is created on the server running Hyper-V and is associated with the virtual Fibre Channel adapter. Additionally, a **World Wide Name (WWN)** is assigned to the NPIV port, which allows all I/O to be redirected to a specific virtual Fibre Channel adapter in the virtual machine.

In Windows Server 2012, Hyper-V connectivity to the Fibre Channel storage is done by using **multipath I/O** (**MPIO**); this ensures continuous connectivity to the Fibre Channel storage from within the virtual machine. In addition to all these great characteristics of the MPIO feature, we can also configure multiple virtual Fibre Channel adapters in a VM, while at the same time, we can also separate each copy of the multiple MPIO paths within the OS of the virtual machine, to connect to the SAN LUNs.

Larger virtual hard disk support (up to 64 TB)

We all loved **virtual hard disk** (**VHD**) because of its simplicity and ease of implementation among its other features/characteristics. But while working with Windows Server 2008 / 2008 R2, we saw a caveat where VHD failed to fulfill the requirement of having a larger virtual hard disk because of its limited maximum size of 2 TB. Usually, people encounter this problem when they run/are running a file server or any other server application that requires a larger amount of disk space.

In Windows Server 2012 Hyper-V, Microsoft introduced a new format of virtual hard disks for virtual machines that is called VHDX. Here "X" represents the extended capabilities of VHD, where a VHDX can now be as large as 64 TB, which is a far bigger size than the original VHD format.

This new format with an extended maximum size addresses all the past problems of building virtual machines with a larger virtual hard disk.

In addition to this, VHDX also provides the following list of benefits over the VHD format:

- It increases performance for applications and workloads, especially on physical disks that have a sector size larger than 512 bytes
- It supports the storage of custom metadata
- It logs updates to the VHDX metadata structures
- It supports larger block sizes for dynamic and differencing disks, which allows the disks to be tuned in to the needs of the virtualized workloads
- It allows you to configure and manage virtual hard disks on a computer running Hyper-V, using Windows PowerShell commands

SMB-based virtual machine storage

Before we go ahead and explain this feature in detail, let me point out a limitation of Hyper-V Windows Server 2008 / 2008 R2, which we all faced in the past. Small- to medium-sized companies faced the biggest problem of making larger disks locally available to Hyper-V server to virtualize more servers and applications from their infrastructure. Due to having a limited amount of local disk space, we always saw ourselves in a bit of a problem. And while dealing with this problem, we all thought of using SMB storage for Hyper-V because of its feasibility and availability, where we could store virtual machines on a file server, but it was not available in earlier versions of the Hyper-V server.

Good news! Windows Server 2012 Hyper-V supports storage based on SMB 3, which could be your Windows file server, for storing data related to the virtual machine, including virtual machine configuration files, virtual hard disks (VHD/VHDX), and virtual machine snapshots (AVHD). This new feature makes it very easy for small- to medium-sized organizations to create more virtual machines, while having limited amount of disk space available on their Hyper-V servers locally.

Okay, we read the good news; now let's read a bit about SMB 3. SMB 3 allows you to use your file server storage for Hyper-V virtual machine placement. This will enable you to store virtual machines based on Hyper-V on the cheaper disks of the file server. While on the one hand it may save some dollars, on the other hand it may affect the virtual machine's storage performance.

Moreover, you can also enhance network performance by using the Hyper-V server's NICs that support the **Remote Direct Memory Access** (**RDMA**) feature. This will enable all the functionalities to work on low latency and CUP, while working at full speed. While using an SMB-based file server as storage for your Hyper-V server, you can have all the benefits that you used to have when using SAN storage for your Hyper-V virtual machine storage.

Virtual machine live storage migration

There are many situations where critical virtual machine storage needs to be migrated from its current storage platform to a different one. This could be because there is a need to migrate the virtual machine's storage from a slow disk to a faster one, or there could be many more reasons. In the previous releases of Windows Server 2008 and Hyper-V, migrating virtual machine storage for running workloads was not possible. And the only solution we had was to bring down the virtual machine to migrate its storage platform.

Windows Server 2012 Hyper-V addressed this problem with all its other features and has now made it possible for customers to perform live migration of virtual machine storage from one location to another. We will see live migration of virtual machine storage in the coming chapter.

Types of Hyper-V virtual storage

In the previous section, we discovered what virtual storage is and how it contributes to the server virtualization architecture. With all the information we got from the previous section about virtual storage, let's now move ahead and see the virtual machine storage options that Hyper-V offers us.

In this section, we will go through different types of virtual machine storage options, such as VHD, VHDX, fixed disk, dynamic disk, differencing disk, and pass-through disk. We will discuss each of them in detail so that you understand all their ins and outs for better planning and sizing.

Each of these virtual storage options has a different set of properties than the others, and the administrator must choose the correct virtual storage that best fits the server operating systems and application needs.

Let's now start by discussing each of these virtual storage options for virtual machines based on Hyper-V.

Virtual disk formats

First we must select the virtual disk format before we go ahead and create the virtual hard disk file. There are two possible virtual disk formats available with Windows Server 2012 Hyper-V; they are VHD and VHDX. Let's first make a short comparison between the two virtual hard disk formats, which will provide us with some quick guidance on making the appropriate selection according to the usage.

Feature	VHD	VHDX
Disk size	Up to 2 TB	Up to 64 TB
Native disk support of 4 KB	Not supported	Supported
Secure offload data transfer	Not supported	Supported

Virtual hard disk (VHD)

After the release of Hyper-V, Microsoft provided its customers with a native hypervisor for their server virtualization needs. But this newly released product had to face challenges for being called an enterprise virtualization platform. And virtual hard disk (VHD) limitation was one of the caveats that customers faced.

There are a few limitations to the VHD format; one is the limited size of the virtual hard disk (which we faced before) and another is the possibility of data inconsistency due to power failures. Virtual hard disk (VHD) is a file-based storage for your virtual machine that is based on Hyper-V; this is a default and basic level of storage functionality for a virtual machine. An administrator can create a virtual hard disk (VHD) file for a virtual machine within Hyper-V for a specific size, where defining the size is mandatory. This VHD file can have a different set of properties based on its type.

A virtual hard disk (VHD) file or file extension is similar to the VMKD file format, which is a VMware virtual machine hard disk extension. VHD files also existed in the earlier versions of server and desktop virtualization software from Microsoft, for example, Virtual PC and Virtual Server.

Virtual hard disk (VHDX)

As we saw, the two main limitations of VHD format based virtual hard disk are size and data inconsistency due to power failure; Microsoft addressed these two main limitations of the VHD file format and introduced a new virtual hard disk format called VHDX. This virtual hard disk format allowed customers to create virtual hard disks of up to 64 TB, where earlier the virtual hard disk format (VHD) only allowed virtual hard disks up to the size of 2 TB. Also, as this new format has a resilient architecture, the possibility of data corruption due to power failure also reduced.

Virtual disk types

The virtual hard disk format decides the maximum size of a virtual hard disk, while the virtual hard disk type decides the functionality and features a virtual hard disk will provide. Microsoft Windows Server 2012 Hyper-V provides four types of virtual hard disks for virtual machines based on Hyper-V. These four virtual hard disk types are as follows:

- Dynamic disk
- Fixed disk
- Differencing disk
- Pass-through disk

You should choose the virtual hard disk type based on your server and application requirements. Each type of virtual hard disk provides different set of disk performance and functionalities, so proper planning is highly important to ensure that you select the right virtual storage for your workload.

Let's now discover each of these storage types in detail.

Dynamic disk

When you create a new virtual machine, and create a new virtual hard disk from **New Virtual Machine Wizard**, the wizard chooses the dynamic disk as the virtual hard disk type for you. Dynamic disks, as they sound, are dynamic; this means they get changed over time or due to the occurrence of certain events. Dynamic disks are the best choice for economic usage of the server's storage. With whatever size of dynamic disk you create, it won't immediately deduct the same amount of disk space from the physical storage of the Hyper-V server but instead will get created with a very small size, and over a period of time, keep growing as you put data and content on this disk. This dynamic growth of a disk is the actual concept behind this type of virtual hard disk.

Since dynamic disks are not of a fixed size and are actually small in size, they cannot deliver a good disk I/O for storage-intensive applications.

Real-world example

Over the years, I have seen many cases where a production workload (VM) has had performance bottlenecks, especially for the disk subsystem of a virtual machine. And among these, in the case of performance problems related to the virtual machine disk subsystem, the majority of times I saw people using dynamic virtual hard disks for their production workloads. And since dynamic disks do not have a fixed size storage for virtual machines, they are not a good choice for disk-intensive applications and server roles. A dynamic disk has another problem of not being able to provide good results for disk fragmentation or other similar activities due to its design. Dynamic disks are good for the testing and research and development types of virtual machines where the performance factor is not very important.

Now let's see how we can create a dynamic disk for a virtual machine.

As we have said previously, when you create a virtual machine via **New Virtual Machine Wizard**, it also gives you the option to create a virtual hard disk for the virtual machine by default. This wizard for creating a new virtual machine, along with the creation of the virtual hard disk, provides a dynamic disk by default, and so the disk type option is not provided as a selection option.

In the following brief steps, we will see how to create a dynamic disk:

1. Open **Hyper-V Manager** from **Administrative Tools**.

2. From the **Hyper-V Manager** snap-in, find the **New** button on the right action pane and click on **Hard Disk**.

3. **New Hard Disk Wizard** will open; it will first ask you to select the hard disk format, which could be either **VHD** or **VHDX**, depending on the size of your hard disk.

4. Then you will be prompted to select the disk type; here we will select **Dynamic Disk**.

5. The next section of **New Hard Disk Wizard** will ask you the name of the virtual hard disk and the location where you want this virtual hard disk to be created and stored.

6. Now the last section of this wizard will ask you the size of the disk you want to create. This section also gives you the functionality to copy content from a physical disk of the server or any other virtual disk that has already been created.

Fixed disk

A fixed disk is like a static disk that has a fixed size and doesn't grow over time if we go on adding content to it. Fixed disks provide better performance as compared to dynamic disks, because when we create a fixed disk of 100 GB, Hyper-V creates a VHD or VHDX file of 100 GB. It should be noted here that creating this 100 GB fixed disk will take a long time as it has to create a VHD/VHDX file of 100 GB, and the larger disk you create, the longer time it will take. A fixed disk allocates a fixed size from the physical storage of the Hyper-V server, and so this big chunk of allocated disk space allows the virtual machine to receive better I/O performance from this type of virtual hard disk.

Fixed disks are always recommended for production workloads because their better performance allows administrators to perform faster read/write operations on virtual disks. Fixed disks are mainly created for virtual machines that run disk-intensive applications, where a high disk I/O is required for virtual machine storage, for example, the virtual hard disk you will create if you are going to virtualize a file sever. Here you will store all the files to the hard disk and so it should be a fixed disk, but at the same time the operating system disk of the file server can be kept as a dynamic disk because there will not be much disk activity on it.

To create a fixed disk, you need to perform the following steps:

1. Open **Hyper-V Manager** from **Administrative Tools**.

2. From the **Hyper-V Manager** snap-in, find the **New** button on the right action pane and click on **Hard Disk**.

3. **New Hard Disk Wizard** will open; it will first ask you to select the hard disk format, which could be either **VHD** or **VHDX**, depending on the size of your hard disk.

4. You will then be prompted to select the disk type; here we will select **Fixed Disk**.

5. The next section of **New Hard Disk Wizard** will ask you for the name of your virtual hard disk and the location where you want this virtual hard disk to be created and stored.

6. Now the last section of this wizard will ask you the size of the disk you want to create. This section also gives you the functionality to copy content from a physical disk of the server or any other virtual disk that has already been created.

Differencing disk

A differencing disk has a parent-child model associated with its architecture. Mainly, it comes into use when an administrator takes a snapshot of a virtual machine, where after creating the snapshot, Hyper-V leaves the first parent VHD intact and creates a new child disk that gets linked to the parent virtual hard disk. Both parent and child disks always have the same disk format; this means that if the parent disk is created as VHD, the child disk cannot be VHDX.

A differencing disk is usually never recommended for production workloads because if you to create a snapshot of a production workload, you will stop writing to the production virtual hard disk. Differencing disks are the same in nature as dynamic disks, where the disk size grows over a period of time as we go on adding more data to the disk; this nature of the disk may not give you good performance for the disk subsystem of the production workload.

Another problem with the differencing disk is that when we create a snapshot of the virtual machine, from that point in time, all the data gets written on to the differencing disk and your parent VHD/VHDX becomes idle and isolated from the new data changes. And in the case of multiple snapshots you will have data written on multiple differencing disks. So if any of the differencing disks (snapshots) get misplaced or deleted, you will lose all the data that was written on it at that particular period of time. So in a nutshell, it is highly recommended not to create a snapshot of a production virtual machine; but if you have taken it already, make sure that you restore it to its parent VHD/VHDX as early as possible.

To create a differencing disk, you may perform the following steps:

1. Previously, we saw the steps for creating other disk types; follow those same steps until we reach the step where we need to select the disk type.

2. When we are prompted to select the disk type, select **Differencing Disk**.

3. The next section of **New Hard Disk Wizard** will ask you the name of the virtual hard disk and the location where you want this virtual hard disk to be created and stored.

4. Now the last section of this wizard will ask you the size of the disk you want to create. This section also gives you the functionality to copy content from a physical disk of the server or any other virtual disk that has already been created.

Pass-through disk

A pass-through disk is a storage type in which an administrator presents a physical hard disk, which is associated or attached to the Hyper-V host server, to the virtual machine as a raw disk. This type of virtual machine storage is called a pass-through or raw disk; in this type of storage, the physical disk or LUN passes through the hypervisor and later to the virtual machine guest system. This physical disk that is associated or attached to the Hyper-V server could be a SAN LUN storage bound to the Hyper-V server, or it could be a locally installed physical hard disk.

To mitigate all these aforementioned risks, administrators prefer to use a pass-through disk as a local disk for highly critical virtual workloads and keep the virtual machine storage on this pass-through disk. As a first step, the pass-through disk is attached or made available to the Hyper-V server; once the disk is available to the server, you have to bring the disk offline before you pass the disk through to a virtual machine available on the same Hyper-V box. We cannot make a partition on the disk available to a virtual machine; it is only the local disk of the Hyper-V server that can be made available as a pass-through disk.

In many cases, admins prefer to use pass-through disks instead of using VHDs, especially if they want their virtual machine to boot from a SAN LUN, or in the case of databases, where an Exchange Server mailbox database can be placed on pass-through SAN LUN disks. Pass-through disks are also suitable for environments where the application's high availability methodology is placed on a build blocks level. In these types of high availability requirements for the application, an administrator needs to bind the same data disks (pass-through LUNs) to another virtual machine, and you are all good to go.

It should also be noted here that pass-through disks don't get included in a backup based on a VSS snapshot. This means that if you have taken a backup of a virtual machine using a VSS-based backup solution, all the pass-through disks of the virtual machine will not be backed up and only the VHD-based/VHDX-based disks will be included in the VSS snapshot backup.

The following steps need to be carried out to provide a pass-through disk to a virtual machine within the Hyper-V server:

1. Open **Hyper-V Manager** from **Administrative Tools**.

2. Take the virtual machine settings that you want to configure and add a pass-through disk.

3. Add **SCSI Controller** from the **Add Hardware** section of the virtual machine settings, or if you wish, you can also add a physical disk to an IDE controller. Then select the hard drive and click on the **Add** button.

4. Once you click on the **Add** button at the controller level, you will be prompted to select the physical hard drive that you want to connect to the virtual machine.

5. After selecting the appropriate disk, you need to connect it to the virtual machine. First click on **Apply** and then click on the **OK** button to commit the changes.

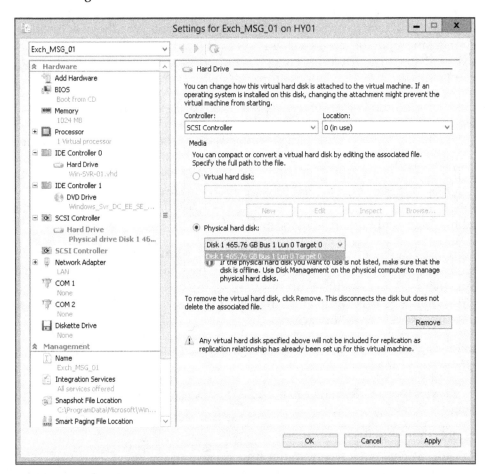

Virtual Fibre Channel SAN

With the release of Windows Server 2012, Hyper-V now offers virtual FC SAN connectivity to virtual machines, to allow virtual machines to connect to a virtual SAN. The administrator first connects a virtual SAN network setup on the Hyper-V server, just like what we would do to create a virtual switch for different network segments. Once the virtual fibre SAN network gets set up, the Fibre Channel adapter can be added to the virtual machine that needs to be associated with the Fibre Channel SAN network.

Hyper-V allows the Hyper-V administrator to configure WWNs and other settings related to Fibre Channel SAN; all these settings can be customized from the virtual machine Fibre Channel adapter or as global settings from the Fibre Channel network of the virtual SAN manager.

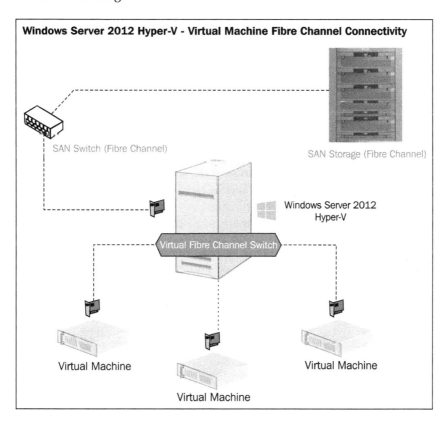

The preceding screenshot describes the connectivity of a standalone Hyper-V server to the FC SAN. In the first phase of connectivity, our Hyper-V server gets connected to the FC SAN switch through a Fibre Channel medium. Then in the second phase of connectivity, we configure the virtual Fibre Channel switch on the Hyper-V server. Once the virtual fabric switch is configured, we can simply add the virtual Fibre Channel adapter to the virtual machine and connect the adapter to the virtual Fibre Channel switch.

Virtual machine storage settings

In this section, we will go through the different sets of available virtual machine settings for storage, where we will see all the available settings that can be customized as per our need.

This section will mainly focus on two types of virtual machine storage settings. In discussing the first type of storage setting, we will understand the different types of storage settings available within Hyper-V virtual machine settings that allow you to add or remove storage from a virtual machine.

In discussing the second type of virtual machine storage setting, we will understand the different utilities that come within Hyper-V for managing and troubleshooting your virtual machine storage.

Now let's go and discover these two types of storage management settings for your Hyper-V virtual machines.

Virtual machine hard disk settings

Virtual machine hard disk settings represent those sets of settings that allow you to add storage to or remove storage from the virtual machine; this may be based on either the IDE controller or SCSI controller. In this subsection, we will cover all these settings that are available to be customized and set.

We will first start with the controllers; there are two types of virtual machine hard disk controllers available on a Hyper-V based virtual machine, as follows:

- IDE controller
- SCSI controller

Now let's discuss each of these controllers in detail.

IDE controller

When you create a virtual machine, the IDE controller is added to the virtual machine by default, and can be used to attach a hard disk and/or DVD drive for the virtual machine to use. It should be noted here that a virtual hard disk containing a virtual machine operating system can only be attached to an IDE controller; you cannot add a virtual hard disk to an SCSI controller for the virtual machine operating system to boot up.

There are two controllers available for an IDE, namely IDE Controller 0 and IDE Controller 1. Other than these you cannot add additional IDE controllers to the virtual machine, and even if you see the **Add Hardware** section, you will not see the IDE controller there. IDE controllers cannot be deleted from the virtual machine, unlike SCSI controllers. In a virtual machine based on Hyper-V, you can only add one DVD drive, and it cannot be added to an SCSI controller. Both IDE and SCSI controllers can be used for configuring and adding a physical disk. In other words they can be configured as pass-through disks.

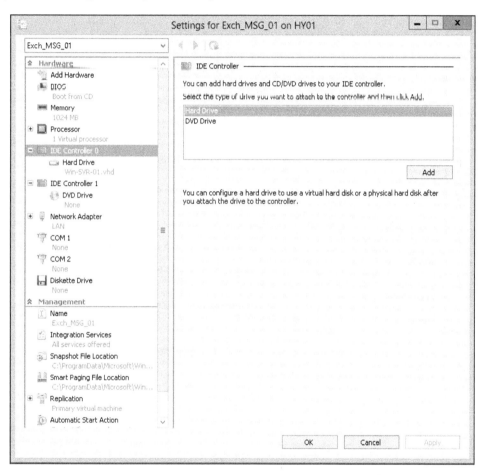

SCSI controller

On a single virtual machine based on Windows Server 2012 Hyper-V, you can add up to four SCSI controllers. SCSI controllers are different from IDE controllers because they require Hyper-V Integration Services to be installed on the virtual machine whereas IDE controllers don't. SCSI controllers can also be configured as pass-through disks. As we mentioned in the *IDE controller* subsection, it is not recommended to add the system drive to an SCSI controller; it should be connected to an IDE controller.

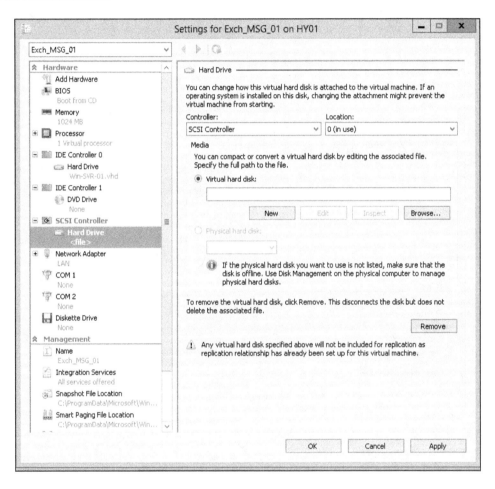

Hyper-V virtual hard disk utilities

Now let's see the other types of Hyper-V virtual machine storage settings; these other types of settings are made through utilities that are wizard based and that manage virtual machine storage. We can also call them the advanced settings for Hyper-V virtual machine storage that allow us to customize VHDs, edit them, and merge them (in the case of differencing disks).

Now let's understand the various features and functions of these utilities in detail.

Edit disk

Edit disk is a wizard-based utility that allows us to edit a virtual hard disk. We can edit both types of virtual hard disks, be they VHD or VHDX. Edit disk is an advanced type of virtual hard disk utility; it can be used for the following functions:

- Compact
- Convert
- Expand

Now let's discuss the functions of each of these functions in detail.

Compact

Compacting a virtual hard disk allows an administrator to shrink the size of the virtual hard disk but doesn't change anything for the storage capacity of VHD/VHDX. There are times when compacting a virtual hard disk becomes necessary, and using the compact feature of edit disk is safer and allows you to free the unavailable storage space on your Hyper-V physical server.

To perform a virtual hard disk compact function, please perform the following steps:

1. Open **Hyper-V Manager** from **Administrative Tools**.

2. From the right-hand side action pane, click on **Edit Disk**.

3. The next step is to locate the disk. You have to browse and select the virtual hard disk (VHD/VHDX) on which you want to perform the disk compacting operation.

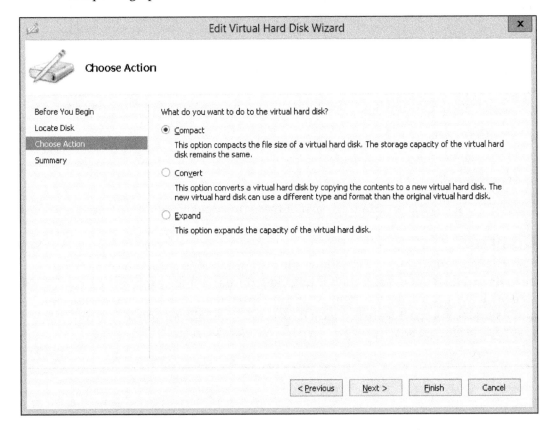

4. In the **Choose Action** section of **Edit Virtual Hard Disk Wizard**, we have to select the action that we want to perform; since in this example we want to compact the virtual hard disk of the virtual machine, select **Compact** and click on **Next**.

5. In the last window, you will be presented with a summary of the disk name and the action you selected to be performed on the disk.

Convert

Another feature that the edit disk utility provides is converting the virtual hard disk for virtual machines based on Hyper-V. Using the edit disk's converting feature, you can convert a virtual hard disk to a different type or different format. This conversion process creates a new hard disk from the one that you wish to convert and keeps the original disk intact. In the disk conversion process, the contents of the original disk are copied and added to the new disk with the format that the administrator selects.

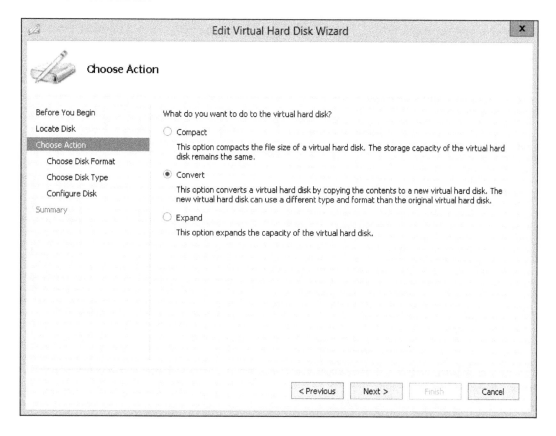

For example, let's say that you have a virtual hard disk for a virtual machine that is currently running as VHD, and due to some size issues with the virtual hard disk, you want to expand the disk; in this case, you might want to convert the disk format from VHD to VHDX, and for this purpose you can use edit disk's convert feature. In this way, you can have a bigger disk with an extended disk capacity.

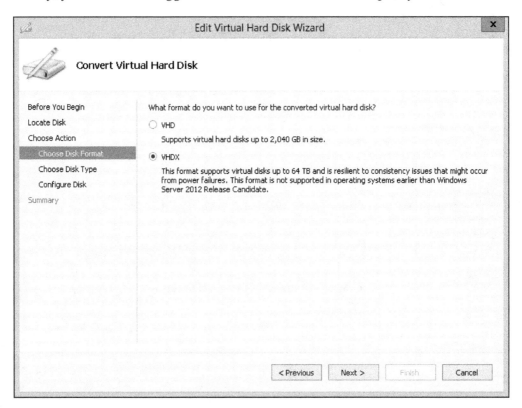

We will continue with the same preceding example. After selecting the disk format to be changed from VHD to VHDX, we also want this virtual hard disk to be a fixed-size disk, because earlier we created this virtual hard disk as a dynamic disk, and it has been noticed that with the dynamic disk, we have been getting a slow response during the peak times of virtual machine usage. So for this requirement, you can select the disk type to be changed from the dynamic to the fixed disk.

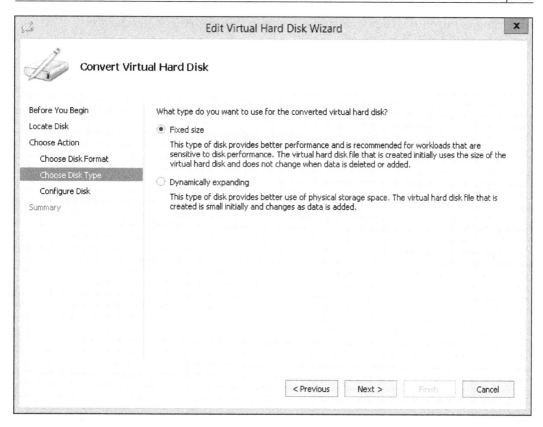

For the process of converting the disk, you can follow the screenshots shown previously. After selecting the intended disk type to be used for the conversion, you can click on **Next** to go to the **Configure Disk** screen and provide the path where you want to create the new disk with all the contents from the original disk; lastly, click on the **Finish** button and wait for the conversion process to kick in.

Expand

This is one of the most widely used features of the edit disk utility, where an administrator can expand an existing virtual hard disk of any type and any format to a new and bigger size. Mostly, administrators use this feature to expand the disk size of a fixed disk, because by their nature, they take the same physical space from the Hyper-V storage; so initially, people create a fixed disk with a smaller size, and later when their data grows and they want to expand the disk size, the disk expansion process comes into the picture.

You can perform the disk expansion process for your virtual hard disk by performing the following steps:

1. Open **Hyper-V Manager** from **Administrative Tools**.

2. Click on **Edit Disk** from your right action pane; this will open the **Edit Virtual Hard Disk Wizard** utility, as shown in the following screenshot:

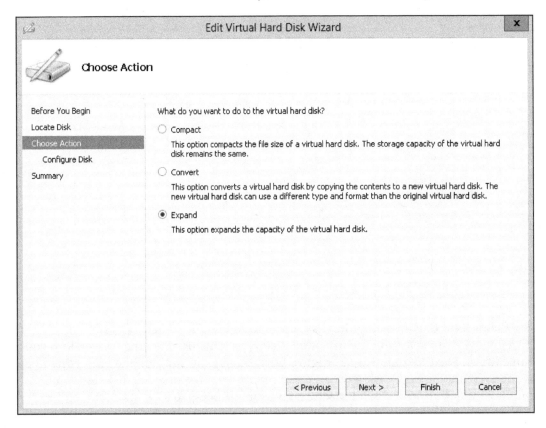

3. On the **Locate Disk** screen, browse to the virtual hard disk for which you want to perform disk expansion and click on **Next** to go to the next window.

4. From the **Choose Action** selection area on the first screen, select the **Expand** radio button and click on the **Next** button.

5. Now on the **Configure Disk** screen, we have to specify the new size of the virtual hard disk that we want. Let's say your virtual hard disk was initially created with 100 GB of space and now you want to expand it to 200 GB; so in the **New size** field from the **Configure Disk** screen, specify the size that you want to keep for the virtual hard disk and click on the **Next** button, as shown in the following screenshot:

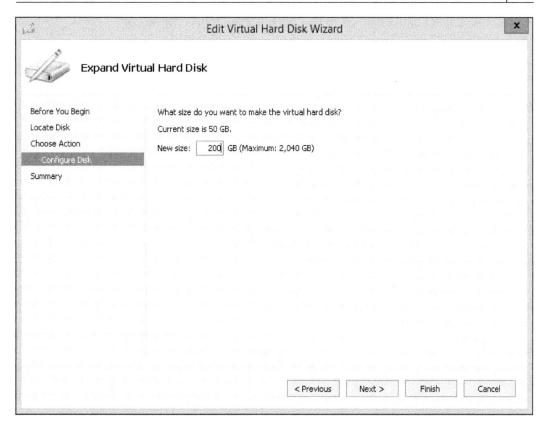

6. Finally, click on the **Finish** button to start the expansion process.

The disk expansion process will take some time and finish with the extended virtual hard disk size.

Inspect disk

The inspect disk utility is a great feature for virtual hard disk files; it is very important and handy while troubleshooting issues related to the virtual hard disk. Let's say you had created a virtual hard disk for your Exchange Server in the past and, after some time, forgotten about the type of virtual hard disk you used; if you want to quickly recall this, you can open the inspect disk functionality, which will tell you about the type of the virtual hard disk.

To use the inspect disk utility, you can perform the following steps:

1. Open **Hyper-V Manager** from **Administrative Tools**.
2. From the right action pane, click on the **Inspect Disk** utility.
3. This opens the file browser window, from where you can browse to the file and select it for inspection.

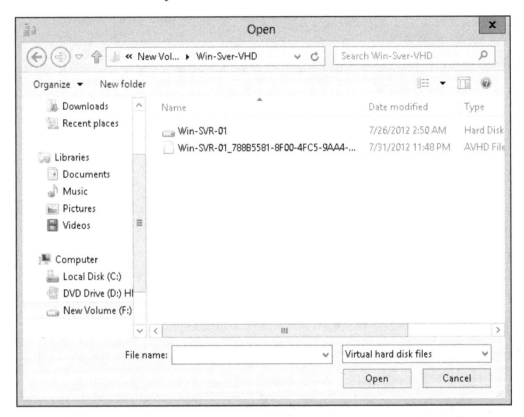

Now here is the beauty of the inspect disk utility. Let's take two examples here; in the first example, we want to inspect the disk type of our virtual hard disk. So in the inspect disk utility, we will browse to the virtual machine folder and select the virtual hard disk we want to know the type of.

Hyper-V gives us the following information about the disk, where we can see the type of virtual hard disk used and the virtual hard disk format:

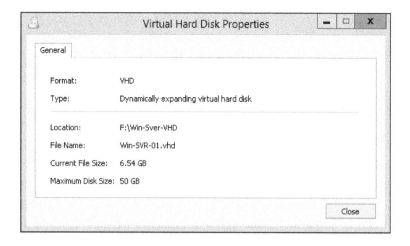

Let's continue with our second example, where we have a virtual machine that we have taken a snapshot of to depict the previous state of the virtual machine before the company's custom-made financial application was installed on it. And now before we merge the snapshot with the parent VHD, the Hyper-V administrator wants to have a look at the parent disk for the differencing disk's chain health before performing the merging process.

So we will check the differencing disk's snapshot file with an AVHD extension by opening the inspect disk utility, and from the browse file window, we will select the AVHD file for inspection; it will give us the following information that the type of the disk is a differencing disk and the format of the disk is VHD, and most importantly, it will give us information about the name and location of the parent VHD file:

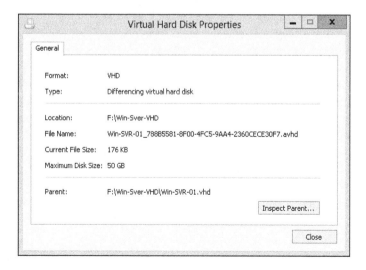

The inspect disk utility also allows us to inspect the parent disk from the same differencing disk inspection report we used to inspect the root VHD or parent VHD. So if we click on the **Inspect Parent**, we will be presented with the following report:

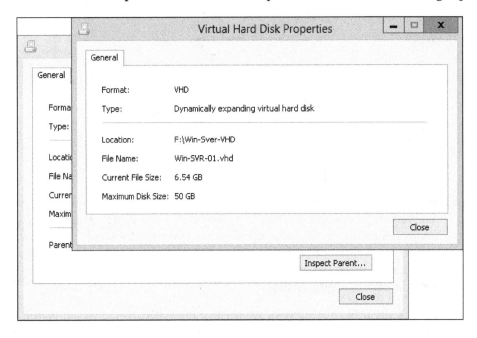

So you can see that our snapshot file has a root VHD or parent VHD located in the same directory, which is a VHD file and a dynamic disk.

Hyper-V storage best practices

Now that we've covered the technical side of the storage you need for your Hyper-V server and virtual machines, before we finish with this chapter, we will discuss the best practices for Hyper-V storage from the perspective of both Hyper-V as a server side and storage for virtual machines. All these best practices that we will discuss in this chapter come from experience in real-world solution designing and troubleshooting. Choosing a wrong storage layout for your critical virtual workload may end up in your highly utilized workload suffering from performance issues, and if you are going to start your first virtualization project after the completion of this book, I would strongly recommend that you pay serious attention while designing your virtual machine storage selection, because with the wrong start you will face bottlenecks in your server's and application's performance and will also be disappointed in virtualization as a practice and a technology.

Virtual storage is an essential part of a virtual machine; selecting virtual machine storage is mainly based on the type of performance and the agility you need to get from it. Over a period of time, it can be seen that server or virtualization administrators won't give much preference and attention to virtual machine storage. They simply think that if a handsome amount of RAM and virtual CPUs have been allotted to a virtual machine, then that's enough; we can get the best performance from them.

But this is not true; the performance of a virtual machine also depends on the types of storage we make available to the virtual machine because, at the end of the day, a virtual machine works in the same fashion as your physical server, so we should not underrate its importance. There are two elements associated with virtual machine storage; one is the type of virtual storage chosen for the virtual machine, which may or may not be appropriate for the intended use of the virtual machine and its workload, and the second element is the type of storage (VHD/VHDX) on which virtual machine data is stored. If either of these is not adequate to take the load of the disk's I/O requirements, the virtual machine storage gets affected, which consequently reduces the performance of the virtual machine, applications, and users connected to these applications.

Let's go through the best storage practices in the following sections one by one, and understand the importance of proper planning and sizing for your virtual machine storage and its performance problems and troubleshooting for these problems.

Dynamic disks are not good candidates for high disk I/O activity

Creating a new virtual machine from Hyper-V Manager, where a given virtual hard disk is created by default, only provides a dynamic disk based virtual hard disk. And if this new machine is going to be a production virtual machine with a disk-intensive application running on it, we would face performance issues with the disk subsystem.

It is strongly recommended, from both theory and real-world experience, that all critical virtual machines, especially ones that mostly get hit by end users for high disk I/O requirements, be created on a fixed disk based VHD/VHDX. When we create a fixed disk based virtual hard disk (VHD), it occupies the same amount of size as the physical disk of the Hyper-V server. It also allows the virtual machine to better expand the Windows process and handle the virtual storage. A dynamic disk, by its nature, grows when you add more content to it and accommodates the virtual machine's load for its disk I/O requirements while the virtual machine is up and running and doesn't have much room available for both the virtual machine and Hyper-V.

We may close this topic by saying that for any part of the production workload related to storage, we have to either go for fixed disks or pass-through disks. If you had the virtual machine configured with too many snapshots or if the VM was configured for a dynamic disk, we would see a serious performance problem for sure.

Differencing disks can lead to data loss

Differencing disks are special types of disks that are different from virtual hard disks (VHD). They have a different file extension, namely AVHD. Each differencing disk has a parent disk associated with it, and we can have a differencing disk that points to a VHD as its parent disk. Differencing disks build a chain in which many differencing disks are interlinked. Okay, now let's see how differencing disks can lead to data loss; for example, if we have multiple differencing disks interlinked with each other, and between the chain of differencing disks, if we lose any of them, all the data written on that disk will be lost. So they are not recommended for production workloads.

Creating a production virtual machine's snapshot with caution

In the preceding recommendation, we saw how differencing disks can lead to data loss; now we will understand what dangers are associated with creating a virtual machine's snapshot for production workloads. Snapshot is a utility in Hyper-V that allows us to create a snapshot or hot backup of a virtual machine at a certain point, which allows us to restore a virtual machine to the same point in time when we created the snapshot.

Let's say you created a virtual machine and installed the operating system; now before you go ahead and install a custom-made application for your finance department, you can take a snapshot of this virtual machine and then install your custom-made financing application. So later on if you find that there is a problem and you need to reinstall the operating system and all the prerequisite software, all you need to do is to restore the snapshot you took before the installation of the custom-made finance application. So without reinstalling everything, you can get the same virtual machine state as when you created the snapshot.

So when we create a snapshot, Hyper-V stops writing to the VHD (parent virtual hard disk) of a virtual machine and creates a new differencing disk with an extension of AVHD, which is a dynamic disk in nature; so from now on whatever data and changes we make to the virtual machine will be stored here on the AVHD. If you take more snapshots of the virtual machine, more AVHDs (differencing disks) will be created and interlinked to each other.

So the problem here is that, first of all, creating a snapshot of production workloads is not a recommended practice, because creating a snapshot stops the use of the original storage of the virtual machine. Let's say that you planned and used good storage for your virtual machine, which provided you with good disk I/O; after creating a snapshot, Hyper-V will stop using your SAN storage or fixed disk and will start writing on these newly created differencing disks, which are dynamic disks in nature and slower than your fast storage.

If you have multiple snapshots, and eventually multiple differencing disks, your virtual machine data will get stored on multiple differencing disks and these disks will be interlinked to each other. So if any differencing disk in the middle of the chain gets corrupted or if you lose it, you will lose all the data that was written on that disk or during that time span when you created the missing AVHD (differencing disk) snapshot.

So with all the information provided here about differencing disks and the snapshot, we recommend keeping the creation of snapshots for the **research and development (RnD)** aspect of your applications.

Pass-through disks are recommended for databases

If your virtual machine is going to have a database, such as Exchange Server or SQL Server, keeping the database and transactional logs on a pass-through disk is recommended. Because of the nature of pass-through disks, they are more reliable and have faster media access storage as compared to traditional, file-based virtual storage.

Pass-through disks are usually provided to the Hyper-V server from external storage providers, such as SAN, NAS, or DAS. These external storage providers have a number of disks installed onto them and thus provide a greater level of fault tolerance and faster disk I/O.

So using pass-through disks is the best practice for a database server, file server, or any other type of virtual machine that you consider critical and that you think requires fast data retrieval for its users, and it is recommended that you configure the virtual machine to have access to a pass-through disk. You can configure pass-through and VHD-based storage in any way you like. For example, if we want to, we can keep the operating system on the VHD disk as part of the local or SAN LUN associated with the Hyper-V server. And in the case of Exchange or SQL database storage, we can place this data on a pass-through disk, which could be the external storage of SAN or DAS disks.

Frequently merging a virtual machine's snapshot

As we said previously, first and foremost we should create a production virtual machine's snapshot only in extreme cases, with caution. And if you create a snapshot of a production virtual machine, it is highly recommended that you merge the snapshot with the parent VHD as soon as you are done with testing or any other purpose that you created it for.

Windows Server 2012 addressed a few of the previous issues that people encountered when using a snapshot of a virtual machine, especially the one where a snapshot can only be restored to a machine in the shutdown state. So now an administrator can perform snapshot restoration even while the virtual machine is up and running. Also, while deleting a snapshot-enabled virtual machine, Hyper-V starts merging the snapshot before it gets deleted from the Hyper-V console.

This best practice will also consolidate your data into one location and provide fast recovery, because if we keep a long chain of differencing disks (that is, many snapshots of the virtual machine), there are chances of losing any of these disks, which may result in loss of data.

Including virtual machine RAM for storage sizing

Over a period of time, I have seen that one mistake people make while sizing their Hyper-V storage is that they forget to keep extra storage available on the Hyper-V server, which is used by the virtual machine for their RAM allocations.

By default if you keep a static RAM of 10,240 MB (10 GB) for a virtual machine, upon invoking the virtual machine, Hyper-V will occupy 10 GB of the physical storage of the Hyper-V server for the virtual machine configuration file, which becomes equal to the virtual memory of the virtual machine.

So the mistake that people mostly make is to add only this extra amount of disk storage needed to run the virtual machine on the Hyper-V server. Creating a larger RAM-based virtual machine requires a large amount of free disk space on the Hyper-V server. So the best practice is to always add the virtual machine's RAM size to the total size of the virtual machine storage required, including the virtual storage of a VM.

External storage migration and Hyper-V pass-through disk availability for VM

Sometimes there may be situations where a storage administrator has to perform the migration of SAN LUNs assigned to various servers, including the Hyper-V server. In this type of situation, we have seen instances where people don't have the documented order and LUN assignment for the virtual machine's pass-through disk. And in the event of configuring a wrong pass-through disk, assigning it to the virtual machine may cause the application running on the virtual machine to not work properly.

For all the best practices for such migration on the SAN and Hyper-V server, I have documented a detailed, knowledge-based article on my blog that I would recommend you all to go through, to see all the information you need to know about these types of planned activities.

The following is the URL of my blog post for the SAN storage migration of a virtual machine that has a pass-through disk configured:

```
http://zahirshahblog.com/2012/01/04/best-practices-for-migrating-
hyper-v-storage-san-luns-for-microsoft-exchange-server-2010-
recommendations-for-migrating-san-luns-for-hyper-v-server-where-
exchange-server-2010-vms-are-using-pass/
```

Virtual machine application and server role placement – best practices

This is a general best practice; here it is always recommended to separate the same application and server roles on different hypervisors and storage. Keeping both VHDs of the same type on the application server's virtual machine may be thought of as keeping all the eggs in the same basket.

Summary

After you complete this chapter, you should understand what virtual machine storage is and what types of virtual machine storage options are available with the Microsoft hypervisor (Hyper-V). We also discussed numerous new virtual storage features added in Microsoft Windows Server 2012 Hyper-V. These new features allow you to use the file server for virtual machine storage and virtual Fibre Channel for virtual machine clustering.

We then covered all the types of virtual machine storage, right from the virtual machine hard disk (VHD) to pass-through disks. We also saw the Hyper-V virtual machine storage settings that allow you to customize the virtual machine's storage settings as per your needs, where we saw the IDE and SCSI controllers for your virtual machine storage. We then covered the two types of utilities, namely edit disk and inspect disk, that come with Hyper-V for virtual machine storage troubleshooting. These two wizard-based utilities provide a handy way for administrators to troubleshoot virtual machine storage and are your toolboxes for compressing and expanding the VHD.

Before finishing with this chapter, we covered the best practices for virtual machine storage, where we mentioned a number of best practices and recommendations for virtual machine storage with reference to the problems related to virtual machine storage. All these best practices will help you choose the correct virtual storage for your VMs.

In the next chapter, we will explore System Center Virtual Machine Manager 2012, which can be used for managing the Windows Server 2012 Hyper-V environment. The next chapter is going to stand out among all the other chapters, because it will provide you with all the basic configuration information for SCVMM for Hyper-V and private cloud deployment. So stay tuned with us.

7

Managing Hyper-V with System Center Virtual Machine Manager

Since the first chapter of the book, we have been exploring Windows Server 2012 Hyper-V as a product and have been discussing how we can take advantage of the available features to use this native hypervisor in Windows Server to virtualize the workload and take advantage of server virtualization.

Some of you must be wondering why we have this chapter in a book solely dedicated to Hyper-V 2012; the answer to that is that it will be handy for you when installing Windows Server 2012 OS on a box and then when adding a Hyper-V role in addition to creating a few virtual machines and keeping them running. But when it comes to an enterprise where hundreds of Hyper-V hosts run hundreds of virtual machines, managing these hosts and guest operating systems becomes challenging. And since a single host runs multiple virtual machines, the reliability factor for a single host becomes more critical because it means that losing a single Hyper-V host can result in losing various virtual machines running on the same host. In this type of situation, an enterprise-level hypervisor and virtual machine management solution becomes a business-critical need of an organization, and therefore knowing about an enterprise host and guest management application becomes a most important skill.

In this chapter we will be going through the different phases of understanding the virtual machine manager; in the first section of the chapter, we will see an overview of the product, and then we will complement it with the new features and capabilities introduced within System Center Virtual Machine Manager 2012 SP1. Then, we will walk through the installation of the product and configuration of basic VMM settings, seeing how to create virtual machines. Last but not least, we will see my favorite feature, which is access to VMM Self-Service Portal. So ladies and gentlemen, please fasten your seat belts because this is going to be an interesting one!

Overview of System Center Virtual Machine Manager (SCVMM)

Microsoft Virtual Machine Manager (VMM) was released as an independent product for managing virtualized workload for virtual machine deployment, management, and maintenance. VMM started providing support for Microsoft hypervisor (Hyper-V), VMware, and Citrix XenServer. If we talk about Hyper-V in particular, VMM introduced a number of features for the management of Hyper-V virtualized workload that were not available with the native tools to manage the Hyper-V virtual machines. With all these capabilities, VMM started getting a good amount of attention from the industry and also helped Hyper-V as a new product available in the market gain customer trust and market share.

Virtual Machine Manager has five major components of architecture, as follows:

- The VMM management server
- The VMM console
- Self-Service Portal
- The VMM database
- The VMM library

Let's understand each of the these key components of VMM in detail.

The VMM management server

The VMM management server is the brain of the VMM architecture; it connects to the hypervisor host and gives it instructions for the various hypervisor- and virtual machine-level tasks. It also talks to providers of computing resources such as networking, load balancers, and storage using **application programming interfaces** (**APIs**) provided by external vendors. The VMM management server directly reads from and writes to its database. When a virtual machine creation task is given to a hypervisor host registered with the VMM management server, VMM directly talks to the management interface of the hypervisor, and after passing the instructions, we can keep track of the status of the task that we have been asked to run.

The VMM console

The SCVMM console can be installed on the same server where the VMM management role is installed, or it can be installed on any other member server. This provides a great level of flexibility for managing a remote VMM server, where an administrator doesn't need to always be connected to the same VMM management server. As, till VMM 2008, the VMM console was the only way to manage the VMM environment, administrators also wished to have a command line and scripting methods available to automate and script various routines and bulk-level additions and modifications as per their needs.

With the release of SC 2012, which is built on top of Windows PowerShell, we are given the flexibility to manage and maintain our SC 2012 and VMM 2012 via PowerShell. This new addition to PowerShell now gives this flexibility to administrators to fully automate and script VMM-related operations using PowerShell.

Self-Service Portal

We introduced System Center 2012 and VMM 2012 as the cloud-focused solution for organizations to build their private clouds for their internal and external customers. Initially, System Center Virtual Machine Manager 2012 (RTM version) provided Self-Service Portal as a built-in feature for organizations to provide the self service experience to their customers. It should be noted here that SCVMM 2012 RTM version had Self-Service Portal included, but later, along with the release of SC 2012 SP1, self service was removed from SCVMM; it has now become a part of SC App Controller 2012 SP1.

The main idea behind this Self-Service Portal is that of the self service experience, like that at a self-service restaurant. Using the same principle, Self-Service Portal allows its customers to get anything done at any time they want. So if your internal finance department wants to get a virtual machine up and running for an urgent need, they can simply browse the Self-Service Portal access provided to them, and according to their package (quota) and size of virtual machine (template) provided to them, they can create it whenever they need to. In this case, they would only be able to see their virtual machine where they created it (on the cloud).

The VMM database

Next, we will see another major component of the VMM architecture, the database where VMM stores the management and asset-level information about various components and objects associated and available within itself. When we install SCVMM, we are asked to specify the Microsoft SQL Server location where VMM will create its database; in this database, VMM keeps track of the information about **configuration items** (**CIs**), including the VMM internal management components and all the integration components associated with VMM.

The VMM library

The SCVMM library is also one of the main components of System Center Virtual Machine Manager. The VMM library can be set up as one of the solution component hosting servers in your SCVMM design, or you can co-locate this role with the SCVMM management server. The VMM library can also be described as a resource store for different types of SCVMM features and components. For example, VMM library is a store for providing access to ISO, VHD, and other SCVMM resources.

All the VMM library resources can be shared between different sets of user roles and clouds.

What's new in SCVMM 2012

To see the list of new features and enhancements of System Center Virtual Machine Manager 2012 SP1, check *Appendix A*, *SCVMM 2012 New Features and Enhancements*.

Installing System Center Virtual Machine Manager 2012

Before we jump right into the installation of SCVMM 2012, let's first check its software and hardware requirements. As a best practice, it is always recommended that you go through the implementation requirements of any product beforehand so you don't need to find required prerequisites or arrange hardware resources for implementation kickoff at the very last moment.

System and hardware requirements

Just like other Microsoft server system products, SCVMM 2012 has a set of hardware and software requirements that should be met before you can install the first SCVMM management or other server roles. There are a number of components of SCVMM 2012, each with its own specific requirements, so if you try to install all the roles and components, you have to install all these required prerequisites on the single physical or virtual machine on which you are planning to host the single SCVMM 2012 implementation.

For our part, we will only be discussing the software and hardware requirements for setting up a single SCVMM server, which will hold all the following SCVMM server roles and components (except the database server, which we kept on a separate server for the SQL Server 2008 R2 installation):

- SCVMM management server
- SCVMM console
- SCVMM Self-Service Portal
- SCVMM library server

For complete SCVMM software and hardware requirements, please go through the SCVMM 2012 Microsoft TechNet documentation at `http://technet.microsoft.com/en-us/library/gg610610`.

System requirements

The following set of system requirements should be met before installing SCVMM management server.

> At the time of writing this book, System Center 2012 SP1 (RTM version) was released for MSDN and TechNet subscribers. You can download this from your MSDN and TechNet subscription.

Systems requirements	Details
OS	Windows Server 2012.
Windows Remote Management (WinRM) 2.0	You can install WinRM as a feature from the server manager.
At least Microsoft .NET Framework 3.5 Service Pack 1	After the installation of the web server role on your SCVMM management server, you can install .NET Framework 3.5.1 as a feature from the server manager.
Windows Automated Installation Kit (AIK) for Windows 7	Windows AIK is available for download from Microsoft Download Center. Once you download AIK, you can launch the autorun from the installation DVD and then install AIK on the SCVMM management server. Also, for Windows Server 2012, we need to install Windows 8 ADT on SCVMM.
SQL Server (database)	• SQL Server 2008 R2 SE/EE/DE – SP2 or later • SQL Server 2012 SE/EE/DE
SQL Server management tools	When you try to install SCVMM 2012, it will ask you to install the SQL Server management binaries, so installing the SQL Server management tools will fulfill the need.

Hardware requirements

The following set of hardware requirements should be met before the installation of SCVMM management server.

The following are the hardware requirements for a small implementation (SCVMM managing up to 150 hosts):

Hardware component	Minimum	Recommended
Processor	Pentium 4, 2 GHz (x64)	Dual-core processor, 2.8 GHz or greater (x64)
RAM	2 GB	4 GB
Hard disk space (without a local VMM database)	2 GB	40 GB
Hard disk space (with a local, full version of Microsoft SQL Server)	80 GB	150 GB

The following are the hardware requirements for a large implementation (SCVMM managing more than 150 hosts):

Hardware component	Minimum	Recommended
Processor	Pentium 4, 2.8 GHz (x64)	Dual-core processor, 3.6 GHz or greater (x64)
RAM	4 GB	8 GB
Hard disk space	10 GB	50 GB

If you are considering a single-server implementation of SCVMM, where the SCVMM management server and library server roles would be placed on the same server, you should have a larger amount of disk space for the SCVMM library.

Installing SCVMM management server, management console, and Self-Service Portal server

After going through the SCVMM software and hardware requirements, we will now drill down to the installation of SCVMM management server, along with the SCVMM console and self-service role on the same server. It should be noted here that, since we are setting up this server for the demonstration of SCVMM 2012 features and capabilities for Hyper-V Windows Server 2012, we are maintaining all the SCVMM server roles and components on the single server. But for all of you who are going to install SCVMM 2012 in production environments, where your SCVMM server is going to manage a vast number of Hypervisor hosts (Hyper-V/VMware/Citrix XenServer), in this type of implementation, I would strongly recommend that you size and plan your deployment such that you keep each role of SCVMM on a dedicated physical or VM machine. After you have installed the required prerequisites on the server, and on the other end your supported version of SQL Server is ready to host the SCVMM database, you may perform the following steps to install SCVMM 2012 management server, management console, and Self-Service Portal server:

1. Mount or insert the Microsoft System Center 2012 SP1 (CTP 2) installation media to your SCVMM server.
2. From the installation media, launch `setup.exe`.

3. From the installation splash screen, click on the **Install** link; this will start the installation process.

4. It is strongly recommended that you enable the checkbox for **Get the latest updates to the Virtual Machine Manager from Microsoft Update**. This will fix any recent bugs found for a product on the relevant operating system platform.

5. On the next screen, you will be presented with the server roles you want to install on the server, if you have run the `setup` utility. For this example we will be installing all the roles, including the VMM management server, VMM console, and VMM Self-Service Portal on the same single server.

6. After the selection of the roles, you have to provide the information about the name of the administrator installing the product, organization details, and last but not least, the product key. If you don't provide the product key during installation, you can provide it later; if you are installing SCVMM 2012 for evaluation purposes, your installation will be valid for a 180-day trial period even without a key.

7. On the next screen, read and accept the licensing agreement of SCVMM 2012.

8. You may join the **Customer Experience Improvement Program (CEIP)** to help Microsoft improve the quality of the product.

9. The next screen will ask you about automatic updates, which will allow you to patch up your SCVMM server. We recommend that you keep automatic updates on, from both the Windows and System Center 2012 perspective.

10. Then, you have to specify the installation directory where you want the installation binaries. We recommend that you keep the application binaries separate from the OS drive.

11. On the prerequisites checker, if there is any prerequisite missing, SCVMM setup will inform you about that. Install any missing prerequisites and re-run the prerequisites checker.

12. If everything goes fine, you will be taken to the next screen, where you have to specify the database server credentials. If you are installing the SCVMM database on the SQL cluster, type the SQL Server cluster name with the proper SQL Server instance name. In addition to this, we also have to specify the correct SQL Server listening port; if you haven't changed the ports on your SQL Server, ignore this.

13. For distributed key management, you will be requested to use an existing Active Directory organizational unit or to create a new one for SCVMM to store the encryption keys. For SCVMM HA implementation, you are required to keep the security keys within Active Directory instead of in a local machine.

14. In the next section, SCVMM will show you all the ports; if there are any requirements to change the ports from the default, you should change the keys as per your need.

    Since we are installing SCVMM Self-Service Portal on the same machine, right after the questions related to SCVMM management server's installation configuration are done, SCVMM asks you about the Self-Service Portal-related configuration settings.

15. On the **Self-Service Portal** configuration screen, specify the SCVMM management server's FQDN, which Self-Service Portal should use to connect.

16. And lastly, provide the Self-Service Portal website port; by default, port 80 is set for SSP, but if you want to change this, you can specify the port here.

17. Before setup is complete and installation begins, you have to specify the library configuration. If you already have an SCVMM library server, you can specify it here; if you don't have an SCVMM library server and are newly installing SCVMM server on your environment, you have to create a new library share. It is recommended that you keep the library share on a separate hard disk other than the OS drive of the SCVMM server.

18. On the last screen, SCVMM shows a summary of all the configuration-related settings you provided.

19. Upon reviewing the entire configuration summary, if you see everything is ok, you can click on the **Install** button to start the installation.

Once the installation is completed, the setup will ask you to open the SCVMM management console. Upon opening the SCVMM management console, you are required to provide credentials.

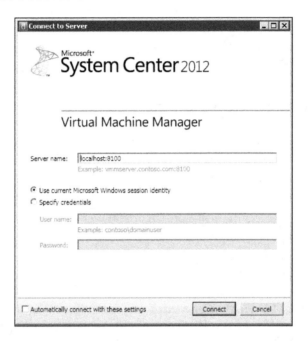

After the successful signing in, we can see the SCVMM management console. Since it's a fresh installation, we cannot see any host or virtual machine inside the SCVMM management console.

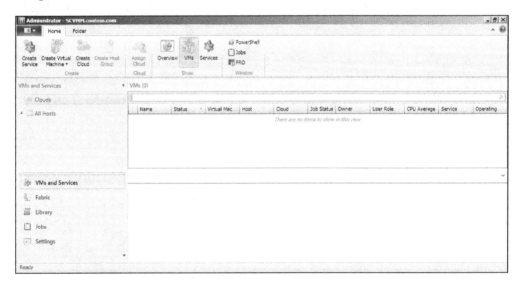

Configuring SCVMM basic settings

To see the complete list of basic configuration settings for SCVMM, please check *Appendix B, SCVMM Management Console Configuration Settings*.

After completing the installation of SCVMM 2012 and understanding the basic management features of SCVMM, we will go through the basic configuration settings required to start managing your Hyper-V infrastructure with SCVMM. As we have said previously, in this chapter we will only showcase the basic features and functionalities of SCVMM for Hyper-V, which will allow us to create virtual machines via SCVMM and manage them.

Creating and managing host groups

Host groups are like containers and help you organize your hypervisor hosts according to the criteria you specify. Let's say, for example, in your environment, you have different virtualization providers, including Hyper-V, VMware, and Citrix XenServers. Within each hypervisor class, you have three hypervisor categories, including critical, general, and research and development hypervisors. So critical business application-based virtual machines are always created on critical category-based hypervisors, and normal, day-to-day applications on general category-based hypervisors. And at last, all research and development related virtual machines are kept on RnD category-based hypervisors.

Now you will wonder whether these host groups are only meant for putting the hypervisor hosts in different containers in SCVMM console or whether there are any other benefits we can get from them. So to answer your question, there are many policy criteria and dynamics available to you in terms of policies, which you can apply to the host group container, which will help you to dynamically scale up and scale down the usage of your virtualized workloads and hypervisors as well.

There are plenty of policies that can be applied to a host group, and by default if you don't customize the policies on self-created host groups, the root-host group policies get in and are applied as the inherited policies from the root host group. The following are the main policies that can be applied to a host group:

- Placement policies (rules)
- Host reservation policies
- Dynamic optimization policies
- Networking
- Storage
- Customization

We will shortly discuss these policies in the *Customizing host group properties* section in this chapter, so first let's see how to create a host group for our multiple Hyper-V hosts.

Creating a host group

To create a host group, perform the following steps:

1. Open the **Virtual Machine Manager** console with administrative privileges.

2. Click on the **VMs and Services** menu in the lower-left corner, or alternatively, you can use *Ctrl + M* as a keyboard shortcut to open the **VMs and Services** menu.

3. In the upper-left corner, under the **VMs and Services** page, right-click on the **All Hosts** container and click on **New Host Group**.

4. Then, give a name to your newly created host group, for example, Hyper-V; if you want to create more hosted groups for your other types of hypervisors, you can create them, and move a hypervisor machine to the host that you want.

Customizing host group properties

Okay, though we have now created a host group for our Hyper-V machines, we will not understand the different policies and customizations available to us. There are many types of policies and customizable settings available that can be applied to a host group. If no customization has been made to a host group, the root host group policies are applicable to all the child host groups.

Let's now drill down to the host group customizable properties one by one.

General

The following are the options under the **General** tab:

*   **Name**: Host group name could be similar to the functionality and features of a hypervisor that will be placed inside.

*   **Location**: The **Location** settings allow us to move the host group from one parent host group to another. When we move a host group from one parent host group to another, the settings of the new parent host group get applied to that host group.

- **Description**: The **Description** is just a field that can distinguish a host group from others. It helps to quickly identify the scope of the host group.

- **File Transfer**: On the **General properties** page, we can see a checkbox that says **Allow unencrypted file transfers (offers improved performance but is less secure)**; if we want increase the performance of file transfers, we would have to uncheck this checkbox, which will offload the encryption overhead and thus will improve file transfer performance.

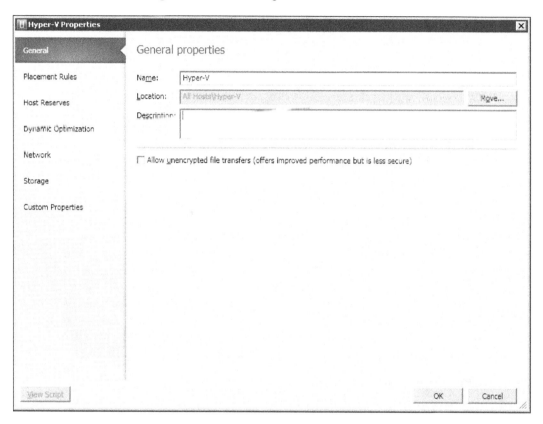

Placement Rules

The placement rules allow SCVMM to make better decisions about placing a virtual machine on a hypervisor host. By default, placement rules inherit from the parent host group, but an administrator can also customize the placement application. To set the placement rules, we first have to uncheck the box that says **Use the placement settings from the parent host group**, and then we can specify our own rules, as described next:

- **Custom Property**: There are a total of ten custom properties available, which can be used to set the placement rules. We can choose any of these custom properties and then set the requirements for the appropriate placement rules.

- **Requirements**: In the **Requirements** settings of placement rules, there are two "must" and two "should" settings available to us, and any two of these four settings can be set with "not". For example, there are four requirement conditions available; one says **Virtual machine must match host** and another says **Virtual machine must not match host**; the other two say **Virtual machine should match host** and **Virtual machine should not match host**.

Host Reserves

The host reserves are like a food stock you always want to save for yourself, which means that there are certain amounts of physical resources you always want to reserve for the host for proper servicing and for healthy operations. By default, just like other properties and settings, the **Host Reserves** settings also get inherited from the parent host group. You can set your defined criteria that you would like for your host physical reserves. If there are no physical resources available for a new virtual machine after reserving the resources for the host, the creation and the placement of a virtual machine will give an error. There are plenty of physical computing resources that can be reserved from the host hypervisor server, as follows:

- **CPU**
- **Memory**
- **Disk I/O**
- **Disk space**
- **Network I/O**

These resources are shown in the following screenshot:

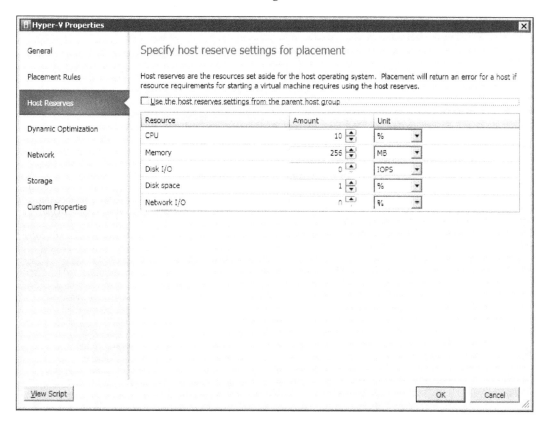

Dynamic Optimization

During the development of SCVMM and System Center 2012, dynamics for a datacenter and virtual machine have always been the focused areas; SCVMM provides a great level of datacenter and cloud dynamics for virtual workloads. Dynamic optimization settings on a host group allow an administrator to set the specific threshold for physical resources before it considers the workload for migration to another host. By default, dynamic optimization settings get inherited from the parent host group. Let's now see each of the optimization settings in detail:

- **Aggressiveness**
    - **High**: This means balance even for small gain. Thus, it results in more live migrations.
    - **Medium**: In the **Medium** case, the gain and number of live migrations performed are in the medium range.

- ○ **Low**: When we set the **Aggressiveness** threshold to **Low**, it balances only for substantial gain. Thus, it results in fewer live migrations.

- **Automatically migrate virtual machines to balance load at this frequency (minutes)**: In the dynamic optimization settings, we are allowed to set the load frequency in minutes before SCVMM performs live migration of virtual machines from one host to another.

- **Thresholds**: Again there are a whole lot of dynamics that can be set for optimizing your SCVMM-catered hypervisors, where we can also set the threshold for the virtual machine. So, if a certain percent of physical resources go down, the virtual machine can be live migrated from one host to another free host.

- **Power optimization**: Power optimization allows an organization to set the specific threshold to optimize the power usage by shutting down unneeded hosts while the workload is low.

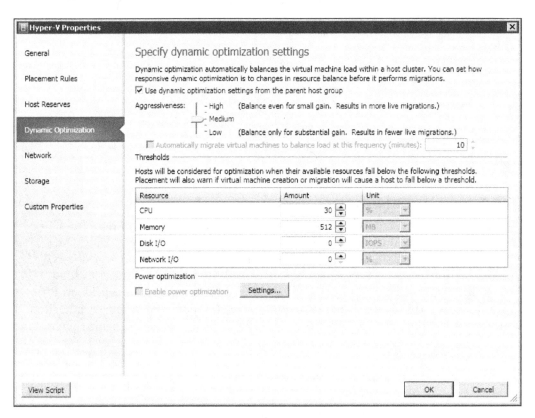

Network

The **Network** settings of a host group allow you to view the network resources that are bound to the host group; by default, these networking resources get inherited from the parent host group. These networking resources are as follows:

- **IP pools**
- **Load balancers**
- **Logical networks**
- **MAC pools**

Storage

The **Storage** settings for the host group can be divided into two parts; in the first part of the storage settings is the summary of storage capacity for hosts in the storage group, and the second part is the allocation of storage to the host group from the storage pools and logical units.

Custom Properties

SCVMM gives you the flexibility of customizing your virtualized environment or private cloud to your own needs, and therefore for every object type inside the SCVMM there are custom properties that are provided. The following is the list of object types for which custom properties are available:

- Virtual machine
- Virtual machine templates
- Host
- Host cluster
- Host group
- Service instance
- Computer tier
- Cloud

Adding a Hyper-V host into SCVMM

In the previous section of configuring SCVMM basic configuration, we created a host group and went through the policies that can be applied and customized for hosts inside the host group. Now in this section of the SCVMM basic configuration, we will discuss the steps for adding a Windows Sever 2012 Hyper-V host into the SCVMM environment.

To add a Windows Server 2012 Hyper-V host, or any other type of hypervisor host, you can perform the following steps:

1. Open the **System Center Virtual Machine Manager** console.

2. Click on the **VMs and Services** menu in the lower-left corner.

3. Right-click on either of the parent host groups as per our requirements — we can create a custom host group as we specified in the previous section — and place the newly added Hyper-V host there. Based on the requirement, click on the default host group or custom one and right-click on **Add Hyper-V Hosts and Clusters**. If you are adding any non-Microsoft hypervisor, you can select the appropriate type of hypervisor to add to the SCVMM.

4. The **Resource location** section of the process of adding hosts into SCVMM asks you the location of the host; if your Hyper-V host is a part of your Active Directory domain, you may select the option **Windows Server computers in a trusted Active Directory domain**. Or, alternatively, you can choose any other option that best fits your scenario.

5. Your credentials are required to add hosts into SCVMM and to authenticate yourself to search for the computer object in the Active Directory domain. You can use the pre-created **Run As Account**, or as per need, you can manually enter credentials.

6. In the **Discovery scope** section, you can either specify Windows Sever computer names and IP addresses, or alternatively define an Active Directory search query. Multiple host names can be entered by separating each server name by writing them on different lines. If required, you can also skip AD verification for your search and addition.

7. Within the **Target resources** selection area, we can select the that we would like to add to our SCVMM environment. You can simply check or uncheck the checkboxes for the server names that are discovered against your search query.

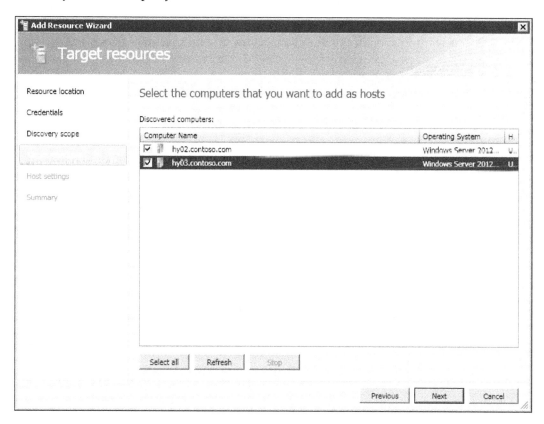

8. In the next step of adding a Hyper-V host to the SCVMM environment, we are requested to specify the host group and the virtual machine placement path for this host. The desired host group can be selected from the **Host group** drop-down list. If the host that is being added into the SCVMM is currently managed by any other SCVMM environment, the **Reassociate this host with this VMM environment** checkbox can also be checked. If you want to specify the default path for virtual machine placement, you can specify the path while adding the host into the SCVMM.

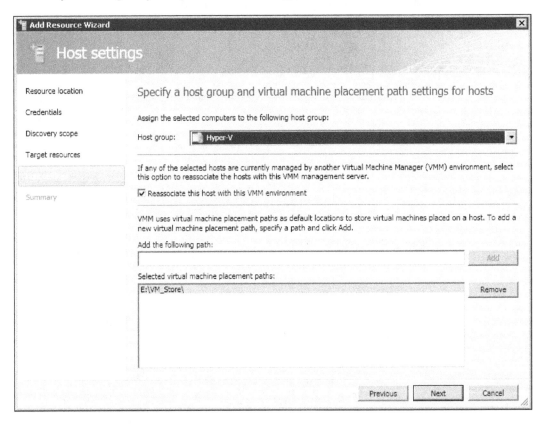

9. Finally, SCVMM provides you with the summary of the selection and the settings you selected for the new host to be added to the SCVMM environment.

So far in this section, we have seen how to create a new host group, customize host group policies and settings for the host, and last but not least, add a Hyper-V host into the host group.

Creating and managing private cloud with SCVMM

In SCVMM, we have been given the luxury of creating virtual workloads either directly on the hypervisors, where we can separate the virtual machines by placing them on different sets of Hyper-V, or by separating the virtual machines and placing them in private clouds. These clouds can be created for departments, group-run companies, or for each customer in the case of cloud service providers.

We are not going to look at the basics of cloud computing or private clouds here because we have already discussed this in detail in *Chapter 1*, *Getting to Know Microsoft Hyper-V*. So, to refresh you memory about cloud computing and private clouds, go back and go through the NIST definition for cloud computing and private clouds.

As we said previously, we can create virtual machines and place them into clouds created within SCVMM, where each cloud has a capability profile that defines the resources and virtual machines the cloud can host and run.

To create a cloud in SCVMM, we can perform the following steps:

1. Open the **System Center Virtual Machine Manager** console.
2. Click on the **VMs and Services** menu in the lower-left corner.
3. Then find the **Clouds** tab in the upper-left corner, right-click on it, and click on **Create Cloud**.
4. In the **General** tab, we have to specify the name of the cloud we want to create, and we can also specify the description of the cloud.

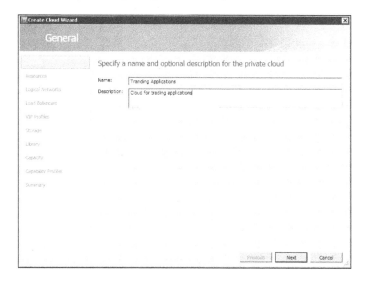

5. In the next tab of the cloud creation wizard, **Resources**, we have to specify the host groups we have created for different hypervisors. For instance, let's say we have created a host group **Hyper-V**, in which we stored all the Hyper-V servers, and we want all the trading applications to run on the Hyper-V server. Accordingly, while creating this cloud for trading applications, we can select the **Hyper-V** host group on the **Resources** tab of the cloud creation wizard.

6. Then, after selecting the host group for the trading applications cloud, we have to select the logical network that will be used as the virtual network switch for the virtual machines based on the trading cloud.

7. The next configuration screen will ask you about the load balancer; if you have a hardware network load balancer in your environment, you can delete and reconfigure it as a base infrastructure for your SCVMM environment, and then you can add it as the network load balancer for the cloud.

8. As part of the network load balancer, the other setting change that SCVMM cloud creation configuration requires you to make is to create the VIP profile. Also, we can separately create the VIP profile in the SCVMM networking section, and the available VIP profile can be chosen from the list of VIP profiles on the **VIP Profiles** configuration screen of the cloud creation wizard.

9. In the next screen of the cloud creation wizard, you will be required to specify the storage classification for this cloud. Storage classification can be separately created from the storage configuration of SCVMM.

10. The SCVMM library is like a toolbox for your virtualized environment and cloud services. All the elements needed for building the virtual machines and cloud services can be found in the SCVMM library. While we create a cloud, we are asked to provide the library server and library share details. By default, we can choose the library server that is added and configured for the SCVMM management server.

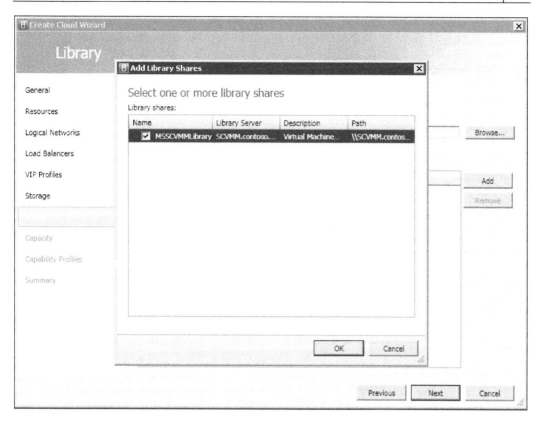

11. The next configuration screen of the cloud creation wizard will ask you about the capacity of the cloud, meaning what computing resources this cloud should have to fulfill its needs, for example, the number of virtual CPUs, storage (disk size), memory (RAM size), custom quota (points), and last but not least, the number of virtual machines this cloud can host. By default, all these values are set as unlimited, but if you want to customize them according to your sizing and capacity planning, you can set the values as per your need.

12. In the last configuration portion of the cloud creation wizard, we are required to set the capability profiles. Capability profiles specify the ability of the cloud to create virtual machines on different hypervisors such as VMware, Hyper-V, and Citrix XenServer.

13. Upon the completion of all the configuration parts, the SCVMM cloud creation wizard will provide a **Summary** screen, which will show you all the details of your selection and configuration for the cloud you are creating.

So in this way, we have created our cloud with all the capacity and capability settings that will allow us to host virtual machines and services on this cloud.

Assigning a cloud to a group of users

In this section, we will now go through the steps of assigning a cloud to a group of users. This set of users can represent a customer, internal department, or set of admins from different teams within the IT department. We can also look at another approach, where we can create clouds for production, quality, and development and assign them to the respective teams and personnel later on.

Assigning a cloud is pretty straightforward; the following are the steps needed to assign a cloud in SCVMM to a group of users:

1. Open the **System Center Virtual Machine Manager** console.

2. Open the **VMs and Services** menu from the lower-left corner, and from the list of clouds in the upper-left corner, right-click on the cloud that you want to assign and click on **Assign Cloud**.

3. After choosing the **Assign Cloud** option from the cloud properties, there will be two options presented to us; we can either assign the cloud to an existing user role, or we can create a new user role for the cloud assignment from the same assigning window. For this example, we will choose an existing user role for the cloud assignment. This user was already created with the name **Data Management Team (Self-Service user)**, as shown in the following screenshot:

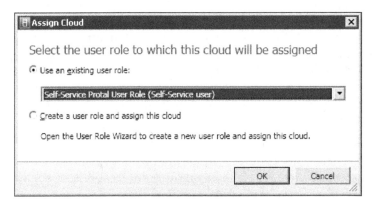

4. After selecting the role, click on the **OK** button to apply the changes.

This way, we have learned the method of assigning a cloud to a single user or a group of users, based on the user role membership.

Creating a virtual machine using the SCVMM console

In SCVMM, virtual machines can be created directly and placed on hypervisors, or you can place them inside the cloud and a single cloud can have multiple virtual machines running and hosted on it.

Since we have gone through all the steps and seen how to build this base infrastructure by means of adding Hyper-V hosts into SCVMM and creating clouds, let's now go through the creation of virtual machines. In this section on creating virtual machines using the SCVMM console, we will be using SCVMM console to create virtual machines, which will directly be placed on Hyper-V hosts.

To create virtual machines via SCVMM console, the following steps need to be performed:

1. Open the **System Center Virtual Machine Manager** console.
2. Click on the **VMs and Services** menu on the left-hand side.
3. Under the **VMs and Services** menu, find the **Hyper-V** node from the upper-left corner, right-click on it, and click on **Create Virtual Machine**.
4. When the new virtual machine creation window opens, you will have to select the source of the virtual machine. This could be **Use an existing virtual machine, VM template, or virtual hard disk**, or if you have none of the existing required elements in your SCVMM environment, you can choose the **Create the new virtual machine with a blank virtual hard disk** option.

Since this is our fresh SCVMM environment, we have neither the hard disk nor the template for creating a new virtual machine. So what we can do here is to create a virtual machine and see how we can create a virtual machine template from this virtual machine later on. It is also a best practice that in your environment, for different types of templates, you create your reference VM, and then make VM templates of this virtual machine. This is easy and meets your exact needs very well.

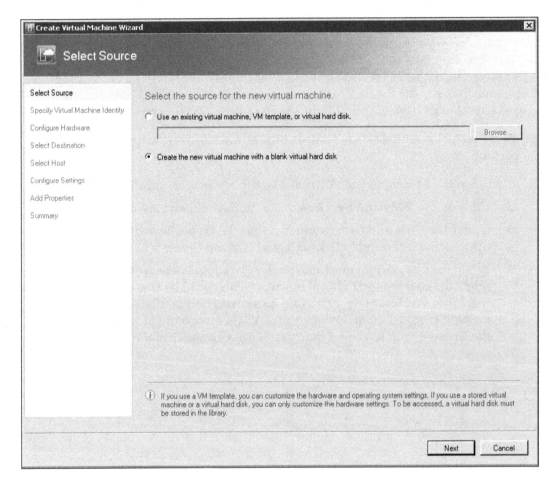

5. On the next wizard screen, you have to specify the virtual machine's identity, when asked to provide the name of the virtual machine, and a few words as the description, which is optional.

6. The next wizard section will take all the information about the virtual machine hardware settings. Here, you have to specify the number of virtual processors and the RAM, hard disk, and DVD drive related information. As per your need, you can add or delete hardware resources, depending on the resources you want this virtual machine to have.

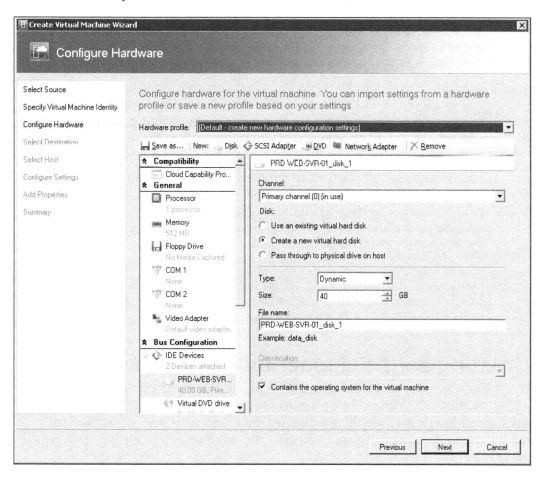

7. After we finish customizing our virtual machine hardware profile, we can move on to the next wizard screen, which is related to selecting the destination of the virtual machine. This means you either want to deploy this virtual machine on a private cloud or hypervisor host or you want to store this virtual machine in the SCVMM library. And since, in this example, we are discovering the method of creating the virtual machine on a Hyper-V host, we will be selecting the **Place the virtual machine on a host** option, which will place this virtual machine on our Hyper-V host.

8. In the next section, the new virtual machine creation wizard will request us to select the host; here, all the hosts that are registered inside the SCVMM will be shown, and each host will have ratings associated to it, based on the available hardware capacity it has for hosting this virtual machine. SCVMM provides the ratings and recommendations that you can follow to select either of the hosts that can accommodate the request.

9. The second section will ask you to configure the location of the virtual machine on the host, along with the preview of the other hardware resources you allocated to the VM, such as networks and virtual hard disks.

10. In addition to all the preceding steps, the next step in the wizard will require you to select a logical network for the virtual machine, and all the available virtual networking switches are shown. According to your needs, you can select the network that you want this virtual machine to be created in.

11. On the next screen of the virtual machine creation wizard, SCVMM will take your inputs about the actions of the host, such as the startup action you want to take when the host gets up and starts running from the down state or how your VM should behave when the running host goes down. In addition to these steps, we have to select the operating system that we are planning to install on this virtual machine.

12. On the last wizard screen, SCVMM will provide you with a **Summary** view, where the entire configuration summary will be presented for your confirmation; if everything looks fine, you can click on the **Create** button to start the virtual machine creation process.

Creating a virtual machine template

While describing the method of creating virtual machines via the SCVMM console, we saw that the SCVMM console gives us the option of creating a virtual machine from a template. Virtual machine templates are an essential part of your service catalogue because, based on your template, you will present the virtual machine package to your internal and external customers. So, let's see how to create a template. One interesting feature of SCVMM is that it allows you to create a virtual machine template from a pre-created virtual machine. The following are the steps for creating a virtual machine template from an existing virtual machine:

1. Open the **System Center Virtual Machine Manager** console.

2. Click on the **VMs and Services** menu from the lower-left corner and click on the Hyper-V host where the virtual machine has been created and made ready for the creation of the virtual machine template from it.

3. To create a virtual machine template from an existing virtual machine, we first need to make sure that the virtual machine is shut down before we start.

4. Find the appropriate virtual machine from the VM list on the host, and right-click and go to the **Create** tab; from there, click on **Create VM Template**.

5. Once you click on **Create VM Template**, you are presented with a warning message for this action that says **Creating a template will destroy the source virtual machine, and any user data on the virtual may be lost**. So, to prevent this loss of data, you may create a clone of the virtual machine that you want to create the virtual machine template for and then create it from the cloned virtual machine. It is your choice whether you want to use the original machine or a cloned machine. For both, the procedure is the same.

Upon your confirmation of the warning message, the VM template creation wizard opens; here, you have to make a series of selections, as follows:

- **VM Template Name**
- **Hardware**
- **Operating System**
- **Library Server**
- **Default path**

All these selections and configurations are just the same as for the creation of a normal virtual machine, where the properties of a virtual machine configuration ask you for the virtual machine template.

At the end of the virtual machine template creation, the wizard will provide you with summary details about the configuration choices and selections you made. The process of creating the virtual machine takes place for some time, and once it is over, you can see the status from the **Jobs** tab. One thing we need to make sure of here is that, once the VM template creation process is completed, we have to go back and take the properties of the VM template and configure the capability profile for the virtual machine template, where we will be selecting the Hyper-V as the capability profile against the hardware profile of the virtual machine.

And the template virtual machine hard disk and template link will be populated in the library, so later on, if you need to create a virtual machine, you will have the template and the virtual machine hard disk shown there for your selection to create the new virtual machine from this precreated settings template.

Access to Self-Service Portal

As we stated earlier, System Center 2012 SP1 has removed the **Self-Service Portal (SSP)** feature from SCVMM. And now, this feature has been added into System Center App Controller 2012 SP1. Although SSP is not part of SCVMM anymore, its basic concepts and features are still the same as before.

In this section regarding access to SSP, we will go through the steps we need to take from the SCVMM side to allow the user access to SSP.

Delegation of SSP rights

To access SCVMM SSP, you need to delegate the rights for SSP. SCVMM provides a great level of delegation of rights from the administration to the support level. Generally, SSP access is granted to support personnel and customers to manage their virtual machines. The process of granting access to SSP can be done from both the SCVMM management console and PowerShell. Let's look at an example of delegating SSP access from the SCVMM console:

1. Open the **System Center Virtual Machine Manager** console.

2. Find the **Settings** tab and click on the button to show further settings.

3. Then, under the **Settings** tab on the left-hand side, select **User Roles** and click on **Create User Role** on the ribbon above.

4. On the initial screen of the **Create User Role Wizard** window, provide the name and description of the role.

5. On the next screen in the user role creation wizard, you will be asked to select a user role profile for this new user role creation. On this screen, whatever user role you select will decide what types of activities and authorities the role member will be able to perform. Since we are creating this role only to delegate the rights to browse SCVMM SSP, we will only choose the **Self-Service User** role among all other roles, as shown in the following screenshot:

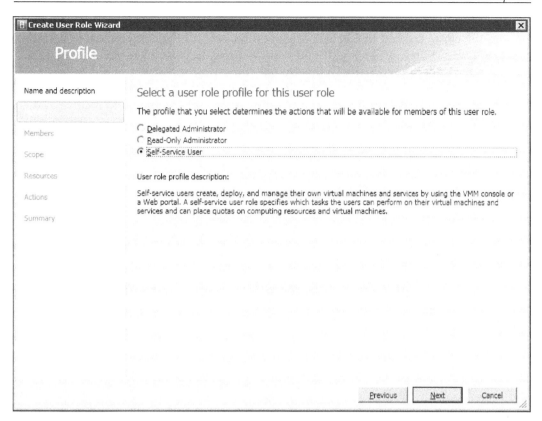

6. On the next screen in the self-service user role creation wizard, the one for delegation of rights for SSP, we have to select the members that we would like to add into this role. As per your need, you can add as many people as you want into this role to allow them to access SSP. We can also create multiple self-service user roles as per our need; here, we can customize the self-service user role to perform the specific operations inside the SSP. We will see this customization of rights on the next screen of the wizard.

7. The next screen is an important screen, where you are prompted to select the cloud created inside SCVMM; you will see all the clouds created inside SCVMM on this list, and if you want to provide your users with access to a specific cloud, you can do this by selecting the appropriate cloud here. At the bottom of the screen, you will see another checkbox for **Show PRO tips**, which will ask you if you want to allow these role members to receive **PRO** (**Performance and Resource Optimization**) tips.

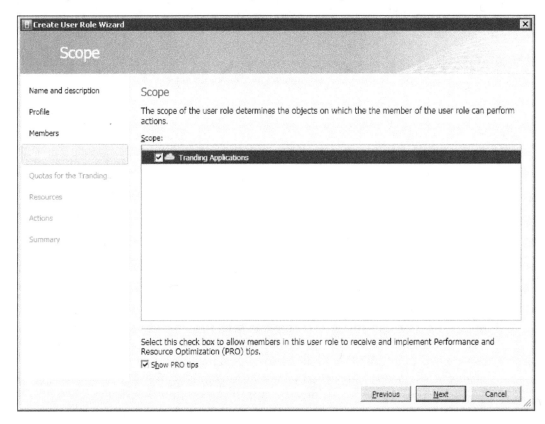

8. Once you select the cloud, on the next screen you will see the quota for the selected cloud that you can use while managing the cloud resources from the SSP.

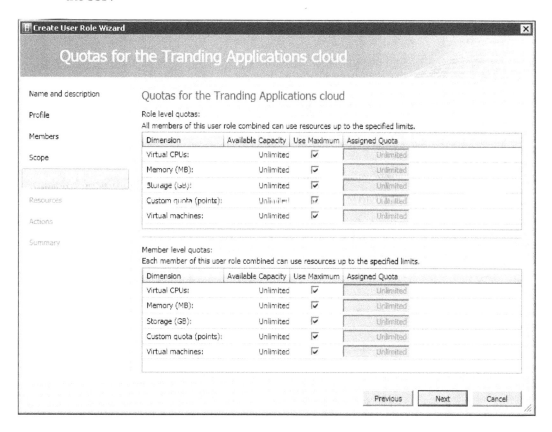

9. SCVMM also provides deep delegation of the rights of your virtualized and cloud environment through the **Resources** tab of the user role creation for SSP, which allows you to even select each cloud resource for which you want to do the delegation of rights. At the bottom of the same wizard screen, you are requested to provide the data path for this user role; if you want, you can also customize this as per your needs.

10. The next screen is the most important screen of this delegation of rights; here we have to choose the capabilities this role will hold. You will find plenty of the activity names that you can choose to add into this user role. Based on your need, add the capabilities you want this cloud user role to have to allow its members to perform the activities for the selected role.

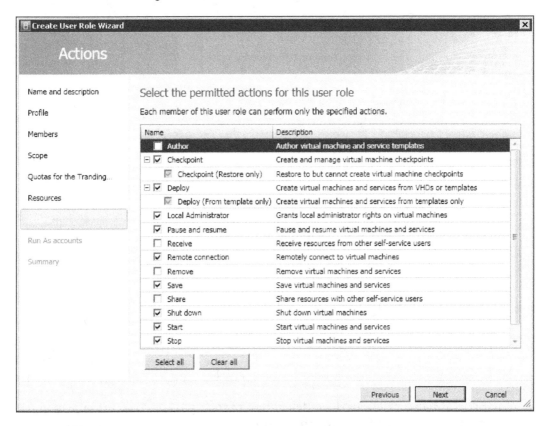

11. To perform the administrative tasks based on the capabilities we select the **Actions** tab of the user role creation wizard, we have to associate the Run As account with this user role. We have to select this option from the **Run As accounts** screen of the user role creation wizard.

12. Finally, SCVMM will provide us with a summary description of the selections we made to create the user role group for our SSP access.

This way, we have created an SSP user role to which we also added the required members that will be delegated for SSP management according to the criteria we described in the self-service user role we created.

After creating the SSP user role and having set the members up correctly, we can now browse the SSP by opening the SSP URL. Note that if you are facing problem with browsing your SSP in the browser, you should check the IIS website settings for your SSP. Open IIS manager on the server and go to the site; from there, right-click on **Microsoft System Center Virtual Machine Manager Self-Service Portal (x64)**. Then go to manage website and click on the **Browse** submenu. This will open your SSP website, where you can easily perform troubleshooting if the site isn't loading.

Creating and managing virtual machines with SSP

So far, we have seen how to delegate the rights for SSP; now in this section, we will go through creating and managing virtual machines within SSP. SSP creates and manages only those instances of virtual machines that are going to be hosted inside the cloud.

Now, let's go ahead and create our first virtual machine within SCVMM SSP. To create a VM in SSP, open the SSP in any website browser and log in with the SSP user role that we assigned to the cloud in the *Delegation of SSP rights* section and perform the following steps:

1. Open the SCVMM SSP URL.
2. To create a new virtual machine, click on **New Computer** in the upper-right corner under the **Creation** action pane.
3. After clicking on the **New Computer** hyperlink, a new, small window will open that will have the name **New Virtual Machine**.
4. In the **New Virtual Machine** window, we select the VM template, and then the other necessary configuration elements, such as the virtual machine name and password.
5. After filling out all the required details for the new virtual machine, click on the **Create** button to start the virtual machine creation process.

All types of virtual machine creation processes take almost the same amount of time, and the progress of the task can be seen at any time from the **Jobs** tab.

Summary

Let's summarize what we accomplished in this chapter. We started with the overview of SCVMM as the product, and then we went through what makes SCVMM 2012 more interesting for Hyper-V and other hypervisors available in the market today. After getting familiar with the product, we went through the step-by-step deployment of the product. Then in the next section, we addressed the basic configuration, which makes your SCVMM environment ready to slowly move towards production. In this section, we saw how to create host groups and clouds, and in addition to this, we also saw how to add the Hyper-V host into the SCVMM environment.

Once our SCVMM environment became fully ready to host the virtual machines for the associated hypervisors, we went straight into creating and managing virtual machines through SCVMM console; in this section, we created and hosted virtual machines on the cloud.

In the last section of this chapter, we moved ahead with explaining the self-service experience by seeing how we can delegate access to SSP for specific cloud resources. In addition to this, we also looked at the steps for creating virtual machines using SSP.

In the next chapter, we will look at Hyper-V high availability and virtual machine mobility features. The next chapter is going to be the longest chapter of our book as it will discuss the majority of the Hyper-V advanced-level features, such as live migration, storage migration, building Hyper-V clusters, and many more.

8
Building Hyper-V High Availability and Virtual Machine Mobility

In this chapter we will have discussions related to Hyper-V high availability and virtual machine mobility, and we will see how we can make our Hyper-V virtual workloads highly available as per downtime. We will also see how we can migrate these virtual resources between Hyper-V hosts without affecting the virtual machine availability.

So far in this book, we have completed seven chapters, and in these seven chapters, we have gone through different architectural and best practices that make sure our virtualized critical workloads and other components related to Hyper-V are configured and working. But any hypervisor product with a single point of failure can cause serious damage to your virtualized critical systems, where corruption of a single-server OS with no high availability can bring down all your virtual machines. Setting up high availability and virtual machine mobility becomes more critical when you start migrating everything from the physical to the virtual environment.

High availability and virtual machine mobility is not only a concern from a disaster recovery or business continuity perspective, but it is also required from the operations and maintenance perspective. Let's assume that your company has a policy that on the third weekend of every month, all the servers and systems should be patched up. So in this case, if you don't have some kind of high availability and virtual machine mobility practice in place, every time you patch your hypervisor server, you will have to shut down all the virtual machines running on it. Only then will you be able to install the patches and restart the server.

Overview of Hyper-V high availability

Let's start this chapter with an overview of Hyper-V high availability. And to get this overview, let's go back in time, to when Hyper-V was first made available to the public right after the release of Windows Server 2012. With this earlier version of the product, Hyper-V was the first initiative of Microsoft that was a built-in server virtualization tool or server role. Initially, Windows Server 2008 Hyper-V used to support only quick migration (we will discuss quick migration and other types of migration later in this chapter) with the support of Microsoft Clustering Services. But there were a few caveats in this high availability approach, such as that using quick migration, an administrator was allowed to migrate a virtual machine from one physical Hyper-V host to another, but with some downtime, due to the unavailability of true shared storage between clusters.

With Windows Server 2008, when we build a two-node failover cluster by using shared storage, it gets set up as an active-passive cluster. This means one node always stays active and the other stays passive. So what happens when an administrator performs a quick migration of the virtual machine from one Hyper-V cluster node to another? This results in saving the virtual machine state on the active Hyper-V node. And then the virtual machine configuration and its storage is moved to the target cluster node. During the migration of the whole of this cluster's resources from one node to another, there is downtime for the virtual machine as it goes into the save state. Once the migration of the required resources is complete, the virtual machine gets restored on the target Hyper-V cluster node. Based on different underlying infrastructure components, this may take longer because of the different dependent components.

The Hyper-V high availability features provided by Windows Server 2008 didn't really help organizations to maintain their highly available Hyper-V environment, but that was not too bad as the product was in the initial maturing state. In Windows Server 2008 R2 — the second release of Windows Server 2008 — Hyper-V 2.0 was made available as a built-in native server virtualization role in Windows Server. With this second release of Windows Server 2008 along with quick migration for Hyper-V, live migration was also introduced; this entirely reshaped Hyper-V virtualization and high availability of the product by allowing migrating virtual machines between Hyper-V hosts without zero downtime. Live migration allowed organizations to move their critical workload during production time while being connected to the virtual machine, and migrate from running on the Hyper-V server to any other Windows Server 2008 R2 in the cluster. Along with live migration, **Cluster Shared Volumes (CSV)** was another feature that was introduced in Windows Server 2008 R2 that helped organizations take advantage of Hyper-V high availability while migrating their virtual workloads between Hyper-V hosts for a planned maintenance window, without any downtime.

Although the live migration and CSV features contributed a lot and helped organizations build Hyper-V HA, there were still a few caveats in the product that customers and the industry wished would be addressed in the next release of Windows Server and Hyper-V. We will discuss this in the upcoming *What's new in Windows Server 2012 for Hyper-V HA and VM mobility* section of this chapter.

Now before we move on to exploring the new features available in Windows Server 2012 for Hyper-V high availability and virtual machine mobility, let's first discuss the challenges we faced with the prerelease of Window Server 2012 and Hyper-V high availability and virtual machine mobility.

Challenges in Hyper-V high availability with Windows Server 2008 R2

As we saw in the previous section *Overview of Hyper-V high availability*, earlier releases of Windows Server, such as Windows Server 2008 or 2008 R2, provided high availability and redundancy features, but with some limitations. Due to these limitations, to manage high availability as a whole for larger enterprises and cloud services providers, these earlier-introduced Hyper-V HA and virtual machine mobility solutions didn't satisfy the need of a true hypervisor-level HA solution. The challenges that were faced in the versions prior to Windows Server 2012 related to HA and Hyper-V VM mobility can be summarized as discussed in the following sections.

Unavailability of flexible virtual machine storage migration

In the releases prior to the Windows Server 2012 release of Windows Server and Hyper-V, if we want to migrate virtual machine storage from one Hyper-V host disk drive to another, the only option available to us is to turn off that particular virtual machine and then perform a normal copy and paste action from one Hyper-V node to another. Due to the unavailability of live storage migration of the virtual machine between Hyper-V nodes, Hyper-V administrators were required to shut down the virtual machine and then move its related storage.

Restrictions on adding more Hyper-V cluster nodes

In Windows Server 2008 R2, at most we could add 16 nodes into a single Windows Server 208 R2 Hyper-V cluster. This limited the customers to extend their Hyper-V cluster to sixteen nodes and after that they had to create another Hyper-V cluster if they wanted to make the remaining Hyper-V nodes highly available as well. So let's say you want to perform a live migration for a critical virtual machine that is running on a clustered Hyper-V, which is low on the physical resources, and want this virtual machine to have more physical resources; you can only find a good Hyper-V candidate within the 16 nodes of the same cluster on which you are hosting this virtual machine, outside of which you cannot perform live migration of this virtual machine.

Virtual machine live migration limitation

This was one of the major limitations that customers and lots of administrators faced in the prerelease of Windows Server 2012 and Hyper-V, where an administrator is only allowed to live migrate a single virtual machine at a time. The time required for one virtual machine to live migrate from one Hyper-V node to another is solely dependent on the resource allocation made for the virtual machine. And since the administrator has to wait for the one virtual machine live migration to finish first and then migrate the others one by one, this cap may sometimes slow down the overall maintenance work cycle.

Another limitation we saw with the pre-release of Windows Server 2012 and Hyper-V was the impossibility of live migrating a virtual machine to a standalone Hyper-V host. Since the live migration feature was only supported for clustered Hyper-V nodes and highly available virtual machines, it was sometimes a bit difficult for small- to medium-sized organizations to set up a highly available Hyper-V infrastructure.

Manual patch management for Hyper-V host nodes

Patching a cluster is always a time-consuming task, because to patch one node you have to move all the virtual machines to other cluster nodes. Patching a cluster node can be more frustrating when moving these virtual machines to other cluster nodes as it slows down the process by limiting the live migration of VMs to one at a time.

Additionally, in the releases prior to Windows Server 2012, patching a cluster node was a manual process, where an administrator had to first install the patches and then download the server after freeing up the server for any cluster resources.

Network-attached storage (NAS) or File Server-based storage for virtual machines

Windows Server 2008 or 2008 R2 Hyper-V didn't allow its customers to keep the **virtual machine storage** (VHD) on network shares such as NAS and File Server. And due to this, customers had to either purchase the local storage for virtual machines, or, if that was not possible, go for SAN; but storing a VHD on a File Server or NAS head was still not possible.

What's new in Windows Server 2012 for Hyper-V HA and VM mobility

Windows Server 2012 Hyper-V contains a number of new features and improvements for Hyper-V high availability and virtual machine mobility. These new features and improvements make it easier for an administrator to maintain a highly available virtualized environment along with optimal usage of hardware resources.

Let's now summarize the new features and enhancements made in Windows Server 2012 and Hyper-V 3.0 for high availability and virtual machine mobility.

Guest machine clustering capabilities with V-Fibre Channel

Windows Server 2012 allows you to connect a virtual machine to your SAN fabric over the fibre channel medium and build virtual machine clusters. This new feature will provide the same level of SAN access over fibre channels that we used to get on physical servers.

Enhanced live migration for mobility of virtual machines

As we discussed in the preceding section, the live migration limitation in the releases prior to Windows Server 2012, where only single live migration was allowed at a time, has been removed in Windows Server 2012. And, live migration network performance optimization allows administrators to perform as many live migrations as they want to start concurrently. The number of live migrations you can perform at a time depends on the network bandwidth and availability of your Hyper-V server.

In addition to the enhancement of live migration, administrators can now select multiple virtual machines and perform live migration; this will queue the live migration of the virtual machine at the failover cluster and each virtual machine will automatically be live migrated one by one to their destination Hyper-V node.

Bigger clusters with more Hyper-V nodes

One of the major limitations of the Windows Server 2008 clustering services platform we saw was the total number of cluster nodes that can be included in a single cluster. Windows Server 2008 R2 allowed only 16 cluster nodes to be added to a single Windows base cluster, which was a fairly small number, and therefore enterprise-level organizations had to manage a huge number of small-scale clusters. This used to increase the administrative overhead of companies.

Windows Server 2012 fixed this problem by allowing organizations to build their base Windows Server cluster with 64 cluster nodes and 8000 virtual machines. In this way, companies such as managed service and cloud service providers didn't have to create too many small clusters and manage different silos for the same administrative needs.

Up-to-date Cluster Shared Volumes and encrypted volumes

Cluster Shared Volumes (CSV) was a great feature introduced in Windows Server 2008 R2, where the concept of making a true shared cluster storage became real with the help of the file-locking technology. How CSV is different from the traditional shared cluster disk is that traditional cluster shared disks are shared between cluster nodes, but only one node can access the disk and data at a time, and only upon the failover of the disk and service is the disk accessible by another node. In the CSV technology, the disk is visible and accessible to all the nodes at all times, and only one node can access one virtual machine hard disk at a time, so we have moved from the whole disk to a file-based locking system.

We will understand more about CSV in the upcoming section of this chapter. After Windows Server 2008 R2 SP1, Windows Server 2012 introduced various new enhancements for CSV 2.0 from both the performance and the management perspective. Some of these new enhancements are as follows:

- Unlike the pre-release of Windows Server 2012 where CSV was a separate feature that needed to be enabled in the failover cluster manager, in Windows Server 2012, CSV is a core feature of the cluster. So now if you want to turn a cluster storage (disk) into a CSV disk, all you have to do is just right-click on the disk and turn it into a CSV.

- Windows Server 2012 further enhanced the working of CSV from both the performance and the integration side, to allow third-party software vendors to integrate and work seamlessly with CSV for various tasks, such as monitoring, backup, and virus protection.

- Apart from CSV, Windows Server 2012 provides a functionality where you can use the Microsoft BitLocker technology to encrypt the cluster disks (volumes) to take your failover cluster security to the next level. There may be situations where a few of your cluster nodes may not be placed in secure datacentres, and due to the highly critical nature of the data available in your cluster volumes, you may not want it to be placed in such a way that someone can look into your cluster node and steal the data. So to make sure such an incident does not occur, you can use the BitLocker feature of Windows Server to encrypt the cluster volumes and disks.

Virtual machine failover and management rules

This feature is one of the most loveable features out of all the other enhancements made in the failover and clustering. Windows Server 2012 now allows you to set rules for your virtual machine failover. So let's say we have two virtual machines, namely Exchange Mailbox Role (**DAG – Database Availability Group**) member server 1 and Exchange Mailbox Role (DAG) member server 2. Now whenever failover happens, we want these two virtual machines to be failed over in a sequence and failed over to the same cluster node. Or in other scenarios, if you have two instances of the same role for any application, you can set rules so that these two instances (VMs) of the application do not fail over to the same node. These rules are called affinity and anti-affinity virtual machine rules.

Understanding Hyper-V high availability and failover clustering core components

In this section, we will be covering the core components for Hyper-V high availability. In this section, we will discuss the basic requirements for setting up high availability for a Hyper-V environment. These core components for setting up a Hyper-V highly available environment that we will be considering are the following:

- Server hardware
- Storage fabric
- Networking fabric

Now let's go ahead and discuss these components one by one and in detail, for their different types and related information.

Server hardware

Your server hardware must be certified for Windows Server 2012 if you wish to set up Hyper-V high availability or clustering. The server you choose should be the same one that you consider suitable for the Hyper-V role in terms of its physical resources. It is not required that the physical boxes you choose for Hyper-V failover clustering and high availability setup be the same in terms of the server model, but the physical resources should be the same. For example, if you have four servers that you are considering to set up as a Hyper-V failover cluster, it doesn't matter if two of them are from one hardware company (HP) and the other two are from a different hardware company (Dell). The main requirements that should be met are as follows:

- Same CPU brand (Intel with Intel, AMD with AMD)
- Hardware-assisted virtualization
- Hardware DEP
- 64-bit capable processor

Cluster storage

In *Chapter 5, A New World of Hyper-V Automation with PowerShell*, we covered many types of storage that we use for operations related to Hyper-V, but in this section about storage fabric, we will discuss a few that were not covered there. The storage types we use for setting up Hyper-V failover clusters and highly available environments are different from the normal Hyper-V storage types; these storage types are as follows:

- Windows failover cluster shared storage
- CSV

Now let's discuss each of these storage types related to the Hyper-V cluster in detail.

Windows failover cluster shared storage

We have been using this type of storage subsystem for quite a long time. Building a Windows failover cluster has always required shared storage between cluster nodes for quorums and other types of cluster-aware applications. Initially, we used to use SAN for this shared cluster storage over a fibre channel medium. But with the passage of time, we saw great innovation in the storage industry when iSCSI SAN hit the industry a few years back, and since it was cheaper than the traditional SAN storage, its use for building clustering became convenient.

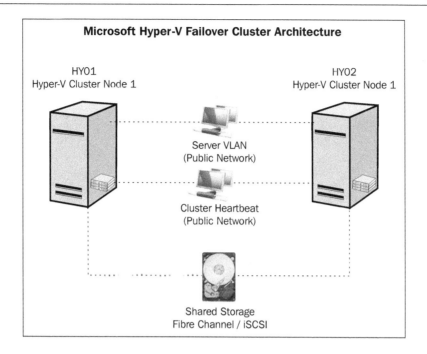

Microsoft Hyper-V Failover Cluster Architecture

HY01
Hyper-V Cluster Node 1

HY02
Hyper-V Cluster Node 1

Server VLAN
(Public Network)

Cluster Heartbeat
(Public Network)

Shared Storage
Fibre Channel / iSCSI

Cluster Shared Volumes (CSV)

The CSV feature was introduced in Windows Server 2008 R2. How CSV works as compared to the traditional cluster disk is different. Before CSV was released, to make the virtual machine highly available, we had to assign a new cluster disk to a virtual machine independently to make sure that in the event of virtual machine failover only the required cluster disk fails over to the destination cluster node. This was needed because at any given point in time only a single cluster node could access a cluster disk (LUN), so at the time of failover, this disk (LUN) had to fail over from the source cluster node to the destination cluster node, which used to make the virtual machine down (paused) for some time and then bring it up. This meant that while using the shared storage for the cluster, we were still lacking full sharing capabilities for the cluster disks.

Another problem with the noncluster shared volume disks was the complexity of managing cluster disks because you had to create separate LUNs and bind them to the cluster storage group in the SAN; and from the server's perspective, for each virtual machine you had to have a separate LUN bound to the cluster nodes storage group.

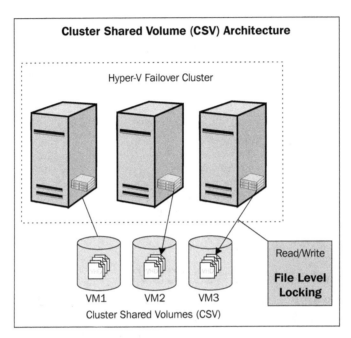

How CSV works

CSV addressed these problems with having true shared storage and solved them by shifting the method of locking a virtual machine storage disk access from the disk level to the file level. This means that with CSV, all cluster nodes see the entire disk all the time, but at any given moment only one cluster node can access the virtual hard disk (VHD) of a virtual machine that is currently running. So let's assume we have four CSV LUNs associated with our group of failover cluster nodes for Hyper-V, as follows:

Cluster disk	CSV volumes	Disk size	VM VHDs
Disk 11	Volume 1	500 GB	VM1, VM2, VM3
Disk 12	Volume 2	500 GB	VM4, VM5
Disk 13	Volume 3	500 GB	VM6, VM7
Disk 14	Volume 4	500 GB	VM8, VM9, VM10

When you enable and add a cluster disk as a CSV, this disk starts showing in `C:\ClusterStorage\Volume1` and so on for other CSV disks. You can rename these CSV names as per your application and disk allocation needs.

In the preceding table, we can see that multiple virtual machines' VHDs are located in a single volume of CSV-enabled disks. So in the case of a failover or the live migration of VM1 from the `HY-SVR-01` node to the `HY-SVR-02` node, VM1 will be moved without any downtime because all the CSV volumes will be accessible from all the Hyper-V cluster nodes, and the difference is that when the VM1 VHD was located on Volume1, only HY-SVR-01 had access to this VHD file, but when we moved the virtual machine to HY-SVR-02, the VHD access was granted and locked for `HY-SVR-02`. Any virtual machine that is run and mounted on a CSV is locked for its running Hyper-V cluster node.

Summary of new features added in Windows Server 2012 CSV

Windows Server 2012 carried forward the CSV features from Windows Server 2008 R2 and added a number of new enhancements, such as an antivirus and backup application in the CSV code to make it more interoperable with your existing application infrastructure, and there are a great deal of features that have been added in Windows Server 2012 that will enhance the performance experience of CSV.

The summary of new CSV 2.0 specific features added in Windows Server 2012 is as follows:

- It supports BitLocker volume encryption for Cluster Shared Volumes.
- It provides multi-subnet support and improved I/O redirection to support block-level I/O and increased performance.
- It improves performance of CSV I/O directing for larger cluster scenario deployments.
- It provides CSV support for memory-mapped files.
- It supports new levels and types of CSV volume repair and maintenance methods, which include copy-offload, defragmentation of CSV volumes, and online corruption repair.
- More server roles are supported now for CSV usage, where earlier Hyper-V was the only candidate that was officially supported. Windows Server 2012 also supports File Server for scaled-out application data.

- Windows Server 2012 has greatly improved its backup capabilities for making VSS-based backup solutions work with CSV, to back up and restore CSV volumes.

- Windows Server 2012 made the CSV 2.0 feature available by default, where all we have to do is enable and add a clustered disk as a CSV disk, while on the other side, Windows Server 2008 R2 requires administrators to enable the CSV feature within Failover Cluster Manager before using it. So, now we have one step less to perform for configuring CSV with the simplified Failover Cluster Manager snap-in.

- It supports **Server Message Block (SMB)** 3.0 file-based storage for Hyper-V.

- With the previous version of CSV in Windows Server 2008 R2, we all suffered re-direct mode access of CSV disk, where taking a virtual machine backup using software-based VSS turned the CSV disk into re-direct mode. And when a CSV disk is in re-direct mode, all the disk I/O goes over a network via the CVS coordinator node. With the Windows Server 2012 CSV 2.0 version, this problem has been resolved. So now when we take a backup, even during production time, using the software-based VSS snapshot provider, the CSV disk doesn't go into re-direct mode.

CSV requirements

Now before we see how to configure CSV volumes to set up a Hyper-V cluster, I would like to summarize the requirements that should be in-place before we configure the CSV volumes. It is essential that you make sure that all the requirements are met before the production servers are configured and started for use in any of your production workload. Any missing requirements may turn your CSV performance or overall operations into a problem state, where not only your cluster operations but also the hosted guest virtual machines will be disturbed.

There are three major key players in the overall functionality of CSV disks for your Hyper-V cluster; they are as follows:

- Server requirements
- Networking requirements
- Storage requirements

Server requirements

The following server requirements are essential for the proper working of CSV:

- **System drive letter**: This is essential because the system drive letter on all the CSV cluster node members should be same. This is required because a CSV volume path gets created in the system drive of the server, so if the second CSV cluster node you are adding, and its system drive letter, is different from the existing cluster nodes, this won't work here.

- **Enabling NTLM**: This is another major requirement from the server-end, that the NTLM authentication protocol must be enabled on all the nodes. By default, NTLM is enabled in Windows Server 2012.

Networking requirements

The following networking requirements are essential for the proper working of CSV:

- **NIC advanced properties**: Clients for Microsoft Network and File and Printer Sharing Services should be enabled on the NICs you are planning to use for your Hyper-V cluster (live migration). These two settings make it possible for the server to use SMB 3.0 on the specified NIC. SMB 3.0 is the default protocol that is responsible for CSV communication between CSV-enabled nodes. Along with the two NIC-specific settings, make sure that the server and workstation services are running and set to start automatically.

- **Teamed NICs**: To sustain a single point of failure, it is recommended to have multiple NICs combined as a teamed NIC and use it for clusters and other NICs such as live migration or clustering. Along with the NIC teaming best practices, it is also recommended that unnecessary NICs be disabled in the failover cluster manager to not be used by the cluster.

- **Network priority**: It is recommended that the cluster-configured network priority not be changed in the cluster configuration.

Storage requirements

The following storage requirements are essential for the proper working of CSV:

- **File System and NTFS**: A CSV disk should always be formatted with NTFS and the disk type should be basic. CSV doesn't support other types of the disk filesystem, such as FAT32. When an NTFS-formatted disk is added as a CSV disk in the cluster, the cluster manager automatically changes the disk file system to **CSVFS**, which is a **Cluster Shared Volume File System**. This is because it allows the server and other operating system components to differentiate the CSV disks from other available storage on the server.

- **CSV and pass-through disks**: CSV disks should always be used for virtual machine storage as VHD and virtual machine configuration files. You should not use a CSV disk as a pass-through disk for virtual machines created on a Hyper-V failover cluster.

 The topic of configuring and adding a CSV disk into a Hyper-V 2012 failover cluster will be covered in the next section on installing and configuring a Hyper-V failover cluster.

Cluster networking

Cluster networking is another core component of a cluster; it plays a vital role in making cluster workload highly available. Cluster networking is usually divided into two parts. The first one is the cluster network that can be accessed by clients for clustered services, and the second part is the cluster private network, which is also referred to as a heartbeat network. A cluster uses the second network for checking the cluster node heartbeat.

In a standard configuration, a Hyper-V server may have the following set of networks for the server and Hyper-V:

Network name	Purpose
Hyper-V Management Network	Monitoring and management of Hyper-V host
Cluster Private Network	Cluster heartbeat and CSV disk
Live Migration Network	Dedicated to live migration network traffic
Server VLAN Network (optional)	The administrator can create a single network for all subnet accesses using the VLAN trunk feature or can create a multiple of each network subnet

In this section, we will not only address cluster public and private networking but also discuss live migration networking and other networking components associated with a Hyper-V failover cluster.

To understand the Hyper-V virtual network switch and networking best practices, please go through *Chapter 4, Understanding Hyper-V Networking,* which covers all types of Hyper-V networking components.

We will be covering the following Hyper-V failover cluster networking components in this section:

- Hyper-V Cluster Public Network
- Hyper-V Cluster Private Network
- Hyper-V Live Migration Network

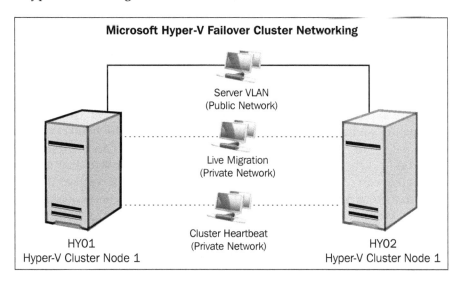

Hyper-V Cluster Public Network

In normal cluster terminology, a public network is referred to as a network on which the client computer connects to clustered services, such as SQL Server NIC that belong to the server VLAN, which allows other applications to access SQL Server. But this is for clusters that usually have one server VLAN membership. What if your cluster needs to have multiple VLAN access? Usually in virtualized environments, a hypervisor host runs many guest virtual machines that are on different VLANs and provides different levels of VLAN access to these guest virtual machines.

Do we need to add these multiple Hyper-V virtual network switches as cluster networks?

The answer is yes, because when you create a highly available virtual machine to be run as a cluster resource on your clustered Hyper-V servers, your Hyper-V cluster needs to have these networks be highly available and part of your clustered networks.

Hyper-V Cluster Private Network

As we mentioned in the preceding section, a normal cluster usually consists of two types of networks; one is the cluster public network on which users and other network applications connect to access the clustered network service, and the second is the private network that the cluster uses for its internal use. This private network is also called a cluster network, because it is internal to clusters only, which means this network doesn't need to be routable and accessible by other nodes or workstations on the network.

Let's assume that you have two Hyper-V nodes and want to configure these two nodes as a failover cluster. Then for their private network, you can directly connect these two machines with a crossover network cable, which will connect one NIC of each cluster node to the other cluster node. And this network can be considered a private network, because in this network there is no one else other than these two cluster nodes that can communicate. It is not required that you connect these two machines with a crossover network cable to set up a cluster private network, you can also connect these two NICs of each cluster node to an external network switch. At the time that you connect these two machines using an external network switch, you will have to make sure whether to segregate their routing and switching domain in the external network switch or use a dedicated network switch for cluster private network connectivity.

Clustering software such as **Microsoft Windows Clustering Services (MCS)** uses the cluster private network for its internal use. By default, users cannot access the clusters on this network, and cluster nodes exchange cluster keep-alive packets between each other (which is also referred to as a cluster heartbeat) that validate the cluster node availability. If any of the cluster heartbeat private network NICs or machines goes down, the heartbeat packets between nodes stop exchanging, and the node that stops responding to the cluster keep-alive heartbeat packets is considered as down. Then the cluster software (MCS) initiates the failover of the cluster resources and clustered applications, and in the case of Hyper-V, moves the virtual machines from the down, unavailable Hyper-V host machine to the preferred failover Hyper-V host machine.

Hyper-V Live Migration Network

Do you need to have a separate network for live migration or can you use a cluster private network for live migrations too? The answer is yes; you can use cluster private network live migration communication between the Hyper-V host and other server, and this decision is solely dependent on your design and the availability of your network or server node supportability. As far as the best practice goes, I would recommend separating your live migration network from the cluster private network because in many circumstances I have seen that network bandwidth allocation and **quality of service (QoS)** can be implemented to provide better speed for the live migration, and if you have the supported infrastructure from cluster hosts and the network fabric, just do it so you can give a better shape to our cluster and live migration communications.

Preparing, creating, and configuring a Hyper-V failover cluster

In this section, we will be covering the preparation, installation, and configuration of Hyper-V high availability and failover step by step with snapshots, wherever they are required to better explain the configuration. Now let's first start with preparing Hyper-V failover cluster nodes.

Preparing Hyper-V failover cluster nodes

For the preparation of Hyper-V failover cluster nodes, we will talk about the three major areas of building a Hyper-V failover cluster. These three areas are as follows:

- Preparing cluster nodes
- Preparing cluster networks
- Preparing cluster disks

Preparing cluster nodes

In this section, we will go through the step-by-step process of installing the Windows Failover Clustering feature and adding the Hyper-V role to the failover cluster nodes.

Let's first start with the installation of the Windows Failover Clustering feature.

Installing the Windows Failover Clustering feature

The following steps are required to install the Windows Failover Clustering feature on the failover cluster nodes:

1. From the main menu bar, open **Server Manager**.

2. In the **Server Manager** window, click on **Manage** in the upper-right corner and click on the first tab **Add Roles and Features**.

3. In the **Add Role and Features** window, click on **Next**, and in the next window, from **Select Installation Type**, select the **Role based or feature based installation** radio button. Then click on **Next**.

4. Then select the server on which you want to install the failover clustering feature from the **Select server from the pool** window, and click on **Next**.

5. Click on **Next** in the **Roles** window, because in this step we will be installing the failover clustering feature, which can be found in the **Features** tab on the next screen.

6. Under the features list, select the **Failover Clustering** checkbox and click on the **Next** button. Then on the next screen of confirmation, install the required features along with the failover clustering feature.

Installing the Hyper-V role

To refresh your memory on installing the Hyper-V role, you can go back to *Chapter 2, Planning, Designing, and Implementing Microsoft Hyper-V*, and see the steps required for installing the Hyper-V role.

Preparing Hyper-V failover cluster networks

In this section, we will configure the network for the Hyper-V failover cluster nodes as specified in the *Cluster networking* section of this chapter.

Creating a cluster public network as a Hyper-V virtual network switch

As mentioned earlier, among all the other types of cluster networks, we only need to create a cluster public network in the Hyper-V virtual network switch because this is the only network that virtual machines would need to communicate to the rest of the network devices and applications.

To create a cluster public network as a Hyper-V virtual network switch in Hyper-V, the steps discussed in the following sections can be performed in order.

Creating an external Hyper-V virtual switch as a cluster public network

The creation of an external Hyper-V virtual switch has already been covered in *Chapter 4, Understanding Hyper-V Networking*. Please go back to this chapter to see the list of steps required for configuring the Hyper-V external virtual switch.

> We have to create the same type of virtual network on each of the cluster nodes with the same name and for the same network port that is configured for the same VLAN. It is important that you pay attention here because if your network name is different in the cluster nodes, when you migrate the virtual machine from one Hyper-V cluster node to another, the different name of the network on the destination cluster node won't allow the virtual machine to start; this is because on this destination Hyper-V cluster node, this migrated virtual machine cannot find the network with the name that is configured in its configuration. So it is highly recommended and required that you configure the Hyper-V network and other settings on the cluster nodes in exactly the same way.

Configuring cluster private and live migration networks

We don't need these two types of cluster networks to be created in the Hyper-V virtual network switch. All we need to make sure about these networks are the following things:

- A cluster private network and live migration network can be the same network, configured for the same physical NIC, but as a best practice it is recommended that you separate them.

- On your live migration network NIC card, you have to make sure that file and printing services are enabled along with the LM Host lookup and NetBIOS.

Configuring external SAN storage connectivity

Before we present the SAN storage to our Hyper-V server, we need to perform various tasks in order to prepare the server to be seen by external SAN storage and to present the **LUN** (**Logical Unit Number**) drives.

1. For the Fibre Channel SAN connectivity, it is required to install SAN HBA card drivers. For iSCSI SAN, configure the dedicated NIC for the IP address and gateway to reach to the iSCSI SAN.

2. For FC SAN zoning, the HBA cards on the SAN switches with the WWN addresses are required.

3. Create the SAN LUNs and assign them to the Hyper-V failover cluster nodes as a group.

Preparing Hyper-V failover cluster disks

Whether it's a planning or an actual configuration, working with cluster disks is always an interesting thing. In this section, we will focus on two types of storage disks; the first one is the cluster quorum disk and the second one is the CSV disk. Once you bind these disks (LUNs) to all the cluster nodes, you have to perform the following steps to configure the cluster storage:

1. Go to any of the cluster nodes and open **Control Panel** | **Administrative Tools** | **Computer Manager**.

2. In the **Computer Manager** MMC console in the bottom-left corner, expand **Disk Management**.

3. Make all the cluster disks **Online** and initialize them.

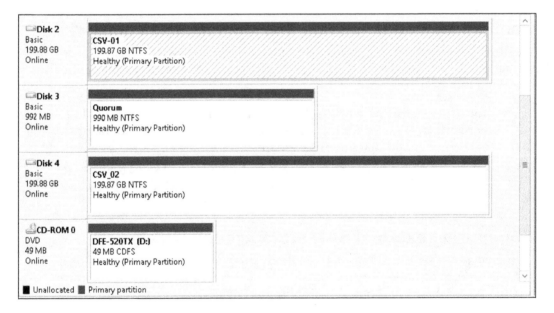

4. Once all the cluster disks have been initialized, format each disk, but don't assign the drive letter to the disk. We can also change the drive letter of any cluster drive from Cluster Failover Manager at any time.

5. Once all the disks have been formatted, bring them offline again on the same node and now move on to each of the other cluster nodes. Then rescan the disks on the node from **Disk Management** by going to the **Action** tab and clicking on **Rescan Disks**. This step will bring all the SAN-assigned LUNs to the node. For testing purposes you can bring the disks online, and you will find that the disks have already been formatted. And if you have assigned the drive letters, you will also see the drive letters assigned to the disks.

If you can see all the disks on all the cluster nodes, as we stated in the preceding steps, it means that your cluster disks are ready and can now be used for creating clusters.

Creating a Hyper-V failover cluster

So far we have prepared our cluster nodes for required server roles and features, such as the Hyper-V role and failover clustering feature of the cluster nodes. After installing these required server roles and features, we configured the public and private interfaces for the cluster nodes in the same manner for each node. And lastly, we configured the cluster storage.

Since our cluster nodes are now ready for creating our Hyper-V cluster on them, before we create a cluster, let's first go and validate these cluster nodes.

Cluster configuration validation

The cluster configuration validation utility is a built-in piece of code in Microsoft Clustering Services available in Windows Server, and it has been there now for quite a long time. The cluster validation utility checks each and every portion of the cluster node, and there are a few dedicated checks for each major component of the cluster, including networking, storage, and server software and hardware compatibility checking of the cluster nodes.

Cluster validation requirement for cluster support

First and foremost, validating your software and hardware environment for creating a cluster is essential, because executing the cluster validation tests against the intended cluster nodes will tell us whether these selected sets of nodes are capable of clustering or not. If the hardware and software environments are not appropriate for clustering, the test will fail and provide us with the details of each failed component. Running cluster validating tests is highly important from the supportability perspective. If you don't perform cluster validation and create the cluster, and if any issues occur later, the first thing any engineer or special Microsoft support will check in the history is if any warnings or errors occurred when the cluster was validated the first time, prior to creation.

Enhanced Windows Server 2012 cluster validation utility

The Windows Server 2012 failover cluster not only offers cluster configuration validation for the major components of a server, such as server software and hardware components (including networking and storage), but also validates your cluster node configuration against the failover cluster role or server role that you have installed on the cluster node. All the Windows Server 2012 server roles that are supported to be set up as failover clusters can now be validated against the supportability of the failover cluster nodes.

If we talk specifically about the Hyper-V role, I am glad to inform you that now while performing cluster configuration validation for the Hyper-V cluster nodes, the cluster validation check based on the Hyper-V role is included as a part of the recommended tests, by default.

Performing cluster validation tests

Ok, now let's start with the cluster validation utility to take our cluster creation setup to the next level. Perform the following steps to validate our cluster nodes for creating the Hyper-V failover cluster:

1. Go to **Control Panel** | **Administrative Tools** and open **Failover Cluster Manager**.

2. Once you open **Failover Cluster Manager**, go to the failover cluster's **Management** pane or, alternatively, you can right-click on the **Failover Cluster Manager** snap-in name in the upper-right corner of the screen and open **Validate Configuration Wizard**.

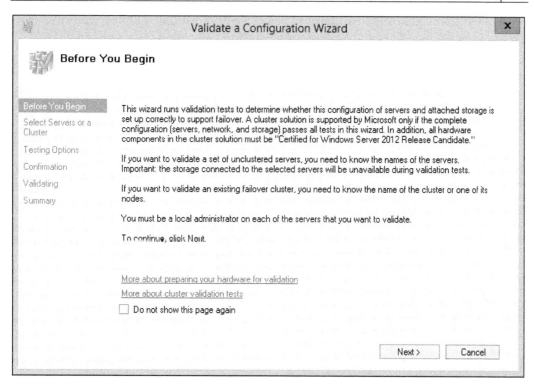

3. On the **Before You Begin** screen, click on **Next**, and you will get the next screen where you can select the cluster nodes that you would like to validate for the cluster configuration. You can browse the cluster servers in the active directory and add them for the cluster validation test. Once you add and select all the cluster nodes for the validation test, click on the **Next** button to go to the next screen.

4. On the next screen, you have to select the test options that you want to execute as part of the cluster configuration validation. You can run a specific test by choosing the second option **Run only test I select**, but the recommended approach is to run the recommended set of tests. Since our cluster nodes have the Hyper-V role installed, if you drill down these recommended tests that the failover cluster manager recommends you test on these selected nodes, you will find that in addition to the core validation test, the Hyper-V role is also added.

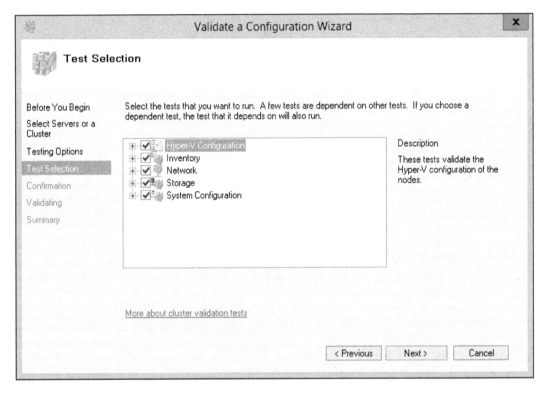

5. After confirming the cluster test selection, we come to the **Confirmation** screen where the cluster configuration validation wizard asks your confirmation to begin the testing. If you say yes, all the selected cluster configuration validations begin testing on all the selected cluster nodes.

6. Once all the testing is completed, the cluster configuration validation wizard generates an HTML report that will tell you about the health of the cluster. If everything is good, you will get an "all green" report and the failover cluster validation utility will allow you to open the cluster creation wizard from the same confirmation summary screen; or, you can alternatively start the cluster creation report later.

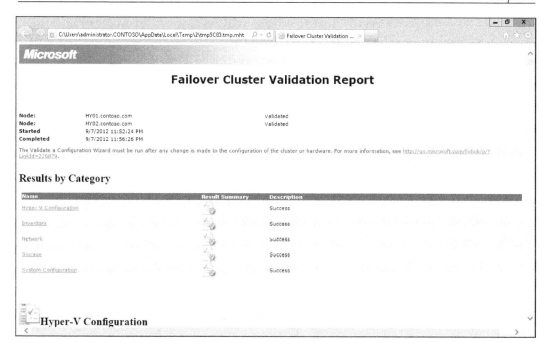

Now we can move ahead with creating our Hyper-V failover cluster because, as we saw with the cluster validation report, our cluster nodes and all other cluster components are ready for formatting this cluster.

Creating a Hyper-V failover cluster

We saw how we can validate our failover cluster nodes to create the Hyper-V failover cluster, and we also looked at the validation report, which says our cluster nodes and their related components are suitable to be used for forming the cluster.

Ok, so now let me take you through the journey of creating our Windows Server 2012 Hyper-V failover cluster.

1. Go to **Control Panel** | **Administrative Tools** and open **Failover Cluster Manager**.
2. From the main **Failover Cluster Manager** console under the **Management** tab, click on **Create Cluster**.
3. On the first screen **Before You Begin**, read all the information presented there for your knowledge and then click on the **Next** button.

4. The next screen **Create Cluster Wizard** will ask you about **Access Point for Administering the Cluster**, where you have to specify the cluster NetBIOS/ DNS name and the corresponding IP address for this name resource for managing the cluster management network. This DNS name and IP address will be used by the network users and applications to connect to this cluster, so you should be careful while configuring these two settings.

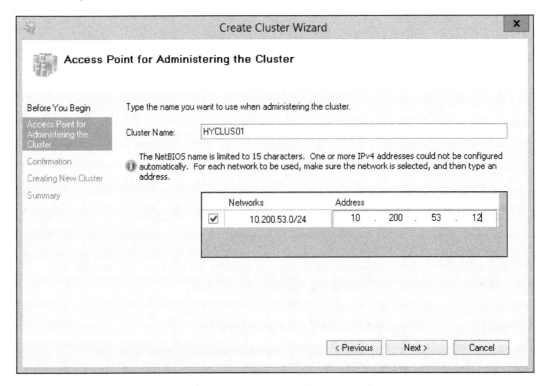

5. On the next screen of confirmation, you will be presented with the confirmation of your settings, including **Cluster Name** and **IP Address**. After your confirmation, if you click on **Next**, the cluster formation process will begin. Click on **Next** if you are ok with the information presented.

6. After this confirmation, the cluster formation process begins and the cluster resources start getting created with the parameters you have defined. It takes a few minutes, depending on the size of the cluster you are creating. Once everything is created in the background, the process will finish and you will get a summary of your cluster creation.

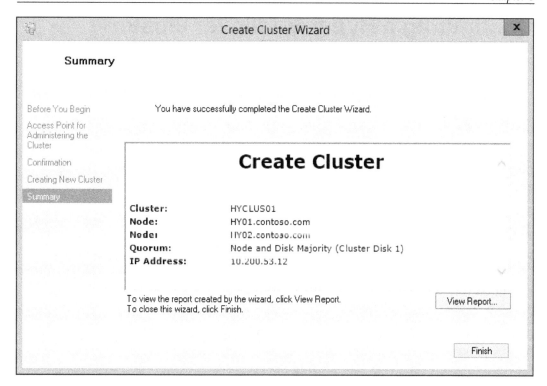

 We can get a report of the cluster we create by clicking on the **View Report** button on the **Summary** page of the cluster creation utility. This is a system-generated report, which tells you about the success of your cluster creation task.

Since our failover cluster has now been created, we will perform some post-installation tasks, such as adding CSV disks to our Hyper-V failover cluster, and a few other tasks. We will see which tasks need to be configured in order to complete our failover cluster configuration.

Configuring a Hyper-V failover cluster

In this section, we will discuss the following configuration settings:

- Adding CSV storage
- Creating a highly available virtual machine
- Creating a Hyper-V replica broker cluster resource

Now let's discuss these three post-configuration items one by one in detail, but please note that these may not be mandatory for your Hyper-V failover cluster and we are discussing them here just to get knowledge about them.

Adding CSV storage

When we prepared these cluster nodes for cluster storage, we also discussed the CSV disks, and since we included and added them in our Hyper-V failover cluster, we should be able to find the CSV disks in our Hyper-V failover cluster storage.

In this section on adding CSVs, we will see how we can add available cluster storage disks into the cluster as CSV disks. It is also imperative for us to complete this step here because in the next section, *Managing Virtual Machine Mobility and Migration*, we need to configure these disks during the Hyper-V live migration with shared cluster storage.

Let's go ahead and add or enable CSVs on our preallocated disks for the CSV role:

1. Go to **Control Panel | Administrative Tools** and open **Failover Cluster Manager**.
2. Once you open **Failover Cluster Manager,** move your mouse cursor to the left-hand side, scroll up and expand the cluster FQDN and then the disk under the **Storage** tab. After clicking on **Disks** under the **Storage** section of the **Failover Cluster Manager,** you will see all the failover clustered disks in your cluster. Here you will also see those disks that are not assigned for any role or cluster resource and that are listed as **Available Storage**. These are the two disks that we initially kept attached to the cluster nodes as CSV disks.

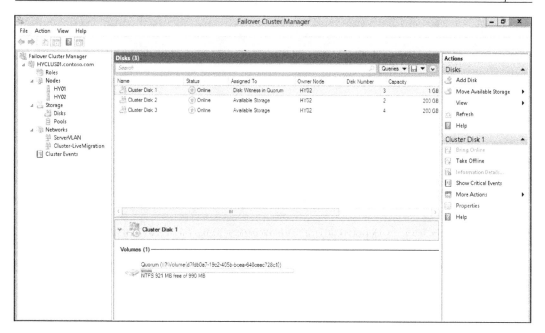

3. Now since we can see the available storage, which we can set as a CSV disk, we have to first make a selection of these two available storage disks and right-click on any one of them, and then click on the **Add to Cluster Shared Volumes** option.

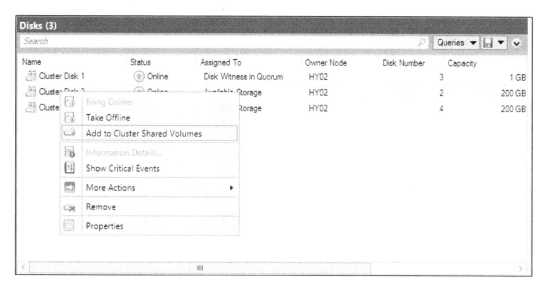

4. After you add both the available storage disks as CSVs, and upon completion of the task, you will see that the status of these two storage disks will be changed to **Cluster Shared Volumes**.

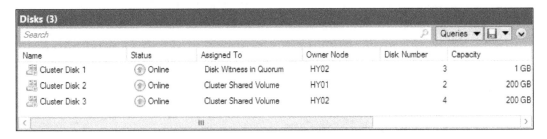

Here, the task of adding the available cluster storage as a CSV is completed, and if you want to verify the same, you can also go to **Disk Management** and check the filesystem, which will be changed from **NTFS** to **CSVFS**, that is the **Cluster Shared Volume File System**. It helps the operating system and other components to differentiate the CSV disks from other disks.

Checking the filesystem of the CSV disks or LUNs in **Disk Management** of the cluster node is one thing you can do, but the easiest way is to go to any of the Hyper-V failover cluster nodes and open the **Explorer** (My Computer), and then open C:. In C:, you should be able to find the ClusterStorage directory. On opening this directory, you should find two volumes, namely Volume1 and Volume2, which are the two disks we set as CSV disks in **Failover Cluster Manager**.

Creating a highly available virtual machine

The third postconfiguration step we have to perform after building the Hyper-V failover cluster is the creation of the highly available virtual machine. Creation of this highly available virtual machine is also a step that verifies what we have built so far. When you build it, you can test the functionality and availability of different cluster and failover capabilities.

Creating a virtual machine within a failover cluster manager is similar to creating a virtual machine in a Hyper-V manager. So let's see the steps for creating virtual machines within a failover cluster manager that will be highly available:

1. Go to **Control Panel | Administrative Tools** and open **Failover Cluster Manager**.

2. In **Failover Cluster Manager**, go to the upper-left corner and expand the cluster FQDN name. Click on the role and go to **Virtual Machines**, then click on **New Virtual Machine…**.

3. On the next screen, **Failover Cluster Manager** will ask you about selecting the target cluster node for virtual machine creation. Select the cluster Hyper-V node and click on **Next**.

4. The next screen of the virtual machine creation wizard is similar to what we did in the Hyper-V manager, but let's keep continuing towards the final creation of the virtual machine. On this screen of the virtual machine creation wizard — the **Before You Begin** page — you can see all the information that you need to know if you are creating a virtual machine for the first time. Click on **Next** on the **Before You Begin** page.

5. On the **Specify Name and Location** screen of the new virtual machine creation wizard, specify the name of the virtual machine and the path for the virtual machine storage and configuration files. Since we will be using this machine later for live migration and other types of failover and migration testings, we will create it on the CSV storage (C:\ClusterStorage\Volume1).

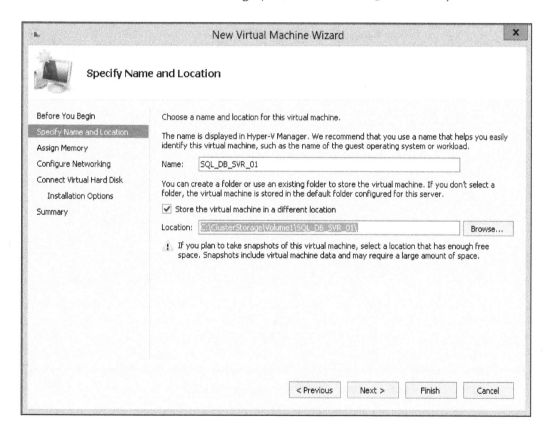

6. On the next screen of the virtual machine creation wizard, you will be required to assign the memory to the virtual machine.

7. Then on the next screen, you will need to set the Hyper-V virtual networking switch to bind the virtual machine network to it.

8. After specifying the networking settings of the virtual machine, you will be required to set up the virtual machine storage, which you can create either now or later. We will create the virtual machine storage at the time of virtual machine creation.

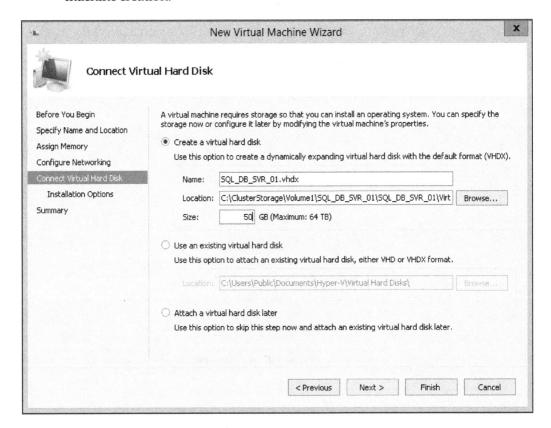

9. In the last setting of the virtual machine creation wizard, you have to define the installation method of the virtual machine's operating system. You can either specify the physical DVD for the Hyper-V failover cluster node or you can specify the ISO image for the operating system.

10. After specifying the operating system's installation method, the wizard shows you the **Summary** page with all the settings and configurations you selected for the creation of this virtual machine. If you are ok with all the information provided on the **Summary** page, click on the **Next** button to begin the virtual machine creation process.

11. Once the creation of the virtual machine is complete, you will be provided with a confirmation on the final screen of the virtual machine creation wizard.

 You might have noticed that in the preceding screenshot of the virtual machine creation wizard, the completion summary screen is showing a warning in the result column; this is because we set the virtual machine operating system installation method as associating an ISO image file of the operating system, and since this ISO image is located on the local folder of one of the Hyper-V cluster nodes, Failover Cluster Manager is saying that this server won't be available if we migrate the virtual machine on the second node. This is a warning and will not harm our virtual machine in any way, so we can ignore it.

12. Once the virtual machine creation wizard is complete, we can turn on the virtual machine from the Failover Cluster Manager.

Creating Hyper-V replica broker cluster resources

If you have already deployed a Hyper-V replica scenario in your Hyper-V virtualization environment, you might be interested in configuring your lately created Hyper-V failover cluster to also use the Hyper-V replica feature. This allows you to replicate your virtual machine from one Hyper-V node to another on the same site or on a different network site. Hyper-V replica is a great feature to make sure that your virtual machines are highly available and also redundant in terms of disaster recovery.

A Hyper-V replica broker allows your Hyper-V failover cluster to participate in virtual machine replication with Hyper-V replica instances. Only one Hyper-V replica broker can be configured on each failover cluster.

To create a Hyper-V replica broker cluster resource for allowing our Hyper-V failover cluster to participate in a Hyper-V replication, we can perform the following steps:

1. Go to **Control Panel | Administrative Tools** and open **Failover Cluster Manager**.

2. In the upper-left corner, expand the failover cluster FQDN and right-click on **Roles**. Then click on the **Configure High Availability** tab.

3. On the **Before You Begin** screen of **High Availability Wizard**, read all the information presented, and once you have read the required information for your knowledge, click on the **Next** button.

4. Then on the next screen **Select Role**, scroll down and select the **Hyper-V Replica Broker** cluster resource and click on **Next**. If you want to read more about the Hyper-V replica broker, you can click on the link shown there.

5. On the next wizard screen **Client Access Point**, we have to specify the DNS name and IP address to create the Hyper-V replica broker resource. This name and corresponding IP address, which you will choose for the Hyper-V replica broker resource, must be different from the Hyper-V failover cluster's name and IP address resource. You can give a new DNS name and IP address and click on the **Next** button.

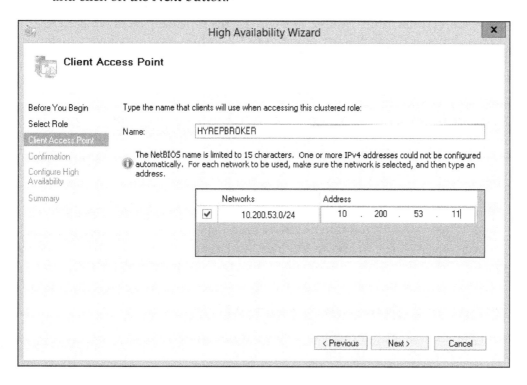

6. The next screen will ask you for a confirmation of the settings you have chosen for creating Hyper-V replica broker resources. If you are ok with the configuration settings, you can click on **Next**; this will commence the process of creating the required cluster resources in the cluster for the Hyper-V replica broker.

7. Once the creation of the required cluster resources for the Hyper-V replica broker is complete, you will get a summary of the task's completion, and from here you can also read the report in the HTML format by clicking on **View Report**.

8. Once the Hyper-V replica broker resource is finally created in the cluster, don't forget to set the properties of the resource and then set the preferred owners of the resource. This is an imperative setting from the failover perspective of a cluster resource.

Managing virtual machine mobility and migration

So far in this chapter, we have completed and achieved many milestones to make our Hyper-V virtualized environment highly available and make it a part of the Hyper-V role. We also learned a great deal about building Windows Server high availability with Microsoft Clustering Services. You can use the same steps that we used to build the Hyper-V cluster for any other type of Windows Server failover cluster, which includes DHCP, SQL Server, IIS, SCVMM, and the list goes on and on. So, this chapter will not only help you to build high availability for the Hyper-V role but also help you to make other services in your organization highly available.

Now let's move ahead with this section, which is an interesting topic to discuss, taking into account the benefits of the Windows Server failover cluster and new features of Hyper-V 2012, where live migration is now not only available in Hyper-V clustered environments, but you can also take advantage of live migration within two standalone Windows Server 2012 Hyper-V servers.

In addition to live migration, we will also cover quick migration for a virtual machine, which is now considered as the traditional method of migrating a virtual machine between clustered Hyper-V nodes. And finally, we will see the new feature added into Windows Server 2012 Hyper-V that is live storage migration.

Virtual machine live migration

Live migration was introduced back in the days of Windows Server 2008 R2 as an additional method of migrating virtual machines between clustered Hyper-V nodes. In the first release of Windows Server 2008 and Hyper-V, the only method of migrating running virtual machines between cluster nodes was quick migration; but the drawback of quick migration was that when you performed a quick migration for a given virtual machine, the Hyper-V and failover cluster saved the virtual machine state only until all the memory pages and the virtual machine storage was dismounted from the source Hyper-V cluster node to the destination Hyper-V cluster node.

Live migration for virtual machines was available in the pre-Windows Server 2012 Hyper-V versions; it contributed a lot to the success of Hyper-V and making it an enterprise hypervisor for server virtualization. However, the limitations of live migration in the previous versions made it a bit tough for enterprises to use this in the case of hundreds of virtual machines.

With Windows Server 2012, Microsoft addressed all the limitations that customers faced with live migration and tried to make it more relaxed and easier for administrators to use it on a larger scale.

Before we go ahead and perform different types of live migrations, let's first understand how live migration works when migrating the workload from one Hyper-V node to another.

Working of live migration

To understand how live migration works, let's divide the live migration into multiple phases, as follows:

1. **Live migration initiation**: When we initiate live migration for a given virtual machine, a session has to be created between a source and destination Hyper-V node. The virtual machine structure gets created in the destination host. The required RAM also gets assigned to this created virtual machine.

2. **Transferring memory pages**: During this second phase of transferring memory pages of the virtual machine, each memory block of 4 KB gets transferred from the source Hyper-V host node to the destination Hyper-V host node. Live migration means everything happens in live motion. When we perform the live migration of the virtual machine, the first thing we do is start migrating the memory pages from the source Hyper-V server where the virtual machine is running, to the destination Hyper-V server.

3. **Delta sync of the memory pages**: In this phase of live migration, all the altered memory blocks are kept in sync with the destination node, and the processor and device state also gets transferred from the source Hyper-V node to the destination Hyper-V node.

4. **Moving the virtual machine storage access to the destination node**: The fourth step involves the transfer of the role of accessing the virtual machine storage and other types of storage to the destination Hyper-V node.

5. **Bringing virtual machine online on the destination Hyper-V node**: In the fifth step, Hyper-V live migration brings the virtual machine online from the destination Hyper-V node. Once this is complete, you will see the node name of the virtual machine's owner getting changed from the previous Hyper-V node to the new destination Hyper-V node name.

6. **Changing the ARP table for the migrated virtual machine**: As a last step, a message is sent to the network switch to change the MAC address for the virtual machine's IP address, to send the network traffic related to the virtual machine to the correct new Hyper-V server.

Requirements for live migration

The requirements for live migration depend on its type. Let's just say that live migration with shared storage would have different requirements than live migration with SMB storage, so to summarize the requirements for live migration, we will lay out the requirements for each type of live migration along with a diagram and explanation.

Live migration type	Requirements
Live migration with shared storage	• A Windows Server 2012 failover cluster with a minimum of two nodes, along with the Hyper-V role installed • Shared storage CSV • Enabled cluster shared storage • As a best practice, dedicated live migration NIC (optional) • A separate network for live migration of data or using the default cluster private network • Enabling the live migration feature on the Hyper-V server for incoming and outgoing live migrations
Live migration without shared storage	• Standalone Windows Server 2012 Hyper-V with at least two nodes for migrating the virtual machine from one Hyper-V node to another • Sufficient standalone storage on the destination Hyper-V node • Based on the live migration settings of the Hyper-V server, the preferred NIC on the server would receive live migration from the other Hyper-V nodes first • Enabling the live migration feature on the Hyper-V server for incoming and outgoing live migrations

Live migration type	Requirements
Live migration with SMB storage	Standalone Windows Server 2012 Hyper-V with at least two nodes for migrating the virtual machine from one Hyper-V node to another
	Windows Server 2012 SMB Share or Windows Server 2012 File Server with required NTFS and sharing permission on the share
	Sufficient standalone storage on the destination Hyper-V node
	Based on the live migration settings of the Hyper-V server, the preferred NIC on the server would receive live migration from the other Hyper-V nodes first
	Enabling the live migration feature on the Hyper-V server for incoming and outgoing live migrations

Enabling live migration on a Hyper-V server

This is a critical requirement as it is mentioned for all types of live migrations in the preceding table. In Windows Server 2012 Hyper-V, an administrator can either allow a Hyper-V server to participate in a live migration or not. This feature can be turned on or off on a Hyper-V server from the Hyper-V server's global settings.

In the following steps, we will show you how we can enable or disable this feature on a Hyper-V server. It should also be noted that the live migration feature is specific to individual servers, and the administrator should enable this on each server one by one before live migration can be initiated between two Hyper-V hosts enabled for live migration.

1. Open **Hyper-V Manager** and click on **Hyper-V Settings**.

2. From the settings pane on the left-hand side, click on the **Live Migrations** tab.

3. Under the **Live Migrations** tab, click on the **Enable incoming and outgoing live migrations** checkbox and then choose the appropriate authentication protocol. We can choose either **Use Credential Security Support Provider (CredSSP)** or **Use Kerberos**.

4. Then we can either dedicate an NIC for live migration traffic on the Hyper-V server by selecting the option **Use these IP addresses for live migration**, which is the preferred and recommended way, or we can choose the **Use any available network for live migration** option for all available IPs and network cards.

5. Now click on **Apply** and then on **OK** to commit the changes.

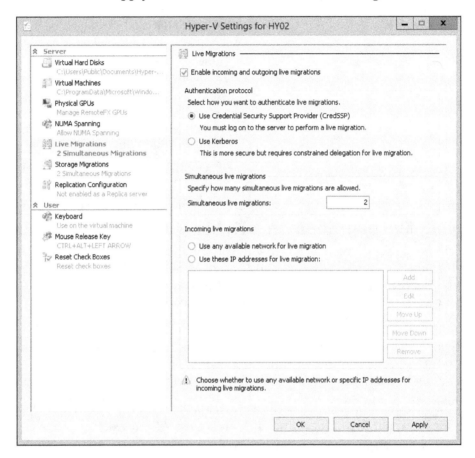

Ok, now we know what live migration is and how it works, so let's get our hands dirty with some real stuff. In this section, we will cover three types of live migration:

- Live migration with shared storage
- Live migration without shared storage
- Live migration with SMB storage

Now let's dive deep into each of the preceding live migration types and understand them.

Live migration with shared storage

Live migration with shared storage means using live migration for the highly available virtual machine created in the Hyper-V failover cluster. And since we use shared storage in the cluster, when we use live migration for clustered virtual machines, it is also called Microsoft live migration with shared storage. There are a few other types of live migrations also available that we will discuss in a short while in the upcoming sections.

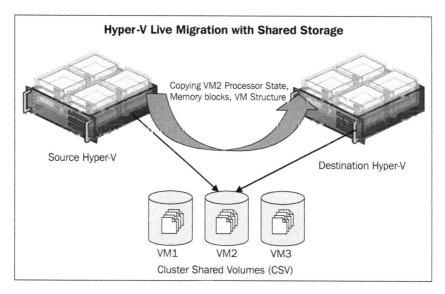

Live migration with shared storage means the use of CSVx, so then we can say that the shared storage is actually the CSV. In the *Preparing, creating, and configuring a Hyper-V failover cluster* section of this chapter, we saw how to add and configure CSVs, which is the primary requirement for using live migration.

So we can say that all the requirements are in place, and we can now use live migration with shared storage. We will simulate all the virtual machine mobility and migration tests with the highly available virtual machine that we created in the *Configuring a Hyper-V failover cluster* section.

To live migrate a highly available clustered virtual machine with shared cluster storage using CSVs, perform the following steps:

1. Go to **Control Panel | Administrative Tools** and open **Failover Cluster Manager**.

2. Then, expand the Hyper-V failover cluster by expanding the cluster FQDN in the upper-left corner.

3. Go to the **Roles** section, and then all the virtual machines and cluster resources will be visible to you. Select any one of the clustered virtual machines for which you would like to perform live migration. Then right-click on the selected virtual machine and go to the **Move** tab. After this, go to **Live Migration** and select either **Best Possible Node** or **Select Node**.

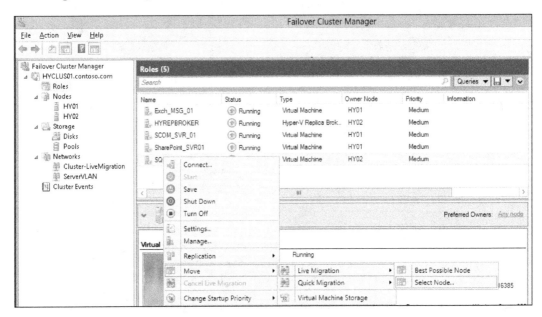

4. If you select the **Best Possible Node** option to migrate a virtual machine, the most preferred cluster resource owner of the virtual machine will be chosen for this. Otherwise if you select the **Select Node** option, the node selection box will be opened, and here we can select the **HY01** node to migrate the virtual machine to this node as we have only two nodes in the Hyper-V failover cluster. Once you select the node and click on the **OK** button, it will kick off the live migration process of the virtual machine.

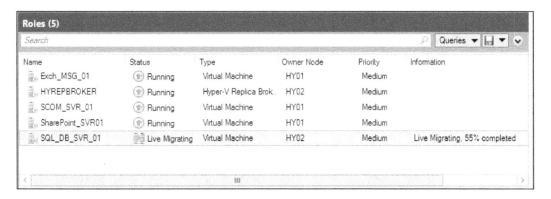

5. In the preceding screenshot, you can see that before starting the live migration the **SQL_DB_SVR_01** virtual machine is running on the **HY02** Hyper-V cluster node, and we can also see the live migration completion status in the **Information** column. Once the live migration is complete, we should see **Owner Node** changed from **HY02** to **HY01**. While the virtual machine live migration is in process, if you went to the Hyper-V node and opened the Hyper-V manager console, you would also see the same information for the **SQL_DB_SVR_01** VM in the **Virtual Machine Status** column.

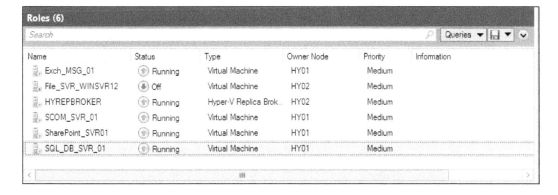

6. As we can see in the preceding screenshot, the **SQL_DB_SVR_01** virtual machine's owner node is now changed from **HY02** to **HY01**; this means that our virtual machine live migration has successfully been completed and we have moved the virtual machine from **HY02** to **HY01**.

Shared nothing live migration

In the preceding type of live migration, we saw how to migrate a highly available (clustered) virtual machine from one Hyper-V cluster node to another. Now we will see another type of live migration, which is the shared nothing live migration. This is a live migration without shared storage. In this type of live migration, the virtual machine is not placed on a shared cluster storage and Hyper-V doesn't care what type of storage you are using. The best part of this type of live migration is that there are no boundaries for this type of migration. For example, we can migrate a virtual machine to a Hyper-V server regardless of its network subnet, be it a domain-joined, workgroup-based, clustered or even a standalone Hyper-V. The only required elements for this type of migration are that the destination server be Windows Server 2012 and that it have live migration enabled to receive live migration from other Hyper-V servers. A non-shared storage is normal storage; it could be a local server disk, a standalone SAN LUN, or any other type of storage that is not shared between two or more nodes.

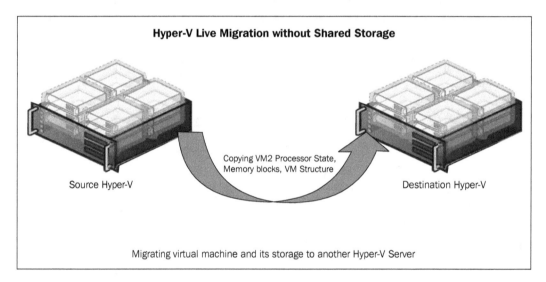

Hyper-V Live Migration without Shared Storage

Copying VM2 Processor State, Memory blocks, VM Structure

Source Hyper-V

Destination Hyper-V

Migrating virtual machine and its storage to another Hyper-V Server

Now let's see how we can perform live migration for a virtual machine without shared storage. The following steps will migrate a non-clustered Hyper-V virtual machine from one Hyper-V host to another:

1. Go to **Control Panel | Administrative Tools** and open **Hyper-V Manager**.

2. Now from the virtual machine dashboard, select the virtual machine that you want to move to another Hyper-V host and right-click on the name of the virtual machine that you want to select for the migration; then, click on the **Move** tab.

 Only a non-clustered Hyper-V virtual machine can be migrated from the Hyper-V manager, and in this type of live migration, we will only see how to migrate a non-clustered virtual machine.

3. Now upon clicking on the **Move** tab of the virtual machine, the virtual machine's move wizard will open. On the first wizard screen, **Before You Begin**, read the information presented, and after reading the information click on the **Next** button.

4. On the next screen **Choose Move Type**, select **Move the virtual machine** and click on **Next**.

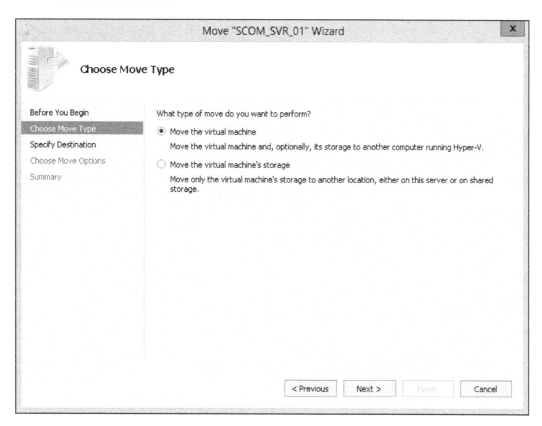

5. The next step of non-clustered virtual machine live migration will ask you to specify the destination Hyper-V server where you are intending to migrate this virtual machine. This allows you to explore the Hyper-V node in the active directory and locate it.

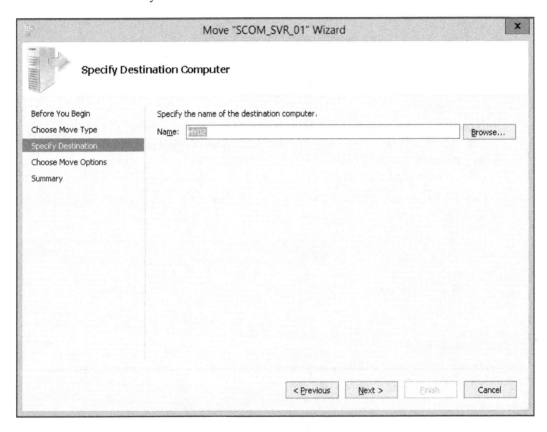

6. The next step of virtual machine migration is **Choose Move Option**. Hyper-V gives you three choices for virtual machine migration, as follows:

    ° Move the virtual machine's data to a single location

    ° Move the virtual machine's data by selecting where to move the items

    ° Move only the virtual machine

According to your choice, you can choose any move option that best fits your needs. For an explanation of this process, we will be choosing the first option that says **Move the virtual machine's data to a single location**.

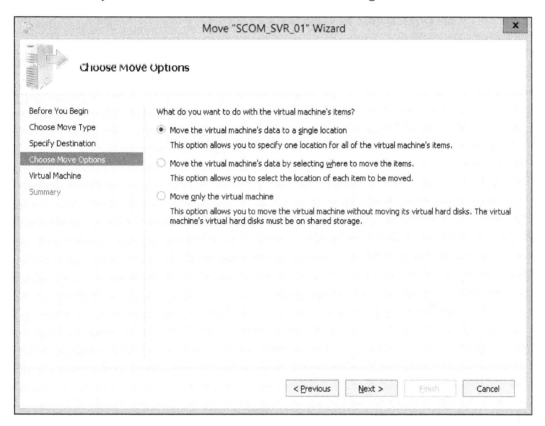

7. After choosing the move option for our virtual machine migration, the next step will ask us to specify the destination location of virtual machine data migration on the destination Hyper-V host. When you click on the **Browse** button to locate and select the location for your virtual machine migration, you will see the drives/disks of the destination server. So if you have already created a folder for your virtual machine migration, it's good, and we will specify it here.

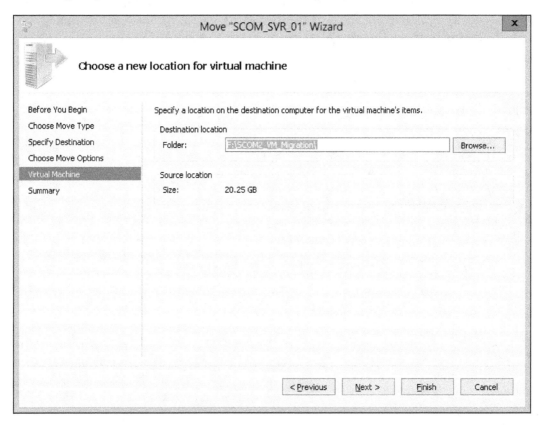

8. After selecting the location for your virtual machine migration for the destination Hyper-V node, click on **Next**.

9. On the last page of the **Summary**, all selections made in the virtual machine migration wizard will be presented to you. If you are ok with the information presented to you, click on **Finish** to begin the process of migrating your virtual machine to the destination Hyper-V node.

Live migration with SMB shared storage

Live migration with SMB storage means when you have virtual machine storage on an SMB file share/server, you can live migrate the virtual machine from one Hyper-V host to another while keeping the virtual machine storage on the same file server. In this type of live migration also we don't need to have a failover cluster in place, just like we saw in the live migration without shared storage. The only difference between live migration without shared storage and live migration with SMB shared storage is that in the live migration without shared storage we keep the virtual machine storage (VHD) on the local server itself, which means that an individual LUN is allocated to a source server or DAS storage, or it could even be the C or D drive of the server, and then we can move this virtual machine along with its storage to the destination Hyper-V server for the same kind of local storage.

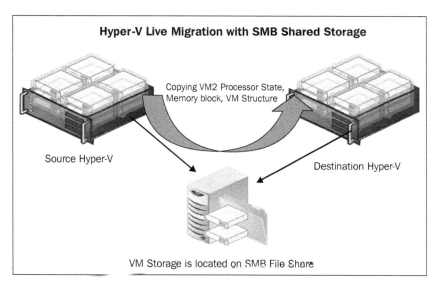

When we perform live migration with SMB storage, the virtual machine storage is located on the SMB file server. This file server is accessible from all Hyper-V nodes because this share or server is available on the network and the share and NTFS permission allows all the servers to access the data in it. So when we perform the live migration of a virtual machine that has storage on this SMB share or file server, we only migrate the data related to the virtual machine configuration to another Hyper-V server. When the live migration process is completed, such as copying the memory pages, the virtual machine gets turned on from this new destination Hyper-V server while accessing the virtual machine storage (VHD/VHDX) from the same SMB share/file server.

Now we will see the steps required to perform live migration with SMB storage.

1. Go to **Control Panel | Administrative Tools** and open **Hyper-V Manager**.

2. Now from the virtual machine dashboard, select the virtual machine that you want to move to another Hyper-V host and right-click on the name of the virtual machine that you want to select for the migration. Then, click on the **Move** tab.

3. Now after clicking on the **Move** tab of the virtual machine, the virtual machine move wizard will open. On the first screen **Before You Begin**, read the information before you begin. After reading the information, click on the **Next** button.

4. On the next screen **Choose Move Type**, select the **Move the virtual machine** option and click on **Next**.

5. The next step will ask you to specify the destination Hyper-V server that you are intending to migrate this virtual machine to. It allows you to explore the Hyper-V node in the active directory and locate it.

6. The next step of virtual machine migration is choosing the move option. Hyper-V gives you three choices for virtual machine migration, which are as follows:

   ° Move the virtual machine's data to a single location
   ° Move the virtual machine's data by selecting where to move the items
   ° Move only the virtual machine

According to your choice, you can choose any move option that best fits your needs. For an explanation of this process, we will be choosing the third option that says **Move only the virtual machine** because we want to keep the virtual machine storage on the SMB share and only move the virtual machine to another Hyper-V standalone node.

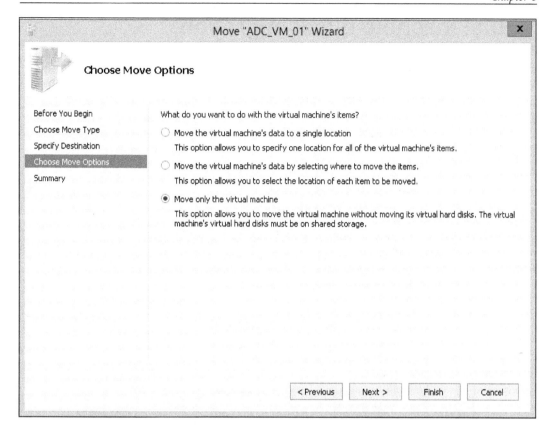

7. After choosing the move option for our virtual machine migration, the next migration wizard screen provides you with a summary of the selections you made to migrate this virtual machine to your intended destination Hyper-V server.

8. If the information presented to you on the summary page is as per your needs and you have confirmed it, click on the **Finish** button. This will start the migration process of the selected virtual machine.

Virtual machine quick migration

Virtual machine quick migration is now considered the traditional method of moving a virtual machine across clustered Hyper-V nodes. Earlier when Hyper-V was released, the only method of making Hyper-V virtual workloads highly available was the quick migration method, because if the primary or — I could use a more appropriate term — Active Hyper-V failover cluster node failed, all the virtual machines running on this server would fail over to the second preferred Hyper-V failover node. The Hyper-V administrator can move the virtual machine between Hyper-V failover cluster nodes using quick migration at any time.

How quick migration works

Now let's take a deeper look at how virtual machine quick migration works. Let's say we follow the same procedure of building the Hyper-V failover cluster that we followed in this chapter. Now we have a fully functional Hyper-V failover cluster containing two Hyper-V failover nodes.

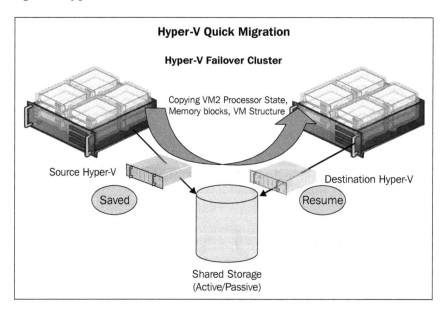

We have created the virtual machine and we want to quick migrate this virtual machine to another Hyper-V node. After initiating the quick migration, perform the following steps in order to migrate the VM from the source Hyper-V cluster node to the destination Hyper-V cluster node:

1. First, the virtual machine on the active Hyper-V failover cluster node, where this virtual machine was running, gets saved in the same state when the quick migration was initiated.

2. In the second step, the virtual machine skeleton gets created on the destination Hyper-V node and the processor state and RAM allocation gets completed.

3. The second phase of the quick migration starts copying the memory blocks from the source Hyper-V node to the destination node.

4. Once all the memory pages are copied to the destination Hyper-V node, the virtual machine storage disk gets dismounted or, in other words, the disk resource gets moved from the source Hyper-V node to the destination Hyper-V node.

5. Upon completing step 4, where the virtual machine storage migration gets completed, the virtual machine from the source machine gets deleted and the virtual machine resource on the destination Hyper-V cluster node is brought up online.

Now since we have understood the concept of quick migration, it's time to see this quick migration in action. In the following section, we will see the steps required to perform quick migration of a virtual machine running on a Windows Server 2012 Hyper-V failover cluster.

Steps to perform quick migration

In this section, we will learn the steps required to perform quick migration for a virtual machine running on a Windows Server 2012 Hyper-V failover cluster. Follow these steps to perform quick migration for a demo virtual machine:

1. Go to **Control Panel | Administrative Tools** and open **Failover Cluster Manager**.

2. Once **Failover Cluster Manager** is opened, expand the Hyper-V failover cluster by expanding the cluster FQDN in the upper-left corner.

3. Go to the **Roles** section. All the virtual machines and cluster resources will be visible to you. Select any of the clustered virtual machines for which you would like to perform quick migration, and then right-click on the selected virtual machine and go to the **Move** tab. Then go to **Quick Migration** and click on either **Best Possible Node** or **Select Node....** In this demo migration, we will see how Microsoft Windows Server 2012 and Hyper-V 3.0 allow us to quick-migrate multiple virtual machines in one shot.

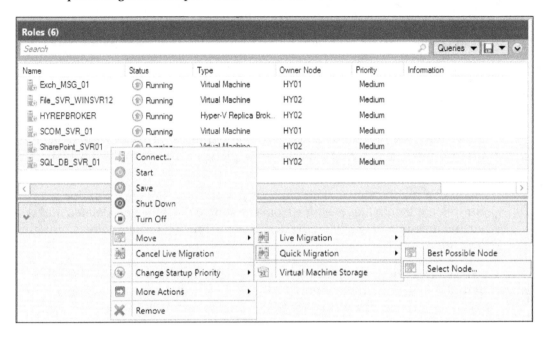

4. If you select the **Best Possible Node** option to migrate a virtual machine, the most preferred cluster resource owner of the virtual machine will be chosen for this; otherwise if you select the **Select Node...** option, the node selection box will be opened, where we will select the **HY01** node for migrating the virtual machine to this node as we have only two nodes in the Hyper-V failover cluster. Once you select the node and click on the **OK** button, the quick migration process of the virtual machines will start.

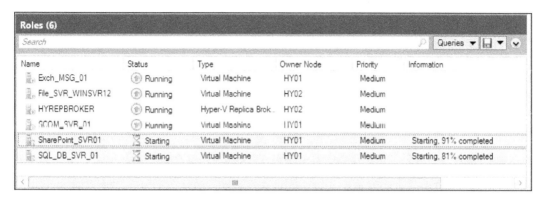

5. As you can see in the preceding screenshot, the selected virtual machines are already stated to be migrating from HY02 to the destination Hyper-V cluster node. To check the status of the quick migration, we can look at the **Information** column in the **Roles** section of the Hyper-V Failover Cluster Manager. Here we can see that 91 percent of **SharePoint_SVR01** is complete and 81 percent of **SQL_DB_SVR_01** is complete.

6. In the preceding screenshot, we can see that **Owner Node** for these two selected and migrated virtual machines is changed to **HY01**. Before initiating the quick migration for these virtual machines, **Owner Node** was **HY02**, and now after migration is complete, **Owner Node** has been changed to **HY01**. In conclusion, the selected virtual machines have successfully been migrated from the **HY02** Hyper-V cluster node to the **HY01** Hyper-V cluster node.

Live storage migration

Now we will look into the virtual machine storage migration feature of Windows Server 2012 Hyper-V. Before Windows Server 2012 Hyper-V, migrating the virtual machine storage required the virtual machine to be shut down because when the virtual machine is up and running, you cannot copy and paste virtual machine storage (VHD) to a new location. Windows Server 2012 Hyper-V addressed this problem and provided very simple steps to migrate the virtual machine storage from one location or Hyper-V node to another location or Hyper-V node.

The virtual machine storage migration process is exactly the same as the live migration without shared be migrating or live migration with SMB storage process, because the processes of these types of live migration provide the flexibility of migrating the virtual machine storage as well, where you can either migrate the virtual machine storage along with migrating the virtual machine settings and other contents or you can individually move the virtual machine storage.

1. Go to **Control Panel | Administrative Tools** and open **Failover Cluster Manager**.

2. Once **Failover Cluster Manager** is opened, expand the Hyper-V failover cluster by expanding the cluster FQDN in the upper-left corner.

3. Go to the **Roles** section. All the virtual machines and cluster resources will be visible to you. Select any of the clustered virtual machines that you would like to perform storage migration for, and then right-click on the selected virtual machine and go to the **Move** tab. Then, click on **Virtual Machine Storage**.

4. Upon opening the virtual machine storage migration wizard, you will see a small window containing all the files and storage related to the virtual machine in particular. If you want to only migrate the virtual machine storage, you should only select the virtual machine VHD or VHDX file, or if you want to completely migrate all types of content of the virtual machine, including snapshots and configuration files, you could select all this other content too. So let's say that we select only the VHDX file for the virtual machine and drag-and-drop it to another folder created in a different CSV volume. As we can see in the following screenshot, the primary and current location of the virtual machine **SQL_DB_SVR_01** is `Volume1`, and we created another folder in `Volume2` called `SQL_DB_Storage_COPY` where we will drag-and-drop the VHDX file. After dragging-and-dropping the VHDX file and other contents to the destination folder, click on the **Start** button to start the migration of the storage and other content to the destination folder.

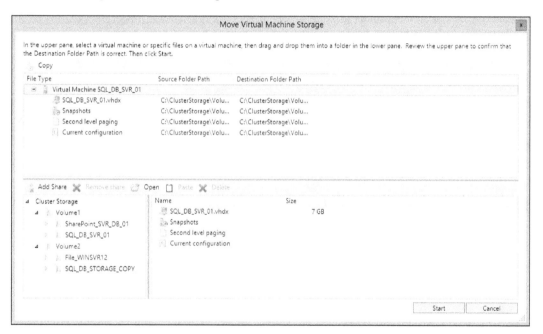

5. After completing the preceding step, you can see the status of the virtual machine storage migration in the **Information** column of that particular virtual machine.

6. Upon completion of the migration, the virtual machine's active storage path gets changed to the destination CSV volume that we defined during the storage migration process. In the following screenshot, we can see that the virtual hard disk location of the virtual machine **SQL_DB_SVR_01** has now been changed to C:\ClusterStorage\Volume2\SQL_DB_Storage_COPY:

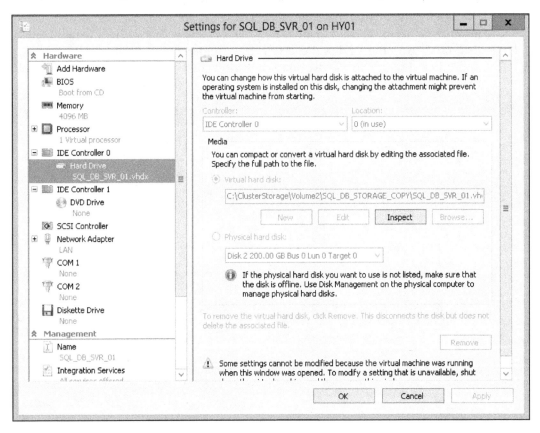

With this exercise, we saw how we can migrate virtual machine storage from one CSV volume to another while the virtual machine is running.

Summary

You must have got an idea that the length and amount of information covered in this chapter was huge; I had this idea at the beginning of this chapter, that it was going to be a lengthy one. Well in this chapter, we covered all the topics related to Windows Server 2012 clustering, Hyper-V high availability, and mobility and migration of virtual machines. We started this chapter with an overview of Hyper-V high availability, in which we first discussed the challenges we faced with the pre-Windows Server 2012 release of Microsoft Clustering Services and Microsoft Hyper-V for building virtual machine high availability and migration features. Then, we looked at the new promising features of Windows Server 2012 and Hyper-V for virtual machine high availability and mobility where we highlighted the few of them that drastically changed the way we mobilize our virtual machines and migrate them, whenever needed, within our Hyper-V virtualized environment.

After completing the overview section, we moved ahead with understanding the core components of Hyper-V high availability and failover clustering. In this section, we covered each and every element of Hyper-V HA building and discussed server hardware, storage fabric, and, last but not least, cluster networking. Once we understood these three major core components of Hyper-V high availability, we discussed how to prepare, create, and configure a Hyper-V failover cluster. In that section, we discussed all the small and large processes of preparing Hyper-V failover cluster nodes and creating Hyper-V failover clusters and configuring them.

Once our Hyper-V failover cluster was ready, we moved on to discuss how we can manage virtual machine mobility and migration, where we discussed three major areas, namely virtual machine live migration, virtual machine quick migration, and virtual machine storage migration. And while discussing all these topics, we ensured that we showed screenshots of the actual steps or configuration utility, so if you carry this chapter along with you while configuring and performing these tasks, it will become easy for you to get the job done.

In the next chapter, we will discuss the best practices and recommended methods for Hyper-V sever security hardening and securing the underlying server infrastructure.

9
Hyper-V Security Hardening – Best Practices

Nowadays, with the increased number of attacks on businesses, security has become a hot topic almost everywhere. Enterprises are more concerned now about both their perimeter and internal security. In Middle Eastern countries, where natural oil and gas is the center of the economy, we have recently seen huge security attacks on the oil and gas sector that caused the targeted companies to lose billions of dollars. And such security attacks that affect the IT infrastructure keeping it shut down for days to weeks have a huge impact on business. While security is important at both client and server ends, it's difficult to find a balanced approach to secure both ends. A well constructed security program for an enterprise ensures that a balanced security approach is in place to safeguard both sides of the network. Many people think that installing antivirus software on the server or client is the ultimate security for their enterprise and that they can then rest, until the time comes to stay late nights at one's desk recovering the system and data after a security breach. Securing a server or a client is itself a complete world. This is because of the increasing number of requirements to allow integration of existing infrastructure with new platforms and applications. This requirement opens a door to new security challenges for infrastructure and application security hardening from the ever-increasing number of security threats and zero-day attacks.

Okay, we have heard about the need for security, which is quite common these days. Let's be specific to our topic, Hyper-V, and discuss why and how security makes itself more important for the Hyper-V role. We saw previously how security plays a vital part in the overall IT service delivery for an enterprise; let's see how security becomes more important for a Hyper-V role, as compared to the other server roles. We can get an idea about this question by simply saying that getting a non-Hyper-V server compromised may end up affecting one service or a component of an application; but compromising a Hyper-V server may result in affecting many different applications and services from your IT service catalogue.

A compromised Hyper-V server may allow an intruder and/or hacker to take control of the system and perform malicious tasks, such as data tampering, deletion of the virtual machine or storage, or changing the behavior of the hypervisor or virtual machine, and could also result in destruction of the entire environment.

Hyper-V and virtualization security pillars

As we understand from the title of the chapter, we will cover both Hyper-V specific and general security best practices and recommendations for securing server systems. Our main goal here will be to understand how we can achieve higher levels of security by implementing both general server security and Hyper-V specific security best practices. Okay, we said general security and Hyper-V level security, but what about the virtual machine-specific security? Well, at the very end of this chapter, we will discuss the security best practices for virtual machines, which will add value to the overall security strategy of Hyper-V virtualized infrastructure.

This virtualization security can also be divided into five major areas, which will ensure a high level of security around our Hyper-V server and the virtual machine running on it. The following are those five major areas of virtualization security:

- Securing Hyper-V base operating system
- Securing Hyper-V virtual network switch
- Delegating of rights for Hyper-V management
- Securing Virtual Machine Storage
- Safeguarding guest virtual machines

Now let's go ahead and discuss each of the these areas of virtualization security.

Since we will be discussing various topics from different domains, such as Hyper-V, Windows Server 2012, and general server management practices, it is impossible for us to cover each topic in full detail, and therefore, we will discuss them briefly, and wherever the details are required, we will provide references to step-by-step guides or knowledge base articles for more information.

Securing Hyper-V base operating system

In this section, we will cover a series of topics that will provide information about how to secure the base operating system for the Hyper-V server role. This section includes topics such as minimizing attack surface, operating system patches, antivirus protection, and last but not least, analyzing Hyper-V server against the security baseline for any vulnerabilities and threats. This information can also be applied to virtual machine operating systems as these are a general security best practices and guidelines for securing the operating system platform.

Minimizing attack surfaces

As a general best practice, it is always recommended to have a single server role allocated on a single box; this practice ensures that there is no extra patching or protection required for maintaining a high level of security. More than one server role assignment for a single box may result in protecting one server role while ignoring other roles and services running on the same box. These unpatched services and server roles may result in opening a door to vulnerabilities and threats, which can affect the overall security and availability of the system. Having the Hyper-V server role running alone on the Hyper-V server box ensures that there will be no extra Windows services or network ports running or opened for any vulnerability, for which we might not have planned or placed a safeguarding strategy. If you have planned on not having extra server roles and services running on your Hyper-V server, running Server Core Edition on your Hyper-V server is the recommended choice. Windows Server Core Edition offers the same functionalities and services and runs only a subset of the basic operating system operations. For example, a server core installed on Hyper-V server doesn't have a GUI available and only hosts the services required to run the Hyper-V role.

 For more information about Windows Server 2012 Core Edition, you can refer to *Chapter 2, Planning, Designing, and Implementing Microsoft Hyper-V*.

Hyper-V management network isolation

Management network access isolation is not only advisable in the Hyper-V case, but it is a general best practice and recommendation for all types of products and services. Now let's first understand what a management network or management network access is. The **management network** is the network on which usually all the administrative-level activities are performed. Let's say if there are hundreds of VLANs created on your core network switch, and apart from the server VLANs, all other VLANs belong to users or the client side.

On all these client or user VLANs you have implemented a strict network compliance and security policy, which disallows computers or workstations that are members of these client VLANs from having administrative-level access to the network servers and devices. So as an administrator, what you will do is to create different VLANs for yourself and other administrators for different levels of security access to these network servers and devices. Usually, this management network that administrators use has a comparatively relaxed security policy, and they have access to all parts of the network.

Since we have now understood the meaning of a management network, let's talk purely about Hyper-V. In the Hyper-V case, as a best practice, we should always manage and maintain Hyper-V administrative level access through the management network. What this means is that we should segregate the service VLANs. The ones that the user connects to, to access services, should always be different from the one that the administrator uses for access to patch the server. Keeping all eggs in the one basket can result in a potential threat to our virtualized environment.

Hyper-V access on all other VLANs or networks should be restricted, and only the management network should have access to Hyper-V administration. This will minimize the risk of an attack from the application or user network side.

Patch management

Patch management, like other best practices, is one of the most important routine activities we should always be carrying our on our servers, no matter what sort of service or operating system version the machine has. The more up-to-date your operating system is, the fewer chances there are of the machine being easily targeted by an attack.

Right after the release of the Hyper-V role for Windows Server 2008, there were bugs found in the product, which were fixed with the hotfixes and service packs provided. These hotfixes are sometimes part of Hyper-V as a product or role, or as a part of the operating system binaries. During the third week of every month, Microsoft releases security updates and patches for the operating system and other products, which fix various bugs in the products. As a preventive measure, we should plan for monthly patch management of our systems. Windows Server 2012 Hyper-V provides a great level of flexibility for planned maintenance of the Hyper-V hosts for patch management, where an administrator can move the virtual machine or its storage to another Hyper-V node or storage while the virtual machine is running and operating. We achieve this feature with live migration with shared storage, live migration without shared storage, and live migration with SMB-shared storage. We can also migrate virtual machine storage with the virtual machine storage migration feature.

Let's take this journey to the next level, where Windows Server 2012 Hyper-V role and failover clustering services provide a wonderful feature, called **Cluster Aware Updating (CAU)**. CAU allows an administrator to automate patch management of Hyper-V failover cluster nodes by configuring CAU to automatically update all the cluster nodes, which will allow you to automatically live migrate the virtual machines from one Hyper-V node to another and then complete patch management by restarting the server. Once the original source server comes back online, CAU automatically performs the failback of the virtual machine to this Hyper-V node and then starts the process with the other Hyper-V cluster nodes. This process is fully automatic and ensures 100 percent availability of the workloads running on these clustered Hyper-V hosts.

For a detailed understanding of **Cluster Aware Updating (CAU)**, visit the following URL:

`http://technet.microsoft.com/en us/library/hh831694.aspx`

Antivirus protection and exclusions

Over a period of time, I have seen that Hyper-V server nodes are always being ignored with respect to antivirus protection because people think a Hyper-V node doesn't need antivirus software installed. This is not true because, like all other server operating systems or server roles we maintain in our datacenter, Hyper-V as a server role also needs to be protected against malicious viruses and attacks. In fact, a Hyper-V role becomes more critical than any other server role. For example, if your IIS web server gets infected by a virus, and as a first precautionary step, you need to remove the IIS web server from the network for maintenance purposes; only your web services will be affected for some time, in this case. But if your Hyper-V server role gets infected with a virus and you have to take down the Hyper-V machine for maintenance, it might also affect the virtual machine running on it.

It is always critical to keep the antivirus software up to date with virus signatures and definitions because any antivirus instance without a proper updating mechanism is just another piece of software installed on the server. Now let's talk about the exclusions that should be made in the antivirus software to restrict the antivirus solution. It has been observed that most of these antivirus solutions make it problematic for the Hyper-V role to work as expected. Especially when it comes to performance-related issues with Hyper-V, it has been seen that unavailability of the antivirus exclusions for the Hyper-V and the Microsoft Cluster Service related components causes these issues for Hyper-V and virtual machines.

The following list of directories and file extensions should be made part of the exclusions in the antivirus software installed on the Hyper-V standalone or Hyper-V failover cluster nodes:

File extensions	File directories
`*.VHD`	`Q:\mscs`
`*.VHDX`	`%Systemroot%\Cluster`
`*.AVHD`	`C:\ProgramData\Microsoft\Windows\Hyper-V`
`*.VSV`	`C:\Users\Public\Documents\Hyper-V\Virtual Hard Disks`
`*.BIN`	`Q:\Cluster\*`
	`*\Cluster\*`
	`C:\Program Files\Hyper-V`
	`C:\ClusterStorage\*`

Best Practice Analyzer for Hyper-V host

The **Microsoft Baseline Security Analyzer** (**MBSA**) tool has been around for quite a long time now. MBSA provided a great set of functionalities for scanning weaknesses and vulnerabilities in a given server. MBSA was there for various releases of the Windows Server operating system, for example Windows Server 2003, Windows Server 2008, and Windows Server 2008 R2. MBSA provided a way to scan a node or a set of nodes by selecting the network range or even a complete Active Directory domain for all the member servers and machines. MBSA allowed selectively scanning Windows server vulnerabilities, such as more than one administrator, missing Windows critical and security patches, IIS vulnerabilities, and so on.

With Windows Server 2012, Microsoft renamed MBSA to Best Practice Analyzer, and it can be run from either Server Manager, BPA utility, or from a PowerShell cmdlet. Using BPA, we can scan a single server role or multiple server roles. It is also now possible to ignore selected scan results for BPA.

For more information about Baseline Security Analyzer in Windows Server 2012, visit `http://technet.microsoft.com/en-us/library/hh831400.aspx` for a detailed description. You can download it from `http://www.microsoft.com/en-us/download/details.aspx?displaylang=en&id=7558`.

Securing Hyper-V virtual network switch

We covered Windows Server 2012 Hyper-V networking in *Chapter 4, Understanding Hyper-V Networking*. It provides detailed knowledge about the network virtualization in Hyper-V, and the new features added to Hyper-V 3.0 as the Hyper-V extensible virtual network switch.

In this section, we will only cover the subtopic of Hyper-V's networking features, which provide the security layer between the virtual machines and active network components. The features we will discuss here share the same networking medium, including the host and other virtual machines running on the host or even running under the same Hyper-V virtual network switch. We will discuss all the security best practices that an organization and an administrator should follow to protect the virtual machine and its running applications from the kinds of danger that can make it difficult for the virtual machine to run in normal mode or that could exploit the data or application and from internal or external threats.

All the information provided in this section will be examined from a real-world standpoint, where we all have seen the importance of these elements, to secure the virtualized networking stack for the protection of both hypervisor and the workload running on it. In this section, we will go through the following subtopics:

- ARP spoofing protection
- DHCP Guard
- Router Guard
- Port mirroring
- Port ACL

ARP spoofing protection

Windows Server 2008 R2 with Hyper-V provided MAC address spoofing, which was a requirement for some scenarios, for example for configuring the Windows NLB cluster on Hyper-V virtual machines. In addition to this example, there are many other places where, due to the application requirements, we use this feature to protect our critical workloads. In this topic, we are not talking about MAC address spoofing, which has existed since Windows Server 2008 R2, but we will discuss the ARP spoofing protection functionality, which is introduced in Windows Server 2012 Hyper-V 3.0 as a value-added feature for protecting workloads from man-in-the-middle type attacks. In this type of attack, an attacker associates a MAC address with the IP address of another machine on the network to pretend to be someone else by sending the ARP message to the network switch to redirect the traffic to himself. This way, the attacker can inspect the network traffic that was destined to reach the original machine.

Unfortunately, just like the MAC address spoofing feature, the ARP spoofing protection feature cannot be enabled on a virtual machine from Windows Server 2012 Hyper-V or Virtual Machine Manager. If you would like to enable this feature for a particular virtual machine or a bunch of virtual machines, we can use a PowerShell script created by one of Microsoft's PFE for private cloud and virtualization solutions team.

You can locate this script at `http://blogs.technet.com/b/virtualpfe/archive/2011/08/02/arp-spoofing-prevention-in-hyper-v-2008-r2-sp1.aspx`

DHCP Guard

Windows Server 2012 Hyper-V introduced numerous architectural enhancements, and among all these enhancements, the security part was the major area in which the product team invested a lot of human resources to make sure that the new version of Hyper-V provides most modern security capabilities to protect virtual machines in the dynamic datacenter and cloud environments.

Let's talk about one of the great security features added in Hyper-V for the virtual machine with which virtual machines can now be protected against fake DHCP instances on the network. This protection feature is called DHCP Guard and can be enabled for a given virtual machine to protect it from unauthorized DHCP scopes running on the virtual stack. When you enable this feature on a virtual machine, you actually tell Hyper-V that this virtual machine is not a DHCP server and thus not to forward DHCP server messages over the network.

Router Guard

Just like DHCP Guard, Windows Server 2012 Hyper-V allows virtual machine administrators to enable the Router Guard feature on the virtual machine, which prevents router advertisement packets and redirection messages from unauthorized virtual machines pretending to be routers. Windows Server has a service called routing and remote access, which provides the basic IP routing capabilities. If Router Guard is enabled on a virtual machine running routing and remote access services that is not intentionally configured as an IP router for different subnets on the network, Router Guard will prevent IP routing advertisements and packets from being sent out from this virtual machine.

This added security layer protects your virtualized networking stack from any malfunctioning virtual machine or misconfigured area of virtualization. By default, all these extra protection layers are not enabled on the virtual machines, so you as an administrator have to enable these features wherever you see them as necessary.

Port mirroring

Security is not a one-time job; it has to be evaluated within a continuous cycle, or better put, it should be part of the development of design, structure, and the daily routine exercise.

As an internal or external penetration testing, to evaluate the strength of the safeguard measures provided for the security of critical workloads, you should always asses the environment and find the weaknesses in your configuration. Windows Server 2012 Hyper-V provides a great feature of port mirroring, which enables network-level troubleshooting and security vulnerability assessment. Port mirroring allows an administrator to have full control on the virtualized networking stack. Port mirroring allows an administrator to configure a virtual machine to perform network communication, for example, receiving both incoming and outgoing packets destined for a particular virtual machine. In this way, this second machine is receiving the network communication that is destined for another machine, to perform analysis and to get insight into network-layer issues. This makes network-based troubleshooting simpler and saves time and money by fixing problems in less time.

With the help of this feature, we can periodically check the network communication destined to our critical workloads, and can find any traffic element that is not authorized or is nonlegitimate for the health of our virtual machine.

Port ACL for network isolation

Windows Server 2012 Hyper-V comes with a lot of great features, but there are a few that make it truly an awesome invention. Port **ACL (Access Control List)** for network isolation and traffic metering is one of these great features, in which the product team invested a lot of effort, to allow organizations to secure their workloads from other virtual machines running on the same host, the same virtual cloud, or even the same physical segment. Now we can configure ACL on the virtual machine to allow traffic to be sent to or received from a predefined destination or source. These ACLs have the same structure as our traditional ACLs, where we can specify the source and destination address with a particular port, on which we want to allow or deny traffic being sent or received.

For more information on Port ACL, visit `http://technet.microsoft.com/en-us/library/jj679878.aspx#bkmk_portacls`.

Delegating rights for Hyper-V management

Delegation of rights to IT operations staff is key to sound management of infrastructure. Delegation of authority also complements the administrative security principles, which say that critical tasks should not be performed by a single person in an organization. From the point of view of the management of IT systems, when a single person performs the entire task for the particular system, it leads to high-risk situations. Delegation of authority allows the administrator to reduce the **total cost of ownership (TCO)** and also improves the quality of the work done. Delegation of authority also trains the internal resources to upgrade their skills and to be part of the ready workforce that is prepared to take over the resources and handle them whenever required.

When we talk about Hyper-V delegation of authority, it becomes more critical because Hyper-V manages a huge part of the system and network infrastructure, so without the proper delegation of authority, managing this huge set of virtual machines (hardware resources), virtual network switches, and virtual machine storage becomes difficult as well as critical. Lack of proper delegation of authority may lead to a disaster, which will not only affect a single server but also multiple workloads running on a single Hyper-V host.

We will discuss two major areas for the delegation of rights between the multiple Hyper-V administrators or virtualization administrators. The first solution we will look at is Authorization Manager, and the second one is SCVMM.

Authorization Manager

Authorization Manager is a framework that allows organizations to use **role-based access control (RBAC)** for different applications and components installed on Windows Server. An administrator can create a set of job-oriented or task-oriented roles for a single user or a group of users to manage a subpart of the responsibility for a given application or server role.

Authorization Manager reads the authorization policies for application and Windows Server roles, which store these authorization policies in the shape of **Active Directory Domain Services (AD DS)**, **Active Directory Lightweight Directory Services (AD LDS)**, XML files, and Microsoft SQL Server instances.

For more information about Authorization Manager, please refer to
`http://technet.microsoft.com/en-us/library/cc726036.aspx`.

Authorization Manager for Hyper-V delegation of authority

We can perform the following steps to delegate the authority for various Hyper-V management tasks for the local or Active Directory users and groups:

1. Open an elevated (**Run as | Administrator**) command prompt, type `azman.msc`, and press *Enter* to open the **Authorization Manager MMC** console; alternatively, we can also add the **Authorization Manager** snap-in in a separate MMC console.

2. Upon opening the **Authorization Manager MMC** console, the next step requires us to add the authorization store of the local Hyper-V instance to open the local authorization store of the Hyper-V server. Right-click on the upper-left corner of the **Authorization Manager MMC** console and click on **Open Authorization Store...**, as shown in the following screenshot:

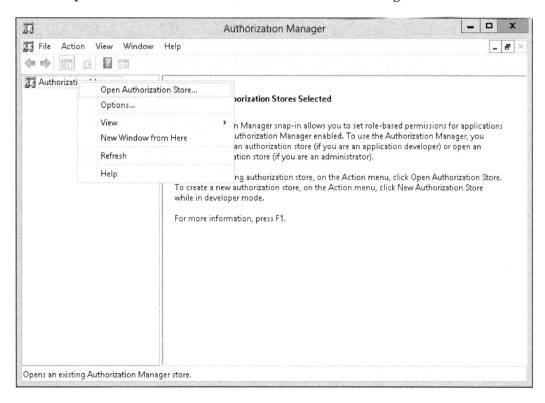

3. We now have to select the authorization store type. By default, Hyper-V gives us the three choices, **Active Directory or Active Directory Application Mode (ADAM)**, **XML file**, and **Microsoft SQL**. For this example, we will select the XML file and will open the `%programdata%\Microsoft\Windows\ Hyper-V\InitialStore.xml` file.

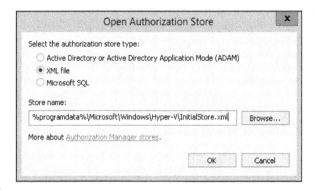

4. Once you browse and open the `InitialStore.xml` file for the local Hyper-V instance, you will see a window similar to the one shown next and the image items and configuration settings will be opened in the **Authorization Manager MMC** console.

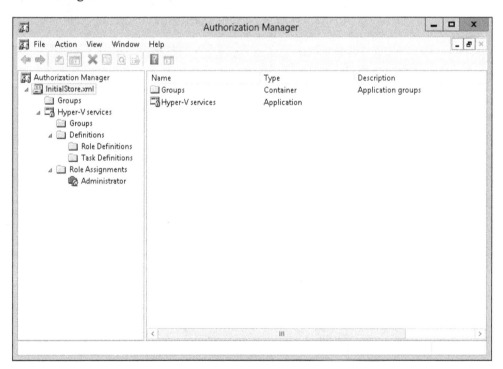

To better understand the Authorization Manager's capabilities and Hyper-V task delegation authority, we will simulate a scenario, where you as an engineer are required to delegate the virtual machine configuration view rights to your level-1 engineers, who are entry-level engineers and are not very well trained. So in this case, you first want them to see the VM configuration, and if they find any problem, you want them to take the request to the level-2 engineers. For this purpose, we have decided to first create task definitions, which can also be called the preset of authorized permissions for the level-1 engineers.

5. To create a task, we will go to the **Task Definitions** tab of Authorization Manager and will right-click anywhere in it and click on **New Task Definition**. This will open a new task definition window. First, we will give a descriptive name to this task and then we will add it. Click on the **Add** button, and in the **Add Definition** window, click on the **Operations** tab and select all the tasks or operations that you would like to allow your level-1 engineers access to.

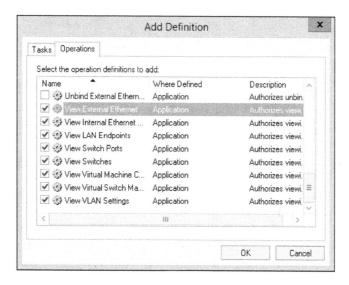

6. After selecting all tasks and operations, click on the **OK** button, and then click on the **OK** button again to close the new task definition window. After completing this task, you should now be able to see the new task definition created in the **Task Definitions** tab of Authorization Manager.

7. Now in the next step, we will create the role definition in Authorization Manager, and there we will add the already created task definition. So, you can say that in the first step, we grouped several tasks that we want our level-1 engineers to be able to perform, and now we are going to create a role that will be bound with this task definition.

8. To create the role definition, we will right-click on the role definition tab in Authorization Manager. We will first give the description name for this role definition, and then we will click on the **Add** button to add the precreated task definition, which will be added from the **Tasks** tab of the **Add Definition** window. Here we should be able to find the precreated level-1 engineer task definition. We will select it, click on the **OK** button, and click on the **OK** button again to close the new role definition window:

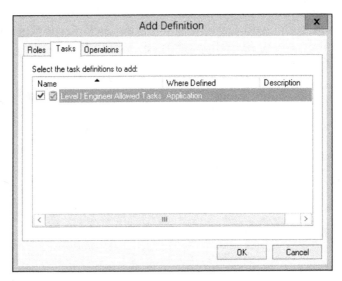

9. To further assign the previously created role definition and task definition to our users or groups, we will now a create role assignment in Authorization Manager. To create the role assignment, we will right-click on the **Role Assignment** tab in Authorization Manager and will click on **New Role Assignment**. Now, from the **Add Role** window, select the role definition we created in the previous step, and click on the **OK** button:

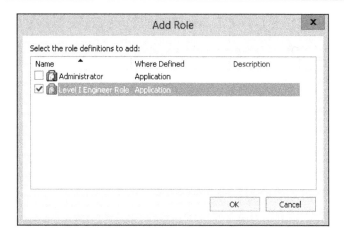

10. Now you will see that, under the **Role Assignment** tab of Authorization Manager, this newly added **Level I Engineer Role** will also show up.

11. To assign the same role to our Active Directory group of level-1 engineers, we will now right-click on **Level I Engineer Role**. We will go to **Assign Users and Groups** and will click on **From Windows and Active Directory...**. This will open the Active Directory browser to locate the required group object to associate it with this new role added in Authorization Manager for Hyper-V role administration delegation. Here we will locate the Active Directory group for **Level I Engineers (Support)**:

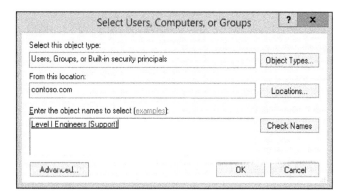

12. After locating and assigning **Level I Engineer Role** to the level-1 engineers' Active Directory group, we have completed the job, and all the group members of the level-1 engineers' Active Directory group should now be able to have access to the task definition we selected in the previous step on this local Hyper-V instance.

Hyper-V delegation of authority with SCVMM 2012

In the previous section on delegation of authority for Hyper-V management, we saw how we can use Authorization Manager to delegate authority for tasks related to Hyper-V operations. But Authorization Manager can only delegate tasks for a standalone Hyper-V instance, and when it comes to enterprise Hyper-V deployment, we cannot use Authorization Manager, and therefore, we need an enterprise-level management solution for Hyper-V management and delegation of authority.

System Center 2012 provides enterprise-class management and delegation of authority for the Hyper-V environment. SCVMM 2012 provides four types of delegation of authority for Hyper-V management, as follows:

- Delegated administrator
- Read-only administrator
- Application administrator (self-service user)
- Tenant administrator

Any of the preceding roles can be chosen for the delegation of authority, which will provide the predefined set of capabilities to the user or the group of users to perform these tasks on either the cloud or a standalone Hyper-V host.

Since we will only be discussing a subpart of SCVMM, we will see this delegation of authority with limited scope.

> If you want to know more about the capabilities of SCVMM 2012 for managing private clouds or Windows Server 2012 Hyper-V, please see *Chapter 7, Managing Hyper-V with System Center Virtual Machine Manager*, or alternatively, to learn particularly about the different delegation roles of SCVMM 2012, you can visit http://technet.microsoft.com/en-us/library/gg696971.aspx.

For an example, we will see the following steps, which will guide us on how to perform the delegation of authority in SCVMM:

1. Open the SCVMM Management console.
2. Click on the **Services** ribbon in the lower-left corner, click on **Security**, and click on **User Roles**. Under **User Roles**, click on the delegated administrator or any other role that you want to delegate to the user or the group of users.

3. Then, on the **Home** tab in the **Properties** group, click on **Properties**.

4. In the **Administrator Properties** dialog box, click on **Members** to access the **Members** page, and then click on **Add** to open the **Select User, Computer, or Group** dialog box.

   Enter a user or Active Directory group of users and click on **OK** to continue. The dialog box verifies that your selections are valid users.

 For more information on delegation of authority in SCVMM, go back to *Chapter 7, Managing Hyper-V with System Center Virtual Machine Manager.*

Securing virtual machine storage

Virtual machine storage is an important element of a virtualized server within your datacenter. Most of the time, we configure virtual machine storage as the virtual machine hard disk, which is a binary file, which gets attached to the virtual machine as its storage. So you can imagine the importance and the criticality of this file; if it is deleted intentionally or unintentionally from the hypervisor, we can say that we have permanently lost the virtual machine.

In this section, we will learn how to protect and secure Hyper-V virtual machine storage. Security is a wide term and mainly has three aspects: confidentiality, integrity, and availability. With respect to this section on securing virtual machine storage, our main concern is the integrity and the availability of virtual machine storage. We don't want somebody to get access and alter the virtual machine hard disk (VHD/VHDX) files, which can result in having replaced or incorrect data for our virtual machine hard disk. It is quite possible for an intruder that gets access to the virtual machine storage to destroy all the virtual machine storage-related data, which will result in the unavailability of the virtual machine and thus make it unavailable for providing services to end users and other integrated applications and systems. Okay, now let's go ahead and talk a little bit about how we can achieve our goal of securing our virtual machine storage on Hyper-V servers.

Specifying the default path for virtual machine storage

As we mentioned previously, virtual machine hard disks, in most cases, are used as virtual machine storage, so protecting these files is a very important aspect of securing the virtual machine storage. When you create a virtual machine and reach the virtual machine storage step of the virtual machine creation wizard, by default, Hyper-V lets you create these virtual machine storage files (VHD/VHDX) in the default virtual machine storage directory of the Hyper-V server, which is `C:\Users\Public\Documents\Hyper-V\Virtual Hard Disks`.

As a security best practice, it is recommended to always change the default virtual machine storage directory to a nonsystem partition, so if something goes wrong with your system partition or the operating system of the Hyper-V server, you will not lose the virtual machine storage files. Now let's see how we can do this:

1. Open **Hyper-V Manager** via **Control Panel | Administrative Tools**.
2. Click on the **Hyper-V Settings** link shown on the right-hand side action pane.
3. Go to the first tab in the list, **Virtual Hard Disks**, and from there, browse to the location where you want to keep the virtual machine storage files by default.
4. After browsing to the location, click on the **Apply** button, and then click on the **OK** button to apply the changes:

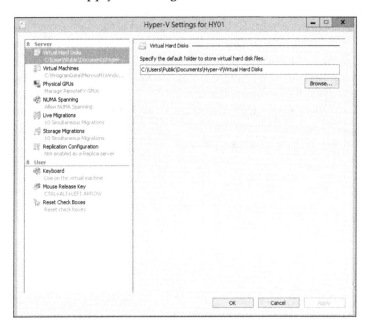

Encrypting virtual machine storage with BitLocker

Encrypting data and making sure that this data is not readable by unauthorized parties is a science, specifically a branch of cryptography. Microsoft BitLocker is a native utility available in the Windows Server and Windows client operating systems for data encryption. BitLocker is now a bit old, and has been around for some time.

Our purpose for discussing the Microsoft BitLocker utility for encrypting data is to use it to encrypt the CSV disk for virtual machine hard disk files and data. Windows Server 2012 introduced a new feature where administrators can now enable BitLocker on the CSV disk level, which will help the organization to maintain a high level of security for its virtual machine storage data. The BitLocker feature can protect Hyper-V host and guest virtual machines in the following ways:

- Enabling BitLocker on the physical disk of the Microsoft Hyper-V host system or other partitions and disks

- Enabling BitLocker on the guest virtual machine for the system or application partition

- Enabling BitLocker on the Cluster Shared Volumes of the Hyper-V failover cluster

As our prime goal here is to discuss the BitLocker feature for use against CSV volumes, let me tell you that unfortunately until now enabling BitLocker on CSV is not a one-step task. Enabling BitLocker on a CSV, can be done with a series of PowerShell cmdlets. We can perform the following steps to configure BitLocker on CSVs:

1. Install the BitLocker feature from server manager on all the Hyper-V failover cluster nodes. To understand BitLocker for Windows Server 2012, you can read the article at the TechNet library URL `http://technet.microsoft.com/en-us/library/hh831713`.

2. Enable and configure BitLocker on the CSV disk for Windows Server 2012 Hyper-V failover cluster nodes. We can perform the steps outlined in the *Clustering and High Availability* article at `http://blogs.msdn.com/b/clustering/archive/2012/07/20/10332169.aspx`.

 Since enabling BitLocker for a CSV disk is not a simple and short configuration step, we will only be discussing it briefly here.

Safeguarding guest virtual machines

In this last section of the chapter, we will now cover the various available best practices to secure the virtual machines running on our Hyper-V server. In this section, we will discuss how an administrator can get help from auditing for access to virtual machines; we will see how we can secure the virtual machine configuration files by changing the virtual machine's default creation path, and then we will see other recommendations such as for path management and filesystem security.

Okay, so let's start with auditing for virtual machines.

Filesystem security for accessing virtual machines

One method of securing virtual machine access is the filesystem-level security for restricting the virtual machine access to authorized personnel. This safeguard can also be helpful for audit trail purposes, where enabling auditing on the virtual machine related files and folders would log the audit trails for compliance and auditing purposes.

This type of filesystem-level security can be achieved with the help of NTFS and sharing permissions, which can protect the virtual machine and its data from any unauthorized access and data tampering.

Especially when it comes to the availability of virtual machines, due to the nature of virtual machine storage, where file-level storage can be on hot share, if no security has been provided for the virtual machine hard disk files (VHD/VHDX), this sensitive data can be deleted with two clicks. And bingo! Your virtual machine storage is lost now, which could be hard to recover after some time.

If your organization is running System Center Virtual Machine Manager, you might also be concerned about the security of your SCVMM library share, and all the content available in this library, which is critical for the smooth working of your virtualized environment. Ensuring that proper security has been placed on the library share and other administrative shares is critical. It is highly recommended that you use dynamic groups or some kind of RBAC when giving access to any part of the infrastructure; RBAC and dynamic groups can be helpful in maintaining the least access privileges methodology in your environment.

Auditing for virtual machine resource access

In the previous section on securing virtual machine access with filesystem and sharing permissions, we saw that controlling file-level access is of utmost importance just like any other security method available and provides secure access to virtual machine data and configuration files. As we know, security is nothing without the proper auditing in place, so we should make sure that proper auditing is happening both failed and successful access, which can be helpful in case of any security breach against the virtual machine.

Enabling auditing for file-level access to virtual machine related data, including the virtual machine storage and its configuration files, can be done by enabling the auditing on the folder where the virtual machine data resides.

In the following exercise, we will walk through the steps required to enable file-level auditing for virtual machine related data access on the Hyper-V server:

1. Go to Hyper-V server, open **Windows Explorer**, and then locate the folder where your virtual machines are placed.
2. On the **File** menu, click on **Properties**.
3. Click on the **Security** tab, and then click on the **Advanced** button.
4. Click on the **Auditing** tab.
5. While performing these operations, you should log in to the machine with administrative credentials. If you are logged on with a user account that doesn't have local administrator rights and if prompted for administrative credentials, click on **Continue**, enter your username and password, and then hit *Enter*.
6. Click on the **Add** button to open the **Select User, Computer, or Group** dialog box.
7. Click on the **Object Types** button, and then in the **Object Types** dialog box, select the object types you want to find. Note that the user, group, and built-in security principal object types are selected by default.
8. Click on the **Locations** button, and then in the **Location** dialog box, select either your domain or local computer.
9. In the **Select User, Computer, or Group** dialog box, enter the name of the group or user you want to audit. Then, in the **Enter the object names to select** dialog box, enter Authenticated Users (to audit the access of all authenticated users), and then click on **OK**. The **Auditing Entry** dialog box gets displayed.
10. Determine the type of access you want to audit on the file or folder using the **Auditing Entry** dialog box.

Here comes the big catch! We should only audit those logs which we really want to see because selecting everything for auditing will generate hundreds of auditing logs, and it may lead to problems with your disk capacity on the source machine.

11. In the **Auditing Entry** dialog box, next to **List Folder/Read Data**, select **Successful and Failed**, and then click on **OK**.

12. You can view the audit entries you enabled under the **Auditing** tab of the **Advanced Security Settings** dialog box.

13. Click on **OK** to close the **Properties** dialog box.

As a best practice, we should also verify our configuration after implementing the preceding exercise to configure auditing for the virtual machine folder container. We can perform a few tests here and check whether the required audit logs are getting logged or not. We can use Event Viewer in Windows Server to check availability for the required audit logs.

Backing up virtual machines

Crashing a virtual machine operating system or an application running inside the virtual machine can result in requiring you to restore a virtual machine to a previous running state. Now there are two ways you can restore a virtual machine to a previous running state in which everything was working just fine. In the first scenario, you can restore a virtual machine snapshot if you have taken it when the machine was working fine just before it crashed. And in the second scenario, you could restore a virtual machine backup that you could have made with any backup application, such as Microsoft System Center Data Protection Manager.

Talking about the first scenario we discussed, taking a virtual machine snapshot is not a recommended choice for production workloads due to how virtual machines work when running under snapshot conditions and also because of the method of restoring from a snapshot. If you take a virtual machine snapshot, at the time of taking the snapshot, Hyper-V stops writing to the original storage of the virtual machine and creates a new dynamic differencing disk, which doesn't provide performance as good as fixed or other types of virtual machine storage. So, running a production machine under snapshot conditions is not recommended. With multiple snapshots, if even a single snapshot is missing, you won't be allowed to complete the chain of differencing disks, and this will result in data loss. Another method of backing up virtual machine configuration and data is to back up the virtual machine configuration and data with a backup solution, which provides Hyper-V aware backup.

For example **Microsoft System Center Data Protection Manager (SCDPM)** is a VSS-based software backup solution available in the market. More information on SCDPM is given in the next chapter. We will not go into virtual machine backups here because we have a complete chapter covering this topic later on in this book. There, we will see the different steps to backing up Hyper-V virtual machines and the best practices for making sure that our critical workloads are backed up properly to deal with any accident.

Summary

In this chapter we covered different aspects of securing Hyper-V server and virtual machines running on it. This chapter was a bit different from the other chapters; we started discussing Hyper-V straightaway and ended with discussing Hyper V functionality and solutions to get it done as per our needs. In this chapter we also saw how we should maintain high security to ensure that all the features and solutions that we saw in the previous chapters are implemented with high availability using the security provided by Windows Server and Hyper-V.

To summarize the topics we covered in this chapter, let's get an overview from the beginning. First, we discussed the physical hypervisor (Hyper-V) level security and learned how we can maintain the base operating system security to make sure that the attack surface is minimized for any potential security threat. Then we completed the best practice section for the base operating system and moved to the discussion of security best practices to secure the Hyper-V virtual network switch. In this section, we covered the new features made available in Windows Server 2012: extensible virtual switch and virtual machine networking capabilities, such as ARP spoofing protection, DHCP Guard, Router Guard, port mirroring, and last but not least, port ACL for virtual machines. With the completion of securing virtual network switch and network security best practices, we continued with the importance of delegation of authority in Hyper-V. We saw how we can use Authorization Manager to ensure that we can achieve the task of role-based delegation of authority on a standalone Hyper-V server. We also looked at the security hardening best practices for Hyper-V virtual machine storage, which plays an important role in the overall security implementation of Hyper-V. At the end of the chapter, we discussed all the security elements that are directly associated with or are within the security of a guest virtual machine running on Hyper-V. In this section we covered filesystem-level security, auditing for virtual machine access, specification of default path for virtual machine configuration files, and last but not least, an overview of the need for backing up virtual machines to deal with any disasters or service interruptions.

The next chapter will be the last chapter of our book, and in it we will discuss Hyper-V backup and recovery methods.

10
Performing Hyper-V Backup and Recovery

This is the last chapter of this book, where we will discuss Hyper-V virtual machine backup and recovery. This discussion on backup and recovery will not include the Hyper-V Replica feature, which was introduced in Windows Server 2012 Hyper-V and was covered in *Chapter 3, Setting Up Hyper-V Replication*, but instead of this we will cover other traditional methods for backing up Hyper-V virtual machines' configuration files and virtual machine storage.

We will divide this chapter into three major areas. In the first area, we will go through the different Hyper-V backup methodologies available around us, and what we have been using from the past till today. This section will include an overview of Hyper-V virtual machine backup methodologies from the very basic options to the advanced ones.

After completing the first section, we will move on to the following topics in this chapter:

- Hyper-V backup considerations and best practices
- Implementing Hyper-V virtual machine backup and recovery:
    - Hyper-V backup and recovery with the Windows Server Backup feature
    - Hyper-V backup and recovery with system center data protection manager

Ok, so let's get to the work and start the chapter with our first topic. Let's get started!

Hyper-V backup methodologies overview

In this section, we will go through various backup techniques. Here, we will not be discussing how to implement these methodologies, but will provide an overview about their existence, and what are the pros and cons of these methodologies around our virtualization ecosystem. Virtualization technology has been there for quite some time now and the majority of the backup methodologies we use these days are based on the traditional file-level and system-management practices. These traditional backup methodologies are still in place for backing up our information systems, including File Servers, Application Servers, Database Servers, and so on.

Copying VHD/VHDX files

This is one of the most used methods of backing up virtual machine data, where one simply copies the current state of the virtual machine hard disk (VHD/VHDX) files from the current Hyper-V storage for the virtual machine to either external storage or a file server. In case of a disaster or virtual machine corruption, administrators can use the earlier copied VHD files with to replace current corrupted virtual machine storage. This protection is a quick fix and takes the virtual machine back in time, to when the virtual machine VHD was copied. If you don't have the most recent copy of the virtual machine VHD, from the current one that has a problem or let's say got corrupted, you might go into an old state of the virtual machine. This workaround doesn't provide virtual machine configuration file backup, so if your running virtual machine is deleted, copying VHD/VHDX files will not help you to restore the virtual machine configuration files, which is a drawback of this type of backup practice.

Problems associated with this practice are mainly time and size, where every time you copy and paste the VHD/VHDX file for a given virtual machine from one location to another (usually from one drive to another or one drive of the source machine to another drive of a remote machine) over the normal network connection, it takes huge amount of time depending on the size of the VHD file(s).

Another problem is the size of the virtual machine hard disk files. Every time you perform this step, either you can overwrite the existing files, but this won't allow you to maintain the version (old state), or you can add the new file into a new or the same directory, which simply needs massive free space for storing these files.

Exporting the virtual machine

Exporting a virtual machine and its data, and keeping a backup, is a fair approach as compared to copying virtual machine storage files. In this method, administrators usually export the virtual machine from one Hyper-V host server to another, mostly when facing limited physical resources. But sometimes it has been noticed that some administrators also use the virtual machine exporting mechanism as their backup feature. That is, whenever virtual machine state-level backup is required, the administrators export the virtual machine configuration files along with the virtual machine storage, and dump the export to a network or location on a separate drive.

To export a virtual machine on a Hyper-V server, perform the following steps:

1. Navigate to **Hyper-V Manager** from **Control Panel | Administrative Tools**.
2. From the main dashboard of the virtual machines, select a virtual machine that you would like to export, and then right-click on it and click on **Export**.
3. In the export wizard, browse the location to either a local hard disk storage or external storage, and specify the location for exporting virtual machine data.
4. After selection, click on the **Export** button to begin the export process.

 It is always recommended to perform a merge of the snapshot of a virtual machine, prior to exporting a virtual machine, either for a virtual machine move process or backup purpose. This technique ensures the correct state of the virtual machine to be exported and imported later on a different Hyper-V server.

When a recovery or backup restore is required, either on the same or preferably on an alternative Hyper-V host, this exported virtual machine gets imported. Some of the disadvantages of this method are similar to the copying virtual machine storage method. The only benefit of this method over copying virtual machine storage files is that with this method, you also back up the virtual machine configuration files. So when you perform recovery, you also get the virtual machine configuration files.

Virtual machine snapshot

Hyper-V snapshot is a utility in Hyper-V, which allows the administrator to create a point-in-time snapshot or a hot-backup copy of the protected virtual machine. Restoring this snapshot or hot-backup of virtual machine can take the virtual machine state with its data to the same point in time when the snapshot was initially created. Compared to the two backup methodologies we discussed earlier in this chapter—copying virtual machine storage files and exporting the virtual machine—creating a virtual machine snapshot is a much more stable and better way to manage the virtual machine backup and recovery. But at the same time, there are few caveats associated with this method.

Let's take a look at the advantage first. When we create a new virtual machine, right before installing a custom-made application, we can take a snapshot that will preserve the virtual machine as a hot backup. And later if we find there is a problem, we need to re-install the operating system, including all the custom application prerequisites.

So in this situation, instead of spending too much time on re-building everything from scratch, all we need to do is restore the virtual machine snapshot, which we took before the installation of the custom-made application. This way, without having to reinstall everything, we can get the same virtual machine state that existed when we created the snapshot.

Ok, we know that this is a good feature, now what is the problem with it? At the time of creating the snapshot, Hyper-V stops writing to the VHD (parent virtual hard disk) of a virtual machine, and creates a new differencing disk with the extension of AVHD, which is a dynamic disk in nature, and from now whatever data and changes you make to the virtual machine, those will be stored here in the AVHD. If you take more snapshots of the virtual machine, more AVHDs will be created and they will be inter-linked to each other.

So what is the problem here? First of all, creating a snapshot of production workloads is not a recommended practice, and that is mainly due to the fact that creating a snapshot stops using the original storage of the virtual machine. So, let's say you plan and use a good storage for your virtual machine, which provides you good disk I/O. But after creating snapshots, Hyper-V will stop using your SAN storage or fixed disk and will start writing on these newly created differencing disks, which are dynamic disks and slower than your fast storage.

In the case of having multiple snapshots, and thus multiple differencing disks, your virtual machine data will split into multiple differencing disks, and as we said these disks will be inter-linked with each other. So, let's say we lose any differencing disks or any of our differencing disks gets corrupted in the middle of the chain, you will lose all the data that was written on that disk or written during that time span when you created the missing AVHD (differencing disk) snapshot.

The Windows Server Backup feature

The Windows Server Backup feature has been there for quite a long time and we all loved it for its simplicity. This is the only choice, when you don't have any other tool available. NTBackup was the old name of the Windows Server operating system backup tool. This NTBackup name was still valid till the release of Windows Server 2003, but with Windows Server 2008/R2, Microsoft changed the name and now we know it as the Windows Server Backup feature or Backup Server Role.

The Windows Server Backup feature cannot be used as an enterprise-wide backup and recovery tool for all types of data and server role, as its main purpose is to provide the ability to back up the critical data from Windows Server operating system for a subset of roles and services. It is your best buddy to work with when a server doesn't have an enterprise-wide and fully capable backup utility or software installed, such as System Center Data Protection Manager.

We will look more closely at the Windows Server Backup feature soon in the up-coming section.

VSS-aware Hyper-V backups

Among all other backup approaches we discussed so far, using a VSS-aware backup solution for backing up Hyper-V virtual machines is the most preferred choice. This feature works hand in hand with both Hyper-V integration Services and Hyper-V VSS writer. VSS-aware backup solutions include Microsoft System Center Data Protection Manager. These software-based VSS backup solutions use client-server architecture, where Hyper-V VSS writer is used from server to client-side to back up the Hyper-V virtual machines. Using a VSS-aware backup solution, we can perform the following two types of backups:

- Virtual machine online backups with Hyper-V integration services
- Virtual machine save state backups without Hyper-V integration services

Now let's discuss each of the preceding types.

Virtual machine online backups using Hyper-V integration services

If the virtual machine has Hyper-V integration services installed and the backup administrator tries to take the virtual machine backup by using Hyper-V VSS writer, the virtual machine will still be running, and a snapshot of the virtual machine and its related data will be created. This method of taking virtual machine's backup is a highly recommended approach, and doesn't cause any availability-related issues for critical virtual machines.

Virtual machine save-state backups without Hyper-V integration services

There are legacy Microsoft and Linux distribution operating systems that cannot have Hyper-V integration services installed. For these virtual machines, even if you use any VSS-aware Hyper-V backup solution, virtual machine backup will change the virtual machine state from the running state to the saved state. This happens due to the unavailability of the Hyper-V integration services.

After we have seen all these traditional and recommended backup approaches, now in the next section we will walk through the Hyper-V backup considerations and best practices, to make sure that our backup system provides a high level of protection and has no major performance or availability impact on the Hyper-V and related components.

Hyper-V backup considerations and best practices

This section is like Cliffs Notes, which we all use while preparing for exams. So before entering into the examination hall, we just go through them to make sure that all the formulas and other important equations are stored in our brain. (Though it slips our head when we see the question paper!). Similarly, Hyper-V backup considerations and best practices are pretty important topics to discuss and retain in the memory, whenever you set up Hyper-V backup. Most of these recommendations and considerations are generic, meaning they are also applicable to all other types of server or data backup we perform on a daily basis in our data center.

Hyper-V backup networking considerations

The networking aspect of architecturing your backup solution for Hyper-V is quite critical in nature. I personally have witnessed various bad networking setups for taking Hyper-V backups, which end up causing severe performance bottlenecks. For every backup solution, a backup window for the data is essential, especially when it comes to tape-based backups. In this case, if any of your scheduled backup jobs does not finish on time, it will make other backup jobs pending and they won't find free slots for tape backup.

When we talk about Hyper-V virtual machine backups, the backup window is quite huge due to the long list of virtual machines available on the hypervisor, which all need to be backed up. These virtual machines are sometimes also big in size, so it takes time to back them up. It is also normal for a hypervisor backup to always be running, because if you have 300 virtual machines running on your Hyper-V failover cluster, it is not possible for you to back up all the virtual machines within one or two days. So, in this case you will also be backing up the virtual machines during production time, and if there is a poor networking layout designed and set up for taking this Hyper-V VM and its data backup, it may end up freezing the client-servicing Hyper-V virtual network switch.

The following are few Hyper-V networking considerations and best practices, which should be followed with any Hyper-V backup design:

- A Hyper-V virtual machine backup should be configured to take Hyper-V virtual machine data backup over a dedicated NIC on the Hyper-V server.

- It is also a good idea to segregate the backup VLAN from the client servicing VLAN.

- There have been a few situations that I came across where I saw that VLANs were created on a firewall and the server VLAN was created in the core layer 2 network switches. So, when the traffic flows in or out from this network architecture, where the firewall interfaces have 100 MB size for data transmit, it causes a huge performance problem. Therefore, it is a good practice to keep both backup and Hyper-V servers in the same core network switch, but separate the client servicing VLAN from the backup VLAN.

- For better performance, it is also advisable to look at the possibility of having multiple NICs on both the backup server and Hyper-V side, so on both sides we will club these NICs and have aggregated bandwidth from all of them. In addition to the bandwidth aggregation, we will also have the flexibility of having NIC failover capability. In the event of having a single NIC, your backup system will be at risk, but having multiple NICs clubbed (teamed) will provide NIC failover for the Hyper-V backup networking.

Hyper-V backup software considerations

The next thing we will cover is the software-side considerations. These software considerations are mainly based on antivirus protection and Hyper-V integration services. Based on the backup software you are using, there could be more software-related best practices that you would have to include in your backup design. Some backup solutions available in the market are fully customizable from the configuration perspective, which allows administrators to tune the performance for data backup and recovery. However, at the same time, there are plenty of backup solutions that claim to be the perfect enterprise-class backup solutions for your environment, but actually don't provide enough customization capabilities.

Hyper-V integration services

Hyper-V integration services play a vital role in the overall virtual machine management and accessibility, and since we have discussed the importance and the use of Hyper-V integration services at many places in this chapter and the previous ones, let's summarize the following about the Hyper-V integration services:

- Always install the Hyper-V integration services for every virtual machine you create either standalone or on a Hyper-V failover cluster.

- Hyper-V integration services allow the virtual machine to participate in the virtual machine backup process. So, if the virtual machine has the Hyper-V integration services installed, any VSS-aware backup solution can take the virtual machine backup without putting the virtual machine in the save state. But at the other end, if the Hyper-V integration services are not available on the virtual machine (due to incompatibility with Hyper-V integration services, or because the administrator forgot to install it), when the VM backup process starts, the backup client agent installed on the Hyper-V server will put the VM into the save state.

Storage considerations

Storage is the big player when it comes to virtualization in the solution planning and designing phase. From a real-world standpoint, I have witnessed many customers, who have under-utilized servers from the memory as well as the processor's perspective. And the main reason these servers stay under-utilized is because the administrator didn't use the disk storage available for creating new virtual machines.

Storage plays an extremely important part in the overall solution design and service scalability of virtualization projects. Nowadays a hypervisor hardware box usually doesn't carry eight to ten disk drives installed because all the virtual machine-related data and storage is usually placed on the SAN/NAS or sometimes JBODs. This new way of using external storage makes the storage availability and scalability more critical for the smooth working of virtualization stack.

 To know more about the Hyper-V storage related stuff, we can go back to *Chapter 6, Insight into Hyper-V Storage*.

We will now discuss a few of the important storage-related design considerations and best practices from the Hyper-V virtual machine backup perspective.

Guest virtual machine storage

The first aspect of virtual machine storage is how Hyper-V presents the storage to a virtual machine and the second important aspect is how the internal virtual machine storage is configured. Both of these aspects have tremendous impact on the virtual machine backup capabilities. The following are best practices and design considerations, which we should keep in the mind while configuring the internal virtual machine storage:

- All virtual machine partitions and drives should be formatted with NTFS.

- The virtual machine disks should not be dynamic disks.

- All the differencing and the parent disks should be in the same location; they could be separated into different folders, but their root folder should be the same.

- It is not a good practice to take snapshots of the production workloads. And if there are situations where you are required to take snapshots of the production workload, it is highly recommended to merge these snapshots to the parent VHD/VHDX. This will ensure that VM is not left to run as a differencing disk (snapshot) for a long time.

- Guest virtual machine VSS backup solutions usually don't back up a pass-through disk, and therefore, it is recommended to configure the guest virtual machine backup for the pass-through disk data.

Implementing Hyper-V virtual machine backup and recovery

After building a solid foundation for our understanding about Hyper-V virtual machine backup methodologies and best practices, we will now move ahead to see things in action. In this section, we will first cover Hyper-V VM backup and recovery with the Windows Server 2012 backup feature. Then, we will go on to see how System Center Data Protection Manager 2012 can help us to back up and recover Hyper-V virtual machines.

Hyper-V backup and recovery with the Windows Server Backup feature

Most of us who have been working with Windows Server from the previous releases are huge fans of the NTBackup, which was a native backup utility for system state, Exchange Information Store, and files and folders. It gave us a nifty way to quickly back up data, whenever needed, and then restore it on the same or any other Windows Server. Some people used to back up the files and folder data, just to avoid keeping this huge amount of data in the original shape so that it wouldn't get infected with viruses.

When we moved from Windows Server 2003 to Windows Server 2008, Windows native backup functionality was not present in the Windows Server 2008 RTM release then, but was later added in the service pack for the product. This new version of NTBackup was now called the Windows Server Backup utility, and is a feature of the operating system that is not available by default, but which the administrators can install whenever it is needed. A series of new features and functionalities was added into this new release of Windows native backup tool. Windows Server 2012 also carried on the same legacy, and introduced numerous new features and capabilities to the product for baking up data and virtual machines from Hyper-V servers.

The Windows Server Backup feature is not an enterprise-wide backup solution. The primary purpose of having such a native backup feature available in Windows Server operating systems was to make sure that important data can be backed up with the basic data and services backup feature. The Windows Server Backup utility also provided VSS-aware backups so that it can back up open files and running virtual machines, without letting them to stop their usage for backing up.

What's new in Windows Server 2012 for the Windows Server Backup feature

Let's now go through few of the new features added in Windows Server 2012 for backing up data and virtual machines on Hyper-V.

Selective backup and restoration of individual virtual machines

In the previous release of the product, if the administrator wants to back up a virtual machine with the Windows Server Backup feature, they have to back up the complete volume. This was because the earlier release of the product didn't allow one to selectively back up or restore a virtual machine to or from the Hyper-V server.

With the improvements in the Windows Server 2012, now it is possible for administrators to selectively back up or restore a virtual machine on the same Hyper-V server.

Backup support for CSVs

The pre-Windows Server 2012 operating systems and Windows Server Backup feature didn't support backing up CSV. But with Windows Server 2012, we can now back up a subset part of the CSV data and virtual machine content.

If we want to perform Hyper-V virtual machine selection for backup by using the Windows Server Backup feature, it won't be possible because CSV-hosted virtual machines are not supported, but at the same time we can back up the virtual machine data from the CSV as a file and folder backup.

In case of the cluster, the Windows Server backup should be configured on all the Hyper-V failover cluster nodes, so in the case of backup and recovery it will be available when the node fails over to another node.

Larger disk volume backup possibility

Prior to Windows Server 2012, it was not possible for the Windows Server Backup feature to back up the volumes larger than 2 TB, and 512-byte sectors were required.

In Windows Server 2012, now it is very much possible for administrators to perform a backup job for a volume that is larger than 2 TB, and we can also use 4 KB sector-size disks for the backup.

Backup retention and backup versioning

These two concepts were not present in the previous releases of the Windows Server native backup feature, which used to cause administrators to script the movement of the old backup data and remove the storage, to avoid the Windows Server Backup feature overwriting the existing in-place backups.

With Windows Server 2012, now backup retention and backup versioning are available, so administrators can offload their burden and can keep multiple copies of the same data, with different versions as well as old and new data.

Installing the Windows Server 2012 Backup feature

For installing the Windows Server 2012 Backup feature to your Hyper-V or any other server, we can either use the GUI method of adding this feature or can also use the Windows PowerShell to add the Server Manager module and then install the backup feature. For this example, we will install the Windows Server Backup feature, using the Server Manager GUI method. So, let's perform the following steps to install the backup feature on one of our Windows Server 2012 Hyper-V servers:

1. Open the Server Manager GUI from the main server manager icon on the left side.

2. Then, click on the **Manage** tab in the upper-right corner, and click on **Add and Remove Feature**.

3. On the first screen **Before You Begin**, click on the **Next** button to move to the **Select Installation Type** screen. On this screen, select **Role-based or feature-based installation** and click on the **Next** button.

4. On the **Server Selection** screen, select the server where we will be installing the backup feature from the server pool. If you want to install on the local machine, it will be selected under the server pool by default. Then click on **Next** to proceed further.

5. Go to the **Features** tab, select the **Windows Server Backup** feature, and click on the **Next** button.

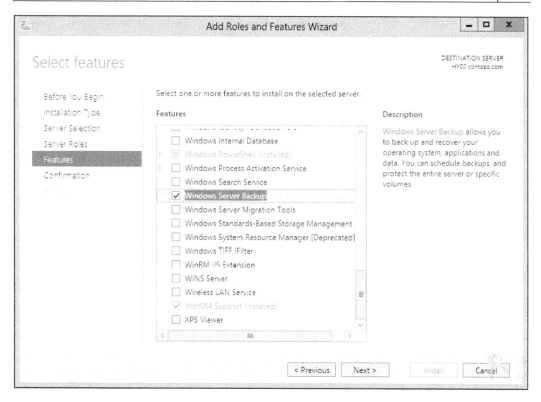

6. Then on the last screen, click on the **Install** button to start the installation of the Windows Server Backup feature on the server. If it is required to restart the server for completing the installation, we can also select the **Restart the destination server automatically if required** option, which will automate the restart of the server.

Configuring virtual machine backups with the Windows Server Backup feature

As we mentioned in the overview section of the Windows Server Backup feature, we cannot back up a virtual machine hosted on CSV disks with the Windows Server 2012 Backup feature. All the other types of virtual machines that have their storage configured on the local storage of the server can be backed up with the Windows Server Backup feature.

Now, let's go ahead and configure the Windows Server Backup feature for backing up a Hyper-V virtual machine running on the local host.

1. to open the Windows Server Backup console, go to the **Control Panel** and then open **Administrative Tools**. From there double-click on the **Windows Server Backup** snap-in to launch it.

2. After launching the Windows Server Backup snap-in, right-click on **Local Backup** in the upper-left corner. For this example, we will take the backup for a virtual machine once, so click on **Backup Once...**.

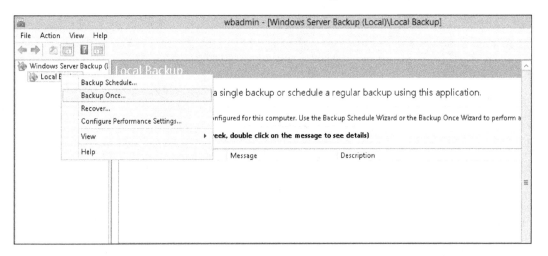

3. Then, we will select the backup options under the **Backup Once** wizard; select the backup option depending on the scenario, and click on **Next**.

4. On the second screen of **Select Backup Configuration**, we will select **Custom** and click on **Next**.

5. Now, it's time for us to select the virtual machine that we would like to back up on this local Hyper-V server. Under the **Select Items** pane, we will drill down the Hyper-V, and from all the listed virtual machines running on this Hyper-V node, we will select **SAP_Portal_VM** as a test candidate to be selected for VM backup.

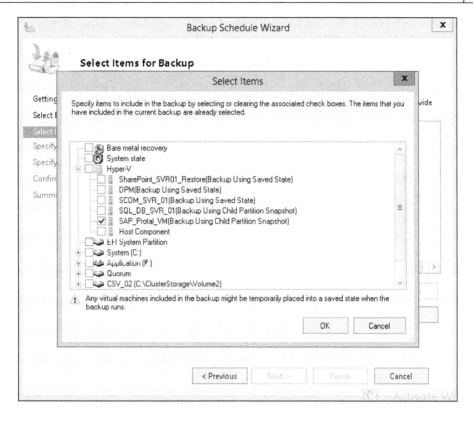

Backup Schedule Wizard ☒

Select Items for Backup

Select Items ☒

Specify items to include in the backup by selecting or clearing the associated check boxes. The items that you have included in the current backup are already selected.

- ☐ Bare metal recovery
- ☐ System state
- ☐ Hyper-V
  - ☐ SharePoint_SVR01_Restore(Backup Using Saved State)
  - ☐ DPM(Backup Using Saved State)
  - ☐ SCOM_SVR_01(Backup Using Saved State)
  - ☐ SQL_DB_SVR_01(Backup Using Child Partition Snapshot)
  - ☑ SAP_Protal_VM(Backup Using Child Partition Snapshot)
  - ☐ Host Component
- ☐ EFI System Partition
- ☐ System (C:)
- ☐ Application (F:)
- ☐ Quorum
- ☐ CSV_02 (C:\ClusterStorage\Volume2)

⚠ Any virtual machines included in the backup might be temporarily placed into a saved state when the backup runs.

OK   Cancel

< Previous   Next >   Finish   Cancel

6. We can click on the **Advanced Settings** button on the **Select Items for Backup** screen and exclude items from the backup selection. Under the second tab of **Advanced Settings**, we can also select which type of backup we want to take from the VSS settings, where two options are given for our choice. The first option is VSS full backup and the second option is VSS copy backup.

> The type of backup that we are using in the preceding steps is a Hyper-V-aware backup, which means it's a virtual machine backup, and in case of disaster to the virtual machine configuration or data corruption, this backup will restore the virtual machine to the same time and with the data form, when it was backed up.

After the selection of the virtual machine, and exclusion of any components if needed, we will have the virtual machine selected for backup.

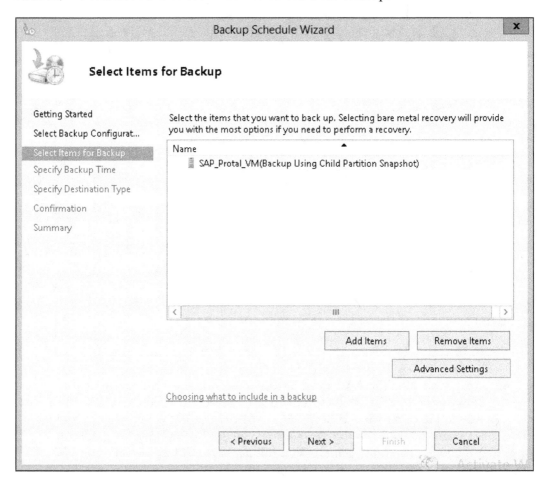

The following are the steps that we need to carry out to complete the backup configuration:

1. Now, we have specified the backup destination where we will store the virtual machine backup data. The Windows Server Backup feature provides two types of backup destination. In the first type, we can keep the destination as the local server to any other disk and in the second type, we can save the data to an SMB file share created on any other server. For this example, we will choose **Remote Shared Folder**.

2. As we said that we will choose remote folder as the backup destination, in the second step, we will specify the remote UNC folder path for the shared location where our backup data will reside. We can also choose the option to inherit or not to inherit the file-level permissions from the source data to the destination data.

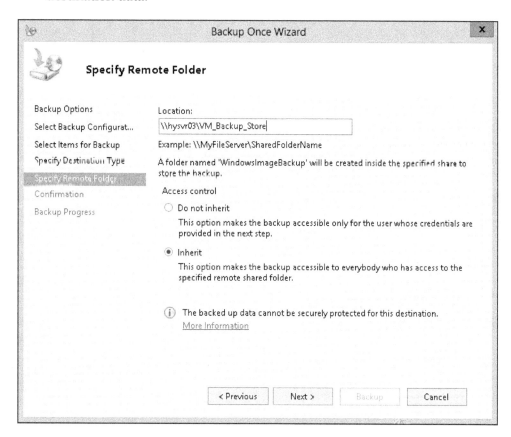

3. On the last **Confirmation** screen, you have the flexibility to start the backup process or keep it for a later time. For our example, we will click on the **Backup** button on this **Confirmation** screen to kick off the backup process of the selected VM.

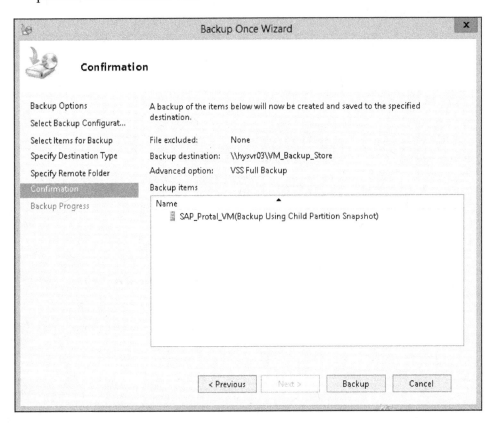

As you can see in the following screenshot, while the Windows Server Backup feature is backing up the virtual machine from the source Hyper-V server, the virtual machine is running, and doesn't get saved. Do you know why? Well the answer is quite simple. As we said in the backup methodology section, if the Hyper-V virtual machine integration services are installed in a virtual machine, the virtual machine will also participate in the backup process and thus doesn't get saved or paused while the VSS-based backup solution backs up the virtual machine data online.

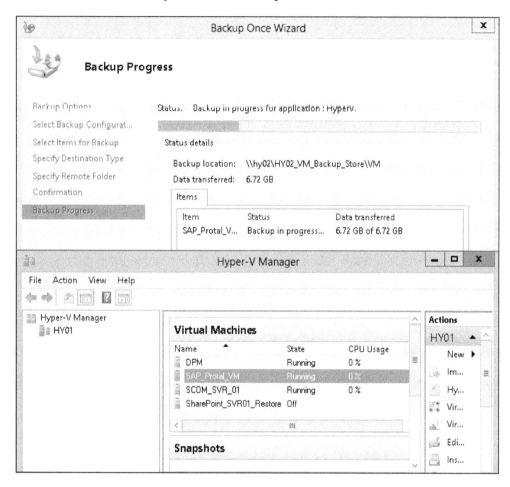

After running the virtual machine backup for sometime, (in this example, we will be backing up 6.72 GB of data, which won't take a long time) in the following screenshot we can see that the Windows Server Backup feature has successfully completed the backup of `SAP_Portal_VM` from the HY01 Hyper-V node.

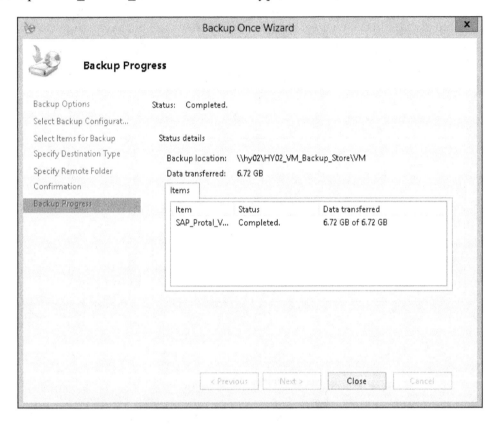

So with this we have completed a virtual machine backup by using the Windows Server Backup feature, which is quite easy to work with, has flexibility to backup critical virtual machines, and comes as a free solution.

Performing virtual machine recovery using the Windows Server Backup feature

In the previous section, we saw how to back up a virtual machine running on Windows Server 2012 Hyper-V host, using the Windows Server Backup feature, which is absolutely free and provides a handy way to the administrator to quickly back up a virtual machine from the Hyper-V host, in the event of unavailability of an enterprise-level backup solution, such as SC DPM.

Now, we will explore the recovery procedures of the Windows Server Backup feature for performing virtual machine recovery in case virtual machine configuration files or data get corrupted. We will perform this recovery on the same Hyper-V node where this virtual machine was previously running and backed up with Windows Server Backup. Ok, so let's start performing this recovery and see the steps required to complete this task.

Before we start the virtual machine recovery, we will perform full deletion of SAP_Portal_VM from the Hyper-V host in our environment, which we backed up in the previous section. To attain this goal, we will remove this virtual machine from both Hyper-V and the storage side (F:), where this virtual machine was located.

1. After deleting the virtual machine SAP_Portal_VM from the both Hyper-V and the disk, we will go to **Control Panel** and from **Administrative Tools**, we will open the **Windows Server Backup** console.

2. From the left-hand action pane, click on **Recover....** This will open **Recovery Wizard**.

3. Since we backed up **SAP_Portal_VM** from the same HY01 Hyper-V host, while recovering the virtual machine, we will select the **This server** option, to specify that the backup is stored on the same server from where we want to read the source.

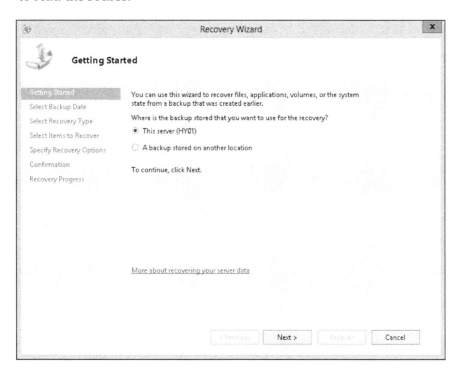

4. On the next **Recovery Wizard** screen, we will select the backup date. It could be possible that you have performed many backups on this server. So you will find many backups on this server and you will have to select the proper backup date to which you want to go back in time for these virtual machines. Select the appropriate backup date and click on **Next**.

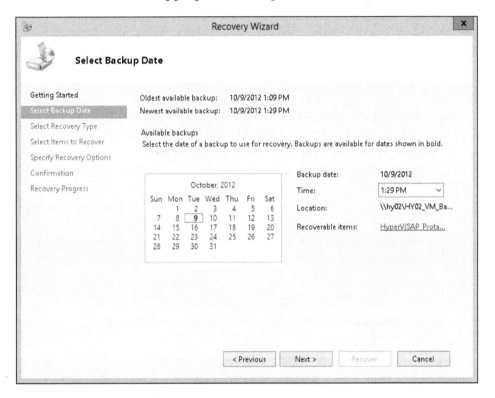

5. The next step will ask you about the backup type. Since we are going to restore a Hyper-V Virtual Machine backup, we will select Hyper-V as the backup type.

6. On the next screen, we will select the backup to restore. Since our `SAP_Portal_VM` has only a single VHDX file as its OS disk, we will select the VHDX file as the only data in the VM selection area.

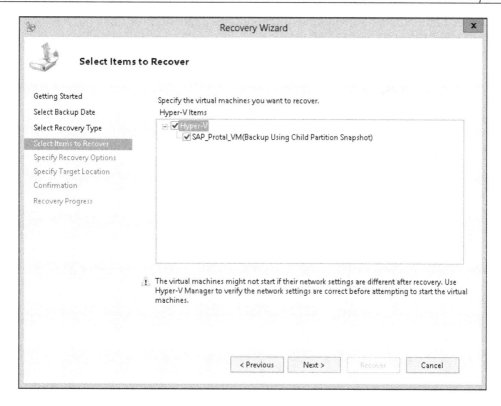

7. The next screen will prompt you about specifying the recovery option. For this example, we will select the **Recovery to original location** option and click on the **Next** button.

8. On the last screen of confirmation, the Windows Server Backup console will provide you a confirmation checkpoint. Upon clicking on the **Recover** button, we start the process of the virtual machine recovery on the same original Hyper-V node, where this virtual machine was running and backed up earlier.

In the following screenshot, you will see that the Windows Backup Server is enumerating the progress of restoring the virtual machine on the HY01 Hyper-V node. This process will restore the accumulated amount of 6.72 GB VM data from the remote backup source to the HY01 backup destination server.

Upon completion of the virtual machine recovery process, Windows Backup Server will provide with you confirmation about the successful restore of the virtual machine as follows:

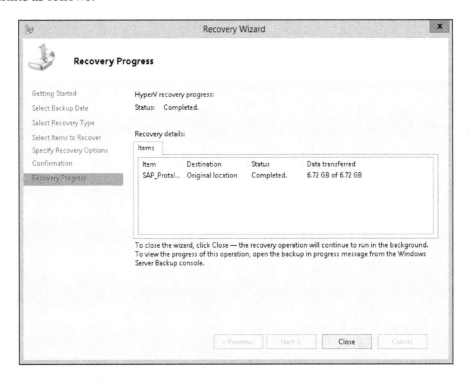

As a proof to see whether the virtual machine has restored successfully or not, we will open the Hyper-V Manager and try to locate **SAP_Portal_VM** in the available virtual machines. As we can see in the following screenshot, after the successful completion of the restore job, **SAP_Portal_VM** is available in the list of virtual machines on the HY01 Hyper-V host node.

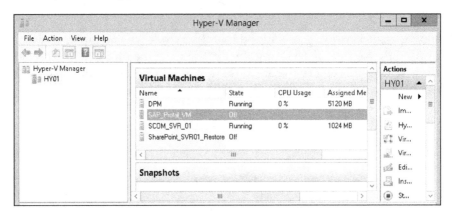

Usually, when we perform the virtual machine backup restore on a different Hyper-V node, due to the different Hyper-V virtual network switch configuration (Name), it makes it impossible for the virtual machine to maintain the IP address or network connection. So, upon opening the virtual machine, you might face errors or no network connectivity. To avoid this, we can employ a best practice here to maintain the names of all the virtual network switches we create on Hyper-V servers in our environment.

For our example, since we restored this virtual machine on the same Hyper-V node from where we backed it up, everything is the same, and when we check the virtual machine configuration after the restore, we see that the virtual machine NIC is configured for the same old and correct Hyper-V virtual network switch.

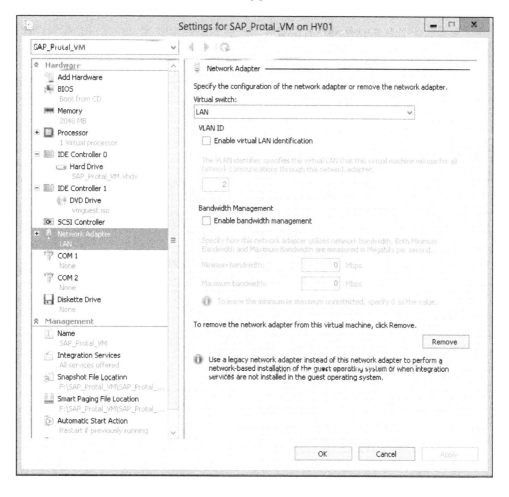

Ok, so we are back in the business now, after restoring the virtual machine with all the configuration and data. I know you would love the Windows Server Backup feature for its simplicity and ability to easily restore the virtual machine backups.

Hyper-V backup and recovery with System Center Data Protection Manager

Microsoft **Data Protection Manager** (**DPM**) has been around for quite a long time. It is famous for its easy and quick protection for Microsoft File Server, SQL Server, and Exchange Server. With the availability of Hyper-V, DPM also provides great support and functionality for Hyper-V virtual machine backup and restore. Initially when DPM was released in 2005, it was a standalone product where customers could buy a number of server and agent licenses for server and application backups. But with the recent changes of Microsoft licensing and addition of DPM to the System Center family, now DPM has become a major part of the Microsoft System Center family product. And as per the current licensing schema of System Center 2012, customers can have DPM running under either the System Center 2012 Datacentre or Standard Edition license.

DPM technical overview

DPM is a server-agent-based solution, where the server sits on one side and on the other side the administrator installs the agent on the server and application that needs to be protected by DPM. Just like other backup software available in the market, DPM doesn't have specific agent binaries for different types of server role or application. DPM has an intelligent agent, which is by default the same binary installation that gets installed on all types of application servers. After installing the agent of the remote application server, DPM server recognizes the installed application on the registered agent installed on the remote servers. For instance, if you install the DPM agent on an SQL Server, and then go on to create the protection group for SQL Server, the DPM protection group creation wizard will show the SQL installed on the server and allow you to select the SQL Server instances and databases for backup and restore purposes.

At the time of writing this book, the current version available is Microsoft System Center Data Protection Manager 2012. Microsoft has also released the System Center 2012 Service Pack 1 beta, which is applicable for DPM 2012 and contains a number of out of the box features for Windows Server 2012 and Hyper-V 3.0 in particular.

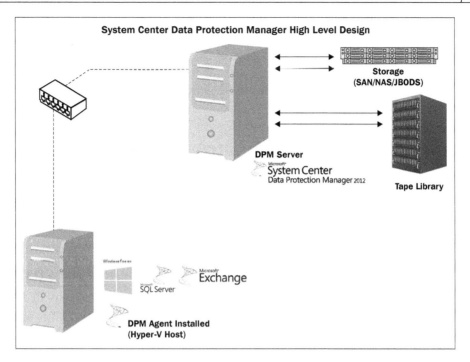

DPM allows organizations to keep the backup data either on **Direct Attached Storage (DAS)**, **Fibre Channel Stroage Area Network (SAN)**, or iSCSI SAN, and also supports tape backup functionality. DPM is a VSS-aware backup solution that provides a great level of flexibility for backing up data that is being used. For instance, if we talk about Hyper-V, DPM administrators can back up the virtual machines running on the Hyper-V host node without getting the Hyper-V administrator to shut down or put the virtual machine into save state during the backup process. Along with all the other features and functionalities, the reporting functionality adds immense value to your service catalogue, where administrators can use the default available reports or custom reports for the backup and recovery of the various protected servers and applications by DPM.

We will now go ahead and explore these new enhancements and features added in DPM 2012 SP1 for Windows Server 2012 Hyper-V 3.0 protection.

Here, it is very important to note that DPM and System Center is a whole big world inside in it, so in this chapter, we will not cover all aspects of the DPM, but would consider the backup and recovery features of DPM. We will also assume that the readers have basic understanding of DPM, and have relative experience for each respective domain within DPM and System Center related family products.

What's new in System Center 2012 Data Protection Manager

Visit `http://technet.microsoft.com/en-us/library/hh848299.aspx` for complete details on the new features of System Center Data Protection Manager 2012.

Setting up DPM base infrastructure

For the DPM protection group, where we will be keeping the protection group backup data either on storage disk pools or tape drives, it is a recommended approach to make the necessary disk or tape drives available before the installation of DPM. Making either of your preferred destination drives available helps setting up the base infrastructure for DPM.

Installing System Center Data Protection Manager 2012

As we said in an earlier note, covering all the bits and pieces of DPM won't be possible. Therefore, we will present just the required information for you to utilize your existing DPM infrastructure for protecting the Hyper-V role. If you don't have DPM setup running in your environment, reading this section you will get enough knowledge about the required resources, which will help you to install and configure DPM 2012 within your environment.

If we summarize the DPM installation methods, it would be as follows:

1. Meet the hardware and software requirements for DPM installation.
2. Run the DPM 2012 setup from the installation binaries.
3. You can use either the locally installed SQL Server or a dedicated SQL Server.
4. Run the prerequisites checker, and if something is missing, fix the prerequisites, and re-run the setup again.

5. For security settings, create a local DPM user account.

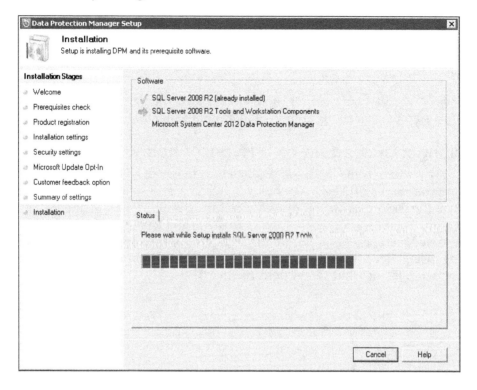

6. After meeting all the requirements, you can roll out the installation, which will take some time to finish with the ready DPM server for your use.

Installing DPM server 2012, like earlier releases, is not that difficult. If your machine meets the requirements, the installation will just flow and everything will be fine.

For more details on the steps for the installation and the requirements for DPM implementation, we can browse to the DPM 2012 TechNet library (`http://technet.microsoft.com/en-us/library/hh758173.aspx`).

To continue with our demo, once the disk is initialized and online on the DPM machine, the next step is to add the disk to the DPM server as the raw disk for the disk-based protection group creations.

Adding disks in the Data Protection Manager for disk-based protection groups

DPM allows the administrator to save the protected data either to tapes or to disks, and particularly for this demo in the chapter, we will choose the disk-based backup of Hyper-V virtual machines.

Visit http://technet.microsoft.com/en-us/library/jj642912.aspx to take a look at the step-by-step configuration of disk storage in DPM 2012.

Installing a DPM agent on a Hyper-V host

Ok, so now we have come far along, and it's time to install a DPM agent on our Windows Server 2012 Hyper-V failover cluster server nodes, for protecting them with the DPM backup and recovery feature. Installing a DPM agent on any of the Windows Servers involves browsing and locating the same domain-based member server within the DPM Active Directory browser, and initiating installation—which will hardly take one or two minutes—depending on the network latency and server performance.

 Visit http://technet.microsoft.com/en-us/library/ hh758186.aspx to find out various methods that can be used to install a DPM agent on Hyper-V standalone and clustered nodes

So far we have completed the DPM agent installation on two of our Windows Server 2012 Hyper-V hosts. In the next section, we will see how we can configure the DPM protection group for our Windows Server 2012 Hyper-V failover cluster nodes.

Configuring Hyper-V backup with DPM protection groups

In this section, we will walk through a step-by-step process of creating and configuring a DPM protection group for the Hyper-V virtual machine backup. Working with DPM protection groups is the same as old times, where you used to drill down the server and select the server roles that you would like to add in the protection for that particular server.

Before we go ahead and see how to create the DPM protection group for a Hyper-V role, let's first understand what types of Windows Server 2012 Hyper-V-based virtual machines and their supported components are supported by DPM for Hyper-V backup and protection groups:

- Protecting Hyper-V highly available virtual machines using CSV storage
- Protecting Hyper-V standalone virtual machines using SMB storage
- Protecting Windows Server 2012 CSV 2.0

We will now move ahead and see the step-by-step configuration for DPM protection groups. This protection group will be created for Windows Server 2012 Hyper-V host nodes that are also clustered and are CSV enabled.

As there is no special configuration required for creating DPM protection groups for standalone or clustered Hyper-V nodes, creation and configuration of the DPM protection group will be the same. The only difference is the selection criteria within the DPM protection group, which we will create for Hyper-V nodes. It is very much possible that your HYCLUS01 Hyper-V cluster node, which has a few clustered virtual machine instances running, and a few running standalone, means that they are not highly available virtual machines. There could be a few others, which have SMB storage used, so the protection group creation will be similar. But the selection of these different types of virtual machines can be done either by selecting them from the same protection group or the administrator can create multiple protection groups for this Hyper-V server, dividing these different types of virtual machines into different protection groups.

> In this chapter, all the backed up and recovered virtual machines have Hyper-V Virtual Machine integration services installed. So whenever we backed up any virtual machine for demo purposes to show you images from the real experience, you must have noticed that, while either the Windows Server Backup feature or DPM was backing up the virtual machine, the virtual machine state didn't get changed from running to saved, because of the integration services that were installed on these virtual machines.

So as a best practice for backing up Hyper-V virtual machines, always look at the possibility of installing the Hyper-V integration to include the virtual machine for VSS participation in Hyper-V VSS-aware backup, which doesn't put the running VM into a saved state.

Protecting Hyper-V highly available virtual machines

In this first example, we will see how we can protect a Windows Server 2012 Hyper-V based highly available virtual machine, which is either created within a Windows Server 2012 Hyper-V failover cluster or added as a standalone machine inside the Hyper-V failover cluster. For this example, the highly available virtual machine we will choose will be having its VHD/VHDX storage located on a CSV. Since this type of virtual machine has storage located on a CSV disk, it is very much ready to be live migrated from and within various failover cluster nodes of the Hyper-V cluster.

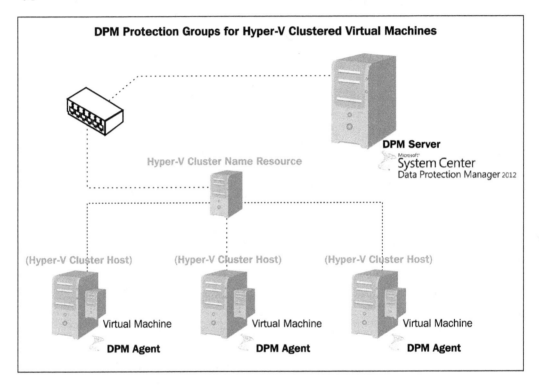

Now let's see the steps that we need to perform to make this type of machine protected with System Center Data Protection Manager:

1. Open System Center 2012 Data Protection Manager 2012 Management Console.

2. Go to the **Protection** tab from the left-hand action menu.

3. Once you are in the **Protection** tab, find the **New ribbon** tab in the upper-left corner, and click on **New**.

4. On the main DPM protection group wizard screen, you can read all the information you need to know about how DPM works. Once you complete reading the informative text, you can click on the **Next** button to proceed.

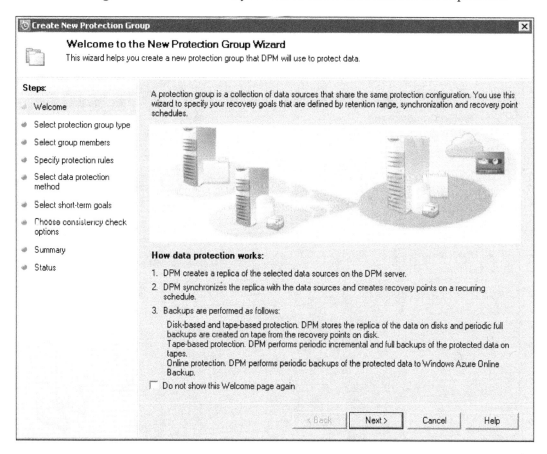

5. The next screen will ask about the type of protection group you want to create, which means whether you want to protect a server or a client base computer. In our example, we will be choosing a server for creating a protection group for Microsoft Hyper-V servers. Select **Servers** and click on **Next**.

6. On the next screen, we will select the virtual machines that are highly available and using CSV storage. For this, we will expand the HYPER-V failover cluster computer icon, and then select all the virtual machines that we want to make part of this protection group. After making the selection, click on the **Next** button to proceed.

For selecting any clustered virtual machine for our protection group, first we need to make sure that the agent is installed on all the clustered nodes. If the virtual machine is using the SMB storage, we need to make sure that the protection agent is also installed on the file share server where the SMB storage location exists.

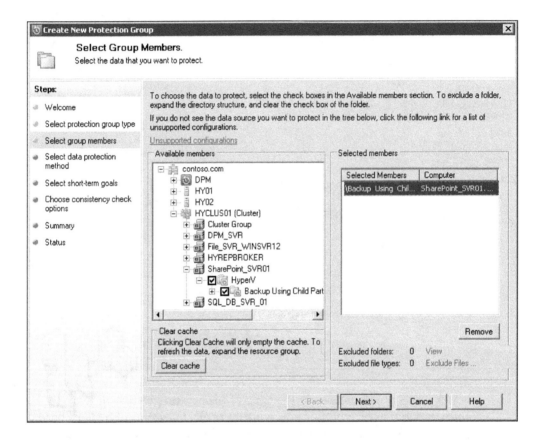

7. The next screen will ask about the protection group name and the type of data protection method to be used for this protection group, which means whether we want this protection group data to be stored on a disk or a tape. It is solely your choice if you want to keep the data on a disk-based subsystem, which could be either a SAN-based LUN or a cheap NAS/JOBODs. We can also set the tape library as the preferred destination for the data store.

8. The next screen will prompt you about the schedule for this backup or protection cycle to run and make sure that you have the data protected on a periodic basis. You can schedule the data backup to be run on either all days of the week or multiple times in a day. In addition to the schedule of the data backup, we can also set the retention settings for the data that is being backed up.

9. Under the **Review Disk Allocation** tab of the screen, we can review the recommended disk allocation; we can also modify the settings as per our choice for the protection group we are creating. By default, the **Automatic growing of this volume** checkbox is selected, which means that if your virtual machine size will increase, you have allowed this protection group to take more from your disk or tape storage.

10. The next step is an important phase of creating the data replica. We are backing up using DPM and we could either use a replica of the virtual machine data over the network — which is a recommended approach in case the data size is not very huge — or we can use another method, where a removable media gathers the initial data for transferring. This second method of using removable media is the best choice for dealing with a massive amount of data you want to replicate with your DPM server. It also gives us the flexibility to either synchronize the data and create the replica as soon as we finish the configuration, or to manually replicate it after the business hours, when the I/O will be reduced to a minimum.

11. The next step is about checking the consistency of the protection group. The first option, which is also the default choice, is to run the consistency check when the replica becomes inconsistent; or if you are concerned about the replica consistency, you can also schedule the consistency check to be run on a periodic basis.

12. The last screen show you a summary of your configuration for the protection group you created, along with the virtual machines and data you selected to be part of the protection group. Within this **Summary** screen, you can also see the schedule you selected for retention time and recovery point creation. Then, you can also see few warnings about the virtual machine, which provide information about the hardware-based VSS snapshot creation of CSV disk for optimal performance and the ILR supportability from the virtual machine storage configuration side. If everything seems fine, click on **Create Group**. This will initiate the creation of the DPM protection group for our VMs.

13. Once the creation of the protection group process gets kicked in, the next screen provides acknowledgement about the status of protection groups. If there are any problems encountered during the creation of the protection group, you will be notified on the **Status** screen. If everything goes fine, you would be able to see the success status of the creation of this protection group.

Protecting Hyper-V standalone virtual machines using SMB storage

In this second type of protection group we create for Windows Server 2012 Hyper-V virtual machines, an SMB file share server will be used as the storage. If we remember from the earlier chapters, where we showed how a Windows Server 2012 Hyper-V virtual machine can use SMB storage, in the same way in this example, we will see how to protect a virtual machine that is using SMB storage for storing VHD/VHDX files.

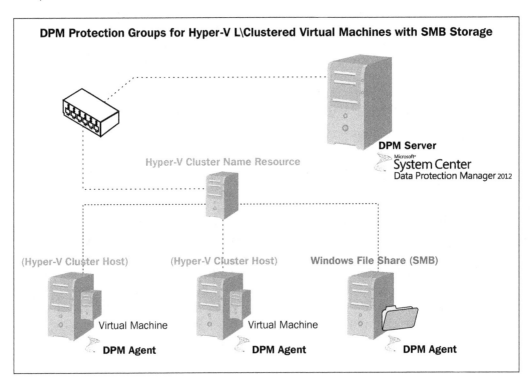

In the preceding screenshot, you can see that there are a few clustered virtual machines that are keeping their storage (VHD/VHDX) files on a Windows Server 2012 SMB file share server. And for protecting these virtual machines, we didn't only install the DPM 2012 management agent on the Hyper-V servers, but also installed the DPM management agent on the SMB file share server, because this is a requirement for incorporating protection for SMB share based virtual machines.

To start with protecting these SMB storage enabled virtual machines, perform the following steps, which are similar to the first protection group example we saw for protecting Hyper-V clustered virtual machines, except the following steps:

1. As specified here, first we will make sure that the DPM management agent exists on all the source servers, including the Hyper-V and SMB file share server.

2. Then, we need to add the custom cluster type, which will enable the DPM management server to recognize the cluster. Because if we are using a non-Microsoft SMB file cluster service, DPM doesn't discover our file share storage automatically. So in this case, if we are using a non-Microsoft file share storage, we will have to edit the registry for the following:

Type	Description
Key	`Software\Microsoft\Microsoft Data Protection Manager\Agent\Cluster`
Value	`PhysicalDiskResourceType`
Data	Type of the non-Microsoft cluster disk service
Type	`REG_SZ`

3. Then from this step, we will follow the same steps as we followed in the creation of the first type of protection group for Microsoft Hyper-V failover cluster virtual machine protection.

4. After completing the entire protection group configuration, just as we did for the first protection group, you can commit the changes, which will start the replica creation process. Upon completion of this, you will be able to see the protection group created for your clustered virtual machine using the SMB storage.

Protecting Windows Server 2012 CSV 2.0

This is the last type of protection group that we will create, for protecting the CSV disks and the data within them. Now most of the critical workloads and even normal ones, on our virtualization platform, are kept on the CSV storage, and that's why CSV and its storage has become an imperative part of our backup agenda.

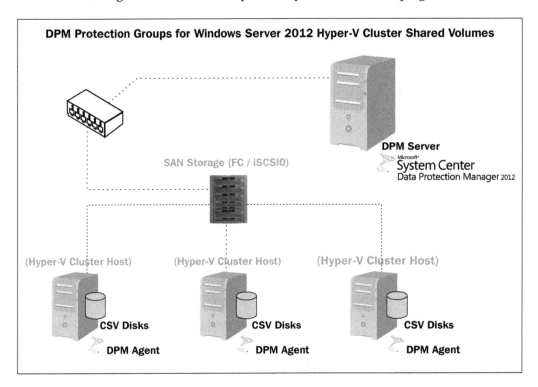

DPM 2012 SP1 also allows organizations to backup their CSV storage volumes directly, and place them either on a disk or tape storage for short or longer periods of time. To protect a CSV disk and its data, we install the DPM agent on all the Hyper-V failover cluster nodes, and then while creating the protection group, we select each CSV to be part of the protection group.

The following are the steps for creating protection groups for Windows Server 2012 Hyper-V failover cluster CSV disks and data:

1. As mentioned here, first we will make sure that the DPM management agent exists on all Hyper-V failover cluster nodes.

2. Then the rest of the steps are the same as before. However, while making the selection for the protection group, we will expand any of the Hyper-V failover cluster node computer accounts, and then under **All Volumes**, we will expand the C:\ClusterStorage\ folder. Now, select either all or some of the cluster shared volumes for the protection group.

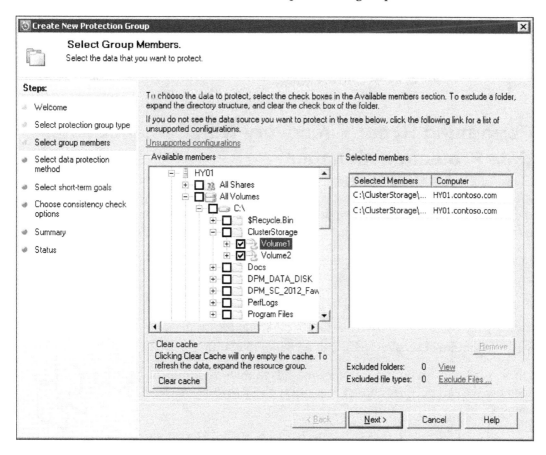

3. After selecting the CSV volume, we will follow the rest of the configuration parameters as we saw in the first protection group creation exercise.

4. Upon reaching the **Summary** screen, if everything looks fine, we will click on the **Create** button, which will start creating the protection group and will also start the replica creation process right after completing the creation of the protection group.

There are few important points, which you should not miss. If we talk about 8 to 16 nodes in a Windows Server 2012 failover cluster, enquiry for a scale of 400 virtual machines may take more than 5 hours to complete.

If we shut down a Windows Server 2012 failover cluster node enabled for CSV disks, this will result in all the virtual machines in the cluster being marked as inconsistent. This will start consistency checks for all virtual machines.

Performing Hyper-V recovery with System Center Data Protection Manager

Microsoft System Center Data Protection Manager 2012 provides server or client recovery models from bare metal recovery to file-level recovery. When it comes to the Hyper-V role, DPM 2012 provides three types of recovery models for customers protecting their Microsoft Hyper-V environments with DPM.

Let's first understand what are these recovery models that DPM supports, and then we will drill down to each of type of recovery model:

- Recover a virtual machine to an original location
- Recover a virtual machine to an alternate location
- **Item level recovery (ILR)** of a virtual machine

Ok, so we know about the recovery models that DPM supports. Now it's time to see how we can perform these types of Hyper-V virtual machine related recovery using DPM.

Recovering a virtual machine to an original location

This is something that makes a Hyper-V administrator's life free from tension, because if the virtual machine from a standalone or Hyper-V failover cluster gets deleted intentionally or unintentionally, DPM administrators can restore the same virtual machine to the point in time when the virtual machine was last synced with the DPM server protection group. DPM can restore a deleted virtual machine from the backup to its original location.

DPM uses Hyper-V VSS writer—just like other types of VSS writers for other applications' backup and restore—for restoring the virtual machine Hyper-V cluster to its original location.

Now, we will see how to perform a recovery using DPM protection group backup. We can perform the following steps for restoring the virtual machine to its original location:

1. Open System Center Data Protection Manager 2012 Management Console.

2. First we will find the **Recovery** tab on the left-hand action menu and then we will expand the **Recoverable Data** hierarchy. Here, we select the name of the virtual machine that we want to recover from the recovery point (backup), drill down the VM name, and click on **All Protected HyperV Data**. After selecting the **All Protected HyperV Data** tab under the VM, right-click on **Backup Using Child Partition Snapshot** and click on **Recover**.

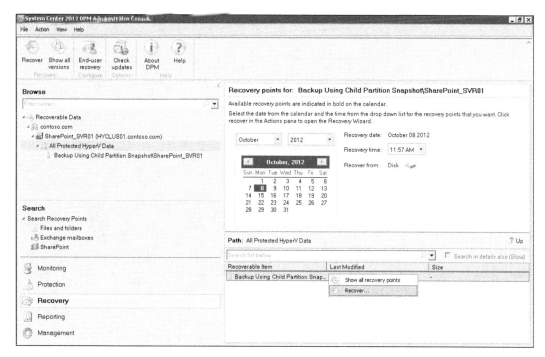

3. Then on the first screen of the recovery wizard, DPM first gives you an insight about the selection we made for recovering the virtual machine or data for our confirmation. If the selection is correct, click on the **Next** button.

4. The next screen is about the recovery type. As we discussed the different types of DPM recovery model, your recovery will be based on the selected model. In our case, we will be selecting **Recover to original instance**. This method will overwrite any file found in the original location of the Hyper-V virtual machine.

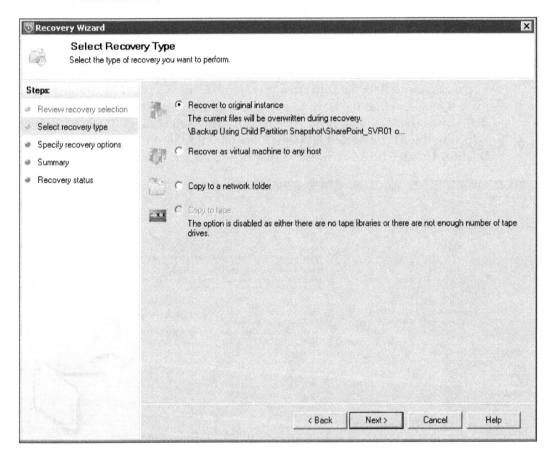

5. On the next screen, you can set the recovery options, such as network bandwidth throttling, SAN recovery, and notification to be sent out as a status report for the administrator.

6. The last screen of **Summary** provides information about the configuration and selections you made for this recovery. If you are comfortable with the information provided here, you can click on the **Recovery** button.

7. Depending on size of the data, recovery will take time and upon completion of the recovery, under the **Recovery Status** tab of the recovery wizard, you will be notified about the successful restoration of the virtual machine.

Recovering a virtual machine to an alternate location

Recovering a virtual machine to an alternate location is another option, which we can use to recover a virtual machine. Sometimes due to issues with the original host or for testing purposes, we restore a virtual machine to an alternative location.

For performing a virtual machine restore to an alternate location by using the DPM protection group backup data, the following steps need to be followed by the DPM administrator:

1. Open System Center Data Protection Manager 2012 Management Console.

2. First find the **Recovery** tab on the left-hand action menu, and then expand the **Recoverable Data** hierarchy. Here, select the name of the virtual machine that we want to recover from the recovery point (backup), drill down the VM name, and click on **All Protected Hyper-V Data**. After selecting the **All Protected Hyper-V Data** tab under the VM, right-click on **Backup Using Child Partition Snapshot** in the **Recoverable Item** list and click on **Recover**.

3. Then on the first screen of the recovery wizard, DPM first gives you an insight about the selection we made for recovering the virtual machine or data for our confirmation. If the selection is correct, click on the **Next** button.

4. The next screen is **Select recovery type**. As we discussed the different types of DPM recovery model, your recovery will be based on the selected model. In our case, we will be selecting **Recover as virtual machine to any host**.

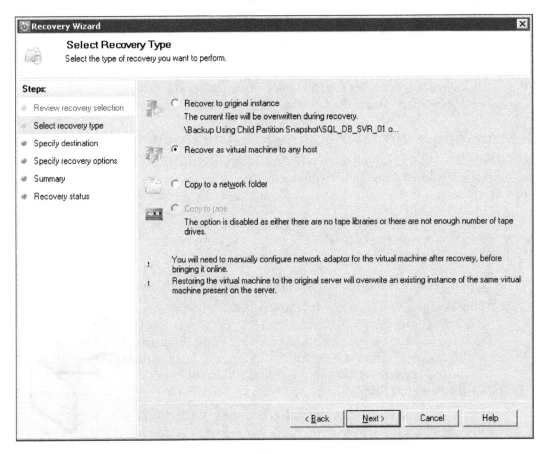

5. In the next step, we will specify the destination for this virtual machine backup restore. Based on the configuration, we can also select to specify the remote storage type on the destination machine. The other two configuration parameters that need to be defined here for the recovery are **Copy destination** and **Recovery Location**.

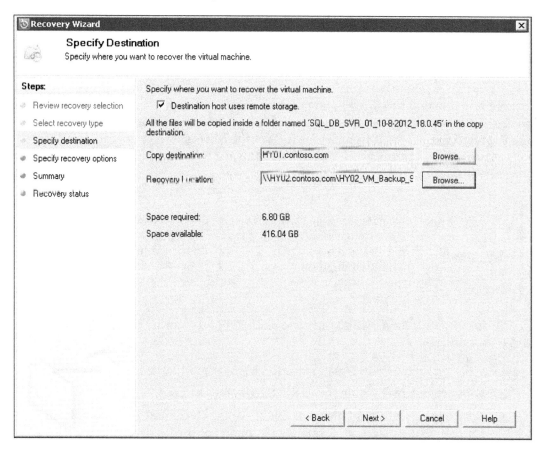

6. On the next screen, you can set the recovery options, such as network bandwidth throttling, SAN recovery, and notification to be sent out as a status report for the administrator.

7. The last screen of summary provides information about the configuration and selection you made for this recovery. If you are comfortable with the information provided here, you can click on the **Recovery** button.

8. Depending on size of the data, recovery will take time, and upon completion of the recovery, on the **Recovery status** tab of the recovery wizard, you will be notified about the successful restoration of the virtual machine.

ILR of a virtual machine

Sometimes there is a situation that requires you to restore a single file or folder from a virtual machine recovery point. In this case, if there is no object-level restore functionality provided by the backup solution, the only choice left with the administrator is to store a complete backup of the virtual machine and get the intended files. DPM 2012 provides ILR for the Microsoft Hyper-V role, where customers could perform the ILR of the files and the folder from Hyper-V virtual machine storage (VHD).

> It should be noted that the DPM ILR feature doesn't support recovery of an item to its original location. And if the virtual machine storage uses differencing disk and base VHD/VHDX on different volumes than the virtual machine configuration files, the ILR feature will not be applicable for this type of virtual machine and its storage.

For performing ILR for a virtual machine using DPM, perform the steps that are listed as follows:

1. Open System Center Data Protection Manager 2012 Management Console.

2. Select the recovery point from the **Recovery** tab.

3. For viewing the actual files and folders in the **Recoverable Items** column for the virtual machine storage, perform one of the following steps:

   ○ Double-click on the item (VHD) for which you want to perform the ILR.

   ○ Double-click on the items (volumes in the VHD) for which you want to perform the ILR.

In the same way as we mentioned for recovering files and folders, we can also recover the VHD and volumes for a given virtual machine, using the DPM ILR feature.

Ok, we talked a lot about Hyper-V primary server virtual machine protection. What about the Hyper-V replica server? Do we need to back up or protect the virtual machines on the Hyper-V replica server? The answer for this question would be backing up restoring virtual machine protection groups for the Hyper-V replica server is not supported with DPM 2012 SP1. While at the same time, you might be able to back up and restore virtual machines from the Hyper-V replica server, still it is not supported by DPM as of now.

Some people ask if we now have the liberty of replicating the Hyper-V virtual machines from one Hyper-V server to another, why on earth should we care about the protection or backup of the Hyper-V virtual machines? So, the answer to this question would be that you don't need to back up the Hyper-V replica server, but there are many requirements for which you want to back up the Hyper-V primary server. These reasons can be summarized as follows:

- You would like to have a long set of retention rage of backup set for a given virtual machine
- Restoring a virtual machine from a past recovery point in time backup
- For a DR drill testing or for any other purpose, you may want to restore a virtual machine state to an alternate destination.

So for all the above reasons, you may still want to protect your Hyper-V primary instances with the DPM server. While, as we said, protection and recovery of Hyper-V replica server is not supported by DPM, you can use the DPM to perform the file-level and system state level backup of Hyper-V replica server.

Summary

In this last chapter of our book, we discussed the importance of virtualized instances running in our data center. In addition to this, we saw the different backup methodologies available at our disposal for backup and recovery of Hyper-V virtual machines. These backup methodologies have been used for virtualization for quite a long time now. With the recent releases of Windows Server 2012 and Hyper-V 3.0, these backup methodologies have now become more mature and been enhanced to cope with the modern virtualized infrastructure.

After covering an overview of the backup methodologies for Hyper-V, we moved on to the Hyper-V virtual machine backup solution design considerations and best practices. In this section, we covered all the major components of a Hyper-V server, including networking, storage, and virtual machine settings. For all these major Hyper-V server components, we laid out the best practices and design considerations, which have a huge impact on the backup and recovery.

In the last section of this chapter, we discussed the implementation side for configuring Hyper-V backup and recovery, using Windows Server 2012 — the Windows Server Backup feature and System Center 2012 Data Protection Manager 2012. In this section we covered both the tools with step-by-step configuration for first setting up the backup of Hyper-V virtual machines and then to perform the various types of virtual machine recovery.

I hope you found this chapter useful and wish you the very best for your first implementation project with Microsoft Private Cloud and Microsoft Windows Server 2012 Hyper-V 3.0.

SCVMM 2012 New Features and Enhancements

Before the release of Microsoft System Center 2012, the previous product suite provided great features for building datacenter dynamics, and helped organizations to automate most of their routine tasks. But still there were a few gaps when it came to the private cloud and managed services. The Microsoft System Center 2012 suite addressed those gaps, which were identified by the industry in the earlier version of the product, and provided great features for datacenter management and building the private cloud on the customers' terms.

SCVMM 2012 in particular is a one-stop shop for all the datacenter and virtualized stack management requirements, where it starts management from the bare-metal deployment of the hypervisor (Hyper-V) to the datacenter optimization. SCVMM works great when it is integrated with the other System Center 2012 suite of products, for better management and automation. Now let's go ahead and understand the new capabilities and enhancements made in SCVMM 2012.

We can summarize the new features and core enhancements in SCVMM 2012 in four major areas, and we will also dig into each of these four areas to understand what new features and enhancements have been made in it.

The following are the new features and enhancements made in SCVMM 2012; let's discover each of them, one by one:

Hypervisor infrastructure management	
HA VMM server	VMM 2012 can be set up as a highly available system with Microsoft Cluster Service. With this new feature in place, organizations can now take full advantage of building highly available SCVMM infrastructures for the management and provisioning of their virtualization platform and private cloud.
Custom properties	VMM has a new feature of custom properties, where an administrator can set custom properties for a given feature; and by means of custom properties, applying and using a specific feature becomes more handy and relevant.
PowerShell	System Center 2012 and all other products are tightly integrated with PowerShell, where all the functions and functionalities you perform within the GUI can be scripted with PowerShell, which provides a great level of flexibility to administrators to script their routine and bulk modifications to their virtualized infrastructure.

Fabric management	
Hyper-V bare-metal provisioning	VMM 2012 allows administrators to perform bare-metal deployment right from SCVMM; whereas in the early version of the product, administrators had to first deploy the OS, then patch the server, and then add the host to the VMM infrastructure. But now you can deploy the operating system right from the VMM itself, and when your system meets all the requirements of your infrastructure, your host will automatically be added to the VMM environment.
Extended support for all major hypervisors	Along with Hyper-V and VMware, now Citrix XenServer also comes under the list of VMM-supported hypervisors. Organizations with a heterogeneous environment can deploy SCVMM, and can manage all these different types of hypervisors in the same way. SCVMM makes it much easier to manage your hypervisors, no matter what vendor you are using and what type of guest virtual machine you are running on them; you can get all the functionalities and features for managing an enterprise-class server virtualization and a cloud environment.

Fabric management	
Network management	As we said, SC 2012 SP1 and VMM 2012 SP1 are cloud-focused tools, where network management functionality has been greatly overhauled along with numerous new features and enhancements added into the network management account. VMM 2012 supports hardware load balancing, VIP profiles, VLAN tagging, static IP pools, and MAC address pools for the virtual machines.
Storage management	Just like network management, storage management can be now done inside VMM 2012 SP1. We can manage the storage LUN management-related activities within SCVMM, which offloads the storage admin part. A storage pool can be attached to VMM, and from there, as per the needs of your virtualized environment, you can allocate and use it wherever you find it necessary.
Update management	Patching up a standalone server has never been so difficult, but patching a Hyper-V cluster node was an immensely difficult task because before you patch up and restart the node, you have to migrate the guest virtual machine to another Hyper-V server. VMM 2012 addressed the cluster Hyper-V nodes, and now VMM 2012 update management is an integrated functionality where VMM now orchestrates the patch management, and allows you to set up baselines to automatically perform the patch management of the host, wherever and whenever it is needed.
Dynamic optimization	According to your need and configuration, VMM 2012 now performs a great level of dynamic optimization of the workload. The scale-in and scale-out features of VMM 2012 for a service deployment group of homogeneous guest VMs can be monitored with **System Center Operations Manager (SCOM)** and at any point in time, optimization of your physical resources can be achieved with a great level of automation.
Power management	With the dynamic optimization and services' deployment within VMM 2012, a great level of power optimization can be achieved, where VMM can turn off an under-utilized host and save power when the load is low; and as per the administrator settings of the scale-in and scale-out features, when VMM sees there is not much load for the service, it may turn off a unnecessary guest, and thus also turn off an under-utilized host to save power.
Cluster management	As we said, VMM 2012 SP1 supports bare-metal deployment, which means that now a new server box gets the OS and patches installed through VMM. It is also possible to add the same box or a number of boxes in the form of a cluster. This new feature of VMM allows organizations to install the operating system.

Cloud management	
Application owner usage	SCVMM enables the self-service usage for an application administrator to author and deploy, manage, and decommission applications in the private cloud.
Capacity and capability	SCVMM provides a great level of control on the capacity and the capability of the cloud rollout within small to large cloud implementations, where controlling the capacity and capability of the individual cloud user and cloud itself is the most important aspect from the service delivery viewpoint. VMM provides capacity- and capability-throttling features for the administrators, so they can set policies and settings on the cloud and the user level to restrict them to use the physical and cloud resources at a certain level.
Delegation and quota	In addition to the capability and the capacity profiles and controlling policies, VMM provides a delegation of rights and quota settings, which apply to both the cloud and the user role, where an extended level of delegation of rights makes it much easier for you to control what level of privileges you want to grant to a user, a department, or an organization for authoring, deploying, and managing cloud resources. Quota is another administrative control available in VMM. Quota can be applied to the usability of different levels of the cloud and physical resources.

Services management	
Service template	Service templates are just same as the virtual machine template. The customization available for service templates allows an administrator to tailor different role-based templates, where integration with other SC 2012 suite products and components makes it more useful for service implementation on the fly with a great level of dynamics and automation.
Application deployment	With all the dynamics and automation, SCVMM 2012 allows organizations to deploy an application as a single instance or as a service. Application deployment usually refers to a tier-based implementation of x number of servers, consisting of frontend tier, middle tier, and the backend tier. In particular, application deployment within SCVMM 2012 refers to the ability to deploy Microsoft SQL Server as a part of the application deployment. SCVMM allows an administrator to deploy SQL Server as an application, and the IIS application as a virtual machine and service. The VMM service deployment feature allows organizations to tailor their service deployment within SCVMM, where this service deployment can also be set as a template; so whenever it is needed, it can be deployed with a few clicks.

Services management	
Custom command execution	While you deploy a service or virtual machine, you have the luxury to execute a particular program or command at any point of time during the deployment and service provisioning.
Image-based servicing	This is another great feature of VMM 2012, where an administrator can also deploy the virtual instances with a preconfigured image. Image-based servicing also helps organizations when it comes to deploying a complex three-tier-based application, in which complex integration and customized application servicing is needed.

B
SCVMM Management Console Configuration Settings

In this section, we will list out all the basic configuration settings available for System Center Virtual Machine Manager. Depending on your scenario and environment, you may not need to configure all of the following configurations for your SCVMM deployment. The following table divides the SCVMM configuration items into four major areas. These areas are considered to be the architectural pillars of the SCVMM base platform.

VMs and services			
Create	**Create Service**	This option allows you to create and deploy single-tiered or multitiered application services.	
	Create Virtual Machine	This option allows you to create a VM from SCVMM and place it either on Hyper-V or cloud.	
	Create Cloud	This option allows you to create clouds; you can create multiple clouds as per your needs.	
	Create Host Group	If you want to segregate your hypervisors, for example, VMware, Hyper-V, and Citrix XenServer, you can create multiple host groups, in which you can place the relevant hypervisors and apply the different policies as per your needs.	

VMs and services		
Cloud	**Assign Cloud**	After creating a cloud, you can assign the cloud to a security group or individual users for creating VMs and managing them.
Show	**Overview**	This option will provide you a summary page inside the SCVMM console and a statistical view of your environment.
	VMs	Clicking on this ribbon button will show all the virtual machines created and placed in the clouds and on hosts.
	Services	Just like the **VMs** button, this will give you information about the deployed services.
Windows	**PowerShell**	This ribbon button will launch the PowerShell window to execute any PowerShell cmdlet.
	Jobs	To see the currently running and recently completed jobs, you can click on the **Jobs** button, which will launch the jobs monitoring window.
	PRO	This is used to open the PRO status report.
Refresh	**Refresh Overview**	This is to refresh the currently launched ribbon data.

Fabric			
Servers	**All Hosts**		As the name suggests, this tells you about all the hosts that have been registered within SCVMM. This option also allows you to add a new host to the SCVMM.
	Library servers		This gives an overview about all the SCVMM library servers installed within your environment for which this SCVMM server has information. Along with seeing the registered library servers, you can also add a new library servers from here.
	PXE Servers		This option displays the **Preboot Execution Environment** (**PXE**) servers registered within SCVMM. You can add a new PXE server from this option as well.
	Update Server		Using this option, you can integrate your **Windows Software Update Service** (**WSUS**) infrastructure with SCVMM for updating virtual machines and hosts.
	vCenter Servers		This option displays available vCenter Servers and provides the option to add a new vCenter server.
	VMM Server		This shows the status of the SCVMM Server environment.

Fabric		
Networking	**Logical Networks**	This displays the logical networks configured in SCVMM and allows you to add a new logical network to be used by the virtual machines.
	MAC Address Pools	This option displays MAC Address Pool and provides the option for adding a new MAC Address Pool.
	Load Balancers	For adding a load balancer, you have to install and configure the load balancer providers component on your SCVMM Server. So install the providers, and restart the service of SCVMM, and then you can add balancers in SCVMM.
	VIP Templates	As part of configuring the load balancer, you would also like to add VIP templates to SCVMM. This option displays them and allows us to add new templates.
Storage	**Classification and Pools**	From this section of the configuration part of SCVMM, you can configure the storage classification and pools for assigning storage to your virtual machines.
	Providers	Just like load balancer, you would also need to install and configure the storage provider in SCVMM.
	Arrays	The array settings are required to configure the external storage, before it can be allocated to the virtual machines.

Library		
Template	**Service Deployment Configurations**	Service deployment configuration is a part of service creation and deployment; this option displays the configured settings for the service deployment within SCVMM.
	Service Templates	You can see the available service templates and create a new one from here.
	VM Templates	Just like service templates, the **VM Template** section of templates allows you to see the existing VM templates and create new ones.
Profiles	**Application Profiles**	This comprises the settings for application deployment as part of the service or virtual machine deployment within SCVMM.
	Capabilities Profiles	This option is used inside the cloud configuration and specifies the allowed and maximum resources allocation a cloud can contain.
	Guest OS Profile	You can have multiple guest OS profiles within SCVMM. A guest OS profile can be used for a virtual machine and the services templates.
	Hardware Profiles	This provides the subset settings for templates.
	Host Profiles	Host profiles are the same as other profiles, where you specify the host-related properties.
	SQL Profiles	As part of service deployment and VM creation, you can set the SQL Server profile; this allows you to deploy SQL Server as an application in the post-OS deployment for a VM and a service.
Cloud Libraries	**Created cloud listing**	This lists all the clouds created within the SCVMM and the profiles assigned to them.
Self-Service Content	**Listing the self-service contents**	This is only for listing the self-service contents.
Library Servers	**SCVMM Library Server**	This shows the library server registered within SCVMM.

Library		
Update Catalog and Baselines	**Update Baselines**	This lists out the update baselines that you have created for your virtual machines.
	Update Catalog	This lists the baselines for your patch management.
Settings		
General	**General**	The **General** settings include the CEIP settings, database connection, library settings, remote control, self-service admin contact, network settings, and last but not least, the guest agent settings.
Security	**User Roles**	This allows you to create customized user roles for the delegation of rights.
	Run As Accounts	You can create multiple **Run As Accounts** for performing various administrative tasks.
	Service Windows	This is just like creating a work schedule in which only you can perform a particular task. You can create a servicing window for your workload from the security configuration area within SCVMM.
	Configuration Providers	This displays the configuration providers that are installed and set up within SCVMM. By default, WNLB is installed and can be seen within the configuration provider list.
	System Center Settings	These settings allow you to connect your virtual machine manager to the System Center Operations Manager.

Index

A

ACL (Access Control List) 303
Active Directory Domain Services. *See* AD DS
Active Directory Lightweight Directory Services. *See* AD DLS
AD DLS 304
address hash 142
Address Resolution Protocol. *See* ARP
AD DS 304
advanced network settings
  bandwidth management 128
  failover TCP/IP 130-132
  hardware acceleration 129
APIs 83, 200
Application-consistent replica 82
application programming interfaces. *See* APIs
architectural pillars, SCVMM base platform
  Fabric 375, 376
  Library 377, 378
  settings 378
  VMs and services 373, 374
ARP 116
ARP spoofing protection 301
Authorization Manager
  about 304
  for Hyper-V delegation of authority 305-309

B

backup and recovery, System Center DPM used 344-345
backup and recovery, Windows Server Backup feature used
  about 328
  features 329, 330
  installation 330
  virtual machine backups, configuring 331-338
  virtual machine recovery, performing 338-344
bare metal hypervisors 23
BCP 21
Best Possible Node option 289
best practices, Hyper-V Replica
  networking 90-92
  security 88-90
  storage 92
best practices, Hyper-V storage 193-197
Browse button 282
business continuity planning. *See* BCP

C

CA 82
CAP 104
CAU 299
central processing unit. *See* CPU
certification authority. *See* CA

DPM
about 344
DPM base infrastructure, setting up 346
technical overview 344, 345
DPM base infrastructure, setting up
disks, adding 348
DPM agent , installing on Hyper-V host
348
System Center DPM 2012, installing
346, 347
dynamic disk 173
Dynamic Host Configuration Protocol. *See*
DHCP
dynamic teaming 141

E

edit disk
compact 183, 184
convert 185-187
expand 187-189
emulated devices 29

F

Fabric
networking 376
servers 375
storage 376
fabric management
cluster management 369
dynamic optimization 369
Hyper-V bare-metal provisioning 368
network management 369
power management 369
storage management 369
update management 369
Failover 82
features, Windows Server 2012 Hyper-V
bigger cluster 240
enhanced live migration 239
Guest machine clustering capabilities 239
up-to-date CSV 240
virtual machine failover 241
Fibre Channel disks 40
Fibre Channel Stroage Area Network. *See*
SAN
Finish button 189

fixed disk
about 174
creating 175
fresh Hyper-V server installation
about 54-56
server manager 56
server manager, using 57-61

G

Get-Command 150
GPU 68
graphics processing unit. *See* GPU
guest virtual machines safeguarding
filesystem security 314
virtual machine resource access, auditing
315
virtual machines, backing up 316

H

hard disk setting, virtual machine
IDE controller 180, 181
SCSI controller 182
hardware acceleration
about 129
IPSEC task offloading 129
single root I/O virtualization 129, 130
virtual machine queue 129
hardware requirements, Hyper-V
disk type, storage 39
memory, storage 41
networking, storage 41
processor 38
storage 39
hardware requirements, SCVMM 2012 204
HID 29
hosted hypervisors 24
host group properties, customizing
custom properties 215
Dynamic Optimization 213, 214
general 210
Host Reserves 212
network 215
placement rules 212
storage 215
human interface device. *See* HID

M

MAC 117
management network 297
MBSA 300
MCS 250
Media Access Control. *See* MAC
microkernel hypervisors 26
Microsoft Baseline Security Analyzer. *See* MBSA
Microsoft Cluster Service. *See* MSCS
Microsoft Management Console. *See* MMC
Microsoft Network Load Balancing. *See* NLB
Microsoft Solution Accelerators
  GRC 50
  IPD 50
  MAP 50
  MDT 50
  MOF 50
Microsoft System Center Data Protection Manager. *See* SCDPM
Microsoft Virtual Machine Manager. *See* VMM
Microsoft Windows Clustering Services. *See* MCS
MMC 30
Monitoring Tools 108
monolithic hypervisors 25
Move tab 279
MSCS 16, 37
multipath I/O (MPIO) 169

N

NAS 239
Native Command Queuing. *See* NCQ
NCQ 39
NDIS 36, 113
NDP 116
Neighbor Discovery Protocol. *See* NDP
Network-attached storage. *See* NAS
Network Device Interface Specification. *See* NDIS
network interface card. *See* NIC
Network settings 215

new features, SCVMM 2012
  cloud management 370
  fabric management 368, 369
  Hypervisor infrastructure management 368
  services management 370, 371
New Hard Disk Wizard 176
NIC 29, 112
NIC teaming
  about 114
  architectural consideration 135, 136
  configuring, for Hyper-V guest virtual machines 143
  configuring, for Hyper-V host 136
  implementing, for Hyper-V host and guest 133-136
  native OS feature 134
  requirements 135
NIC teaming advanced settings
  load-balancing mechanisms 141
  NIC teaming mode 140
NIC teaming configuration, for Hyper-V host
  advanced settings 140
  steps 136-139
NIC teaming mode
  dynamic teaming 141
  static teaming 141
  switch dependent 141
  switch independent 140
NLB 132
Non-Uniform Memory Access. *See* NUMA
NPIV 168
N_Port ID Virtualization. *See* NPIV
NUMA 69

O

OLTA 36
OLTP 36
online transaction analysis. *See* OLTA
online transaction processing. *See* OLTP

P

parent partition 27
pass-through disk 176, 178
patch management 298

Second Level Address Translation. *See*
    SLAT
Self-Service Portal 201. *See* SSP
Server Core 62
server hardware 242
Server Message Block. *See* SMB
service-level agreement. *See* SLA
services management
    application deployment 370
    custom command execution 371
    image-based servicing 371
    service template 370
settings
    general 378
    security 378
Show-Command 153
Single root I/O virtualization. *See* SR-IOV
SLA 81
SLAT 31
SMB 168, 246
software requirements, Hyper-V
    about 42
    disk space 44
    memory 43
    operating system versions 43
Specify Name and Location screen 265
SR-IOV 114
SSP
    accessing 228
    delegating 228-232
    used, for virtual machine creating 233
    used, for virtual machine managing 233
Standard replica 82
static teaming 141
storage area network. *See* SAN
Storage settings 215
storage setting, virtual machine
    about 180
    disk utilities 183
    hard disk settings 180
synthetic devices 29
System Center DPM
    features 346
    used, for Hyper-V recovery performance
        358
System Center Operations. *See* SCOM

System Center Virtual Machine Manager.
        See SCVMM
system requirements, SCVMM 2012 203
system requirements, Windows Server 2012
        PowerShell 3.0
    CLR 155
    .NET Framework 155
    WMI 155
    WS-Management 3.0 155

T

Task Definitions tab 307
TCB 25
TechNet URL 159
technical overview, Hyper-V Replica
    broker 87
    change tracking 87
    network module 87
    Replication Engine 87
total cost of ownership (TCO) 304
trusted computing base. *See* TCB

U

usage scenarios, for Hyper-V management
    about 156
    cloud management 158
    research and development environments
        157
    virtualized datacenter management 157

V

V2P 19
V2V 20
vDevices
    about 29
    emulated devices 29
    plugin devices 29
    synthetic devices 29
    virtual machine bus 30
VHD
    about 99, 166
    benefits 169
VHDs 21

Thank you for buying
Windows Server 2012 Hyper-V: Deploying Hyper-V Enterprise Server Virtualization Platform

About Packt Publishing

Packt, pronounced 'packed', published its first book "Mastering phpMyAdmin for Effective MySQL Management" in April 2004 and subsequently continued to specialize in publishing highly focused books on specific technologies and solutions.

Our books and publications share the experiences of your fellow IT professionals in adapting and customizing today's systems, applications, and frameworks. Our solution based books give you the knowledge and power to customize the software and technologies you're using to get the job done. Packt books are more specific and less general than the IT books you have seen in the past. Our unique business model allows us to bring you more focused information, giving you more of what you need to know, and less of what you don't.

Packt is a modern, yet unique publishing company, which focuses on producing quality, cutting-edge books for communities of developers, administrators, and newbies alike. For more information, please visit our website: www.packtpub.com.

About Packt Enterprise

In 2010, Packt launched two new brands, Packt Enterprise and Packt Open Source, in order to continue its focus on specialization. This book is part of the Packt Enterprise brand, home to books published on enterprise software – software created by major vendors, including (but not limited to) IBM, Microsoft and Oracle, often for use in other corporations. Its titles will offer information relevant to a range of users of this software, including administrators, developers, architects, and end users.

Writing for Packt

We welcome all inquiries from people who are interested in authoring. Book proposals should be sent to author@packtpub.com. If your book idea is still at an early stage and you would like to discuss it first before writing a formal book proposal, contact us; one of our commissioning editors will get in touch with you.

We're not just looking for published authors; if you have strong technical skills but no writing experience, our experienced editors can help you develop a writing career, or simply get some additional reward for your expertise.

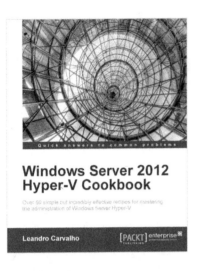

**Windows Server 2012
Hyper-V Cookbook**

Over 50 simple but incredibly effective recipes for mastering
the administration of Windows Server Hyper-V

Leandro Carvalho   [PACKT] enterprise

Windows Server 2012 Hyper-V Cookbook

ISBN: 978-1-84968-442-2   Paperback: 304 pages

Over 50 simple but incredibly effective recipes for mastering the administration of Windows Server Hyper-V

1. Take advantage of numerous Hyper-V best practices for administrators

2. Get to grips with migrating virtual machines between servers and old Hyper-V versions, automating tasks with PowerShell, providing a High Availability and Disaster Recovery environment, and much more

3. A practical Cookbook bursting with essential recipes

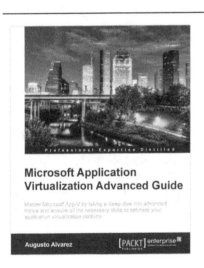

**Microsoft Application
Virtualization Advanced Guide**

Master Microsoft App-V by taking a deep dive into advanced
topics and acquire all the necessary skills to optimize your
application virtualization platform

Augusto Alvarez   [PACKT] enterprise

Microsoft Application Virtualization Advanced Guide

ISBN: 978-1-84968-448-4   Paperback: 474 pages

Master Microsoft App-V by taking a deep dive into advanced topics and acquire all the necessary skills to optimize your application virtualization platform

1. Understand advanced topics in App-V; identify some rarely known components and options available in the platform

2. Acquire advanced guidelines on how to troubleshoot App-V installations, sequencing, and application deployments

3. Learn how to handle particular applications, adapting companys' policies to the implementation, enforcing application licenses, securing the environment, and so on

Please check **www.PacktPub.com** for information on our titles

VMware ThinApp 4.7 Essentials

ISBN: 978-1-84968-628-0   Paperback: 256 pages

Learn how to quickly and efficiently virtualize your applications with ThinApp 4.7

1. Practical book which provides the essentials of application virtualization with ThinApp 4.7

2. Learn the various methods and best practices of application packaging and deployment

3. Save money and time on your projects with this book by learning how to create portable applications

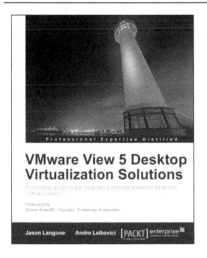

VMware View 5 Desktop Virtualization Solutions

ISBN: 978-1-84968-112-4   Paperback: 288 pages

A complete guide to planning and designing solutions based on VMware View 5

1. Written by VMware experts Jason Langone and Andre Leibovici, this book is a complete guide to planning and designing a solution based on VMware View 5

2. Secure your Visual Desktop Infrastructure (VDI) by having firewalls, antivirus, virtual enclaves, USB redirection and filtering and smart card authentication

3. Analyze the strategies and techniques used to migrate a user population from a physical desktop environment to a virtual desktop solution

Please check **www.PacktPub.com** for information on our titles

www.ingramcontent.com/pod-product-compliance
Lightning Source LLC
LaVergne TN
LVHW062301060326
`32902LV00013B/2002